5/19

The America's Cup

Dodd, Mead & Company

New York

The
America's
Cup

An Informal History

Ian Dear

First published in the United States of America in 1980
by Dodd, Mead & Company, Inc.
79 Madison Avenue, New York, N.Y. 10016

ISBN 0–396–07848–6

Library of Congress Catalog Number 80–65596

Printed in Great Britain by
Fakenham Press Limited, Fakenham, Norfolk

Contents

Illustrations

Black and white

Colour photographs

Line drawings

Acknowledgements

My first thanks go to the New York Yacht Club Library Committee, and the Club's Librarian, Mr Hohri, for their invaluable help; and to Olin Stephens for reading the galleys and for making several very helpful comments as well as correcting some factual errors. He quite rightly questioned my statement that the tank tests on *Easterner*'s hull showed her to be the fastest of the 1958 contenders, and the truth of this must now be open to doubt.

I would also like to thank the many authors who have previously written about the America's Cup. Where they have been quoted I have acknowledged both author and title in the text, but I also read many books which I have not quoted from at any length but which gave me the flavour of what it is like to be involved in the America's Cup. Outstanding among these were: *The Summer of the Twelves* by Carleton Mitchell, *A View From The Cockpit* by Robert Bavier, *Defending the America's Cup* by W. Carrick and Stanley Z. Rosenfeld, *Showdown at Newport* by Jeff Hammond, *The America's Cup: Challenge from Down Under* by W. Baverstock, and *Challenge '77* by Ted Jones.

My thanks, too, to Marianne Wright for undertaking the awful task of typing the manuscript, and to my wife, Wendy, for reading the proofs. Paul Darling took my constant pestering for photographs with good humour and patience, and my thanks go also to Brock Studios, Gerald Lenanton, Graeme Andrew, Robert Harding Associates, and Arthur Knapp Jr for their help with the photographs.

Sources for illustrations not acknowledged after their captions are listed below: 13, 14, 15, 26, 29, 30, 35 (both pictures), 40, 43, 58, *Lawson's History of the America's Cup*; 45, 46, 138 (right), 152 (inset), 159 (both pictures), 160 (above), 163, *Australian Seacraft*; 63, 92, 94, 115, 116, Arthur Knapp Jr.

Author's preface

I have sub-titled this book *An Informal History* because it does not pretend to be an exhaustive treatise on the subject and because I have deliberately dwelt on what I consider to be the more entertaining aspects of the race's history. I believe what makes the story of the America's Cup so extraordinary is not so much which yacht tacked when, but who said – and did – what to whom, and why. But I have not neglected technical detail, nor, I hope, neglected accuracy for the sake of readability. If I have not covered every leg of every race it is because I found those particular races boring – many were – and because there were more entertaining aspects of that particular challenge to write about. Wherever possible I have gone back to the original sources, most of them in the New York Yacht Club, and have, I believe, found something new to say about most of the early challenges. Of the 12 metre challenges, there are other writers more knowledgable than I. But because my theme is one of continuity and comparison – and as I have tried to show the history of the Cup as a whole – I believe I have taken a different viewpoint from other writers on these later challenges. Finally, I have kept statistics and dimensions either at the back of the book or in the captions so that figures and tables don't interrupt the narrative.

The Cup

The Cup is in fact not a cup at all as its bottom is open. It was an ordinary 100-guinea silver trophy offered by the Royal Yacht Squadron to the winner of the race round the Isle of Wight on 22 August 1851. It was made that same year, on the Squadron's orders, by Messrs R. & S. Gerard, of Panton Street, London. It was often subsequently called the Squadron Cup, the Queen's Cup and even Lipton's Cup, but its correct name, from the time of the first challenge, was the America's Cup. It is 27 inches high, weighs 134 ounces, and is firmly bolted down to a plinth in the New York Yacht Club.

The five syndicate members of *America*, the first winners of the Cup, passed it amongst themselves on their return from England and though obviously proud of it – they displayed it on the dinner table in their houses, and during other social functions – they thought at one time about having it melted down so that each owner could have a medal struck from it in commemoration of the race. However this idea was dropped and George Schuyler, one of the members of the syndicate, suggested the Cup be presented to the New York Yacht Club as an international trophy to be raced for by foreign clubs. The others agreed and, in May 1852, a letter was drafted and signed, except by Hamilton Wilkes who was ill abroad and had to grant power of attorney to a friend. But apparently the letter was not sent, and only some five years later did the Cup and the terms for racing for it arrive at the Club. The terms for the conveyancing of the Cup to the Club – they became known as the original Deed of Gift – were dated 8 July 1857, and read:

Any organized yacht club of any foreign country shall always be entitled through any one or more of its members, to claim the right of sailing a match for this cup with any yacht or other vessel of not less than thirty or more than three hundred tons, measured by the custom-house rule of the country to which the vessel belongs.

The parties desiring to sail for the cup may make any match with the yacht club in possession of the same that may be determined by mutual consent; but in case of disagreement as to terms, the match shall be sailed over the usual course for the annual regatta of the yacht club in possession of the cup, and subject to its rules and sailing regulations – the challenging party being bound to give six months' notice in writing, fixing the day they wish to start. This notice to embrace the length, custom-house measurement, rig and name of the vessel.

It is to be distinctly understood that the cup is to be the property of the club, and not the members thereof, or owners of the vessel winning it in the match; and that the condition of keeping it open to be sailed for by yacht clubs of all foreign countries upon the terms laid down, shall forever attach to it, thus making it perpetually a challenge cup for friendly competition between foreign countries.

Two weeks later the Club wrote to all foreign yacht clubs and invited 'spirited contest for the championship' and promised all challengers 'a liberal, hearty welcome, and the strictest fair play'. But in 1860 the American Civil War began and it was not until it was well over that anyone eschewed interest in challenging.

The first four challenges – those of 1870, 1871, 1876 and 1881 – were governed by this original Deed of Gift, and there are those, as will be seen, who thought these races the only legitimate ones for the Cup. However, in December 1881 it was decided to alter the terms of the Deed of Gift. The Cup was returned to George Schuyler, by then the only surviving member of the original syndicate, who returned it with a second Deed of Gift in January 1882.

The next three challenges – 1885, 1886 and 1887 – were held under the terms of this second Deed of Gift, but then after the 1887 challenge George

Schuyler was again asked to receive back the Cup and to agree to a third Deed of Gift. This third deed was not just a letter but a legal document. It raised a storm of protest and the legality of the Club's actions was eventually questioned.

Finally, after the Second World War the Club went to the Supreme Court to ask for the deed to be altered to enable the Cup to be raced for by 12-metres. The Supreme Court ruled that it could be so altered.

How it all began

1851

1851 was not only the year of the first America's Cup race – though, of course, it was not called that at the time – but the year of the Great Exhibition in London. The two events may seem unrelated but in fact the latter sparked off the former when some English businessmen wrote to their New York counterparts suggesting that a New York pilot boat come over for the Exhibition, berth up the Thames, and show how fast it could really go – for the speed of the pilot boat was already renowned. This suggestion must have caused a good deal of interest in New York, and word that the Americans were indeed thinking of sending over a vessel came to the ears of the Earl of Wilton, then Commodore of the Royal Yacht Squadron. He, naturally, in common with all the British nobility of that time, had nothing to do with trade: his interests were sporting and the thought of having a foreign yacht (especially an American one at a time when there was little love lost between the two nations) to race against no doubt caused the blue blood in his veins to course faster.

His note to the Commodore of the recently founded New York Yacht Club, John C. Stevens, was phrased with impeccable courtesy and only the phrase that he would 'be very glad to avail myself of any improvements in shipbuilding that the industry and skill of your nation have enabled you to elaborate' makes the modern reader feel the noble earl's motives were not entirely sporting. He was not, of course, so vulgar as explicitly to suggest that the visitor should race, merely saying the Americans would be welcome if they decided to come.

As it happened the earlier correspondence had encouraged Stevens to form a syndicate with other members of the New York Yacht Club (NYYC) to build 'the fastest yacht afloat' so that by the time he received Lord Wilton's letter the yacht, to be called *America*, was already on the stocks. He was able to

Commodore John C. Stevens

reply to that effect, adding that 'we propose to avail ourselves of your friendly bidding and take with good grace the sound thrashing we are likely to get by venturing our longshore craft on your rough waters', thereby, with true American straightforwardness, letting the noble earl know that they knew why they were being asked and that it was nothing to do with the Great Exhibition. It appeared

13

George Steers

that Stevens, who had introduced cricket to his countrymen, understood the wiles of the English and felt that a modest attitude was the best one to display. But the truth is that he and the members of his syndicate, his brother Edwin, George L. Schuyler, J. Beekman Finlay, Col. James A. Hamilton, and Hamilton Wilkes, didn't feel modest at all. Why should they? They, along with their fellow yachting countrymen, were confident that their yacht designs were well in advance of the British – not because the latter were denied knowledge that the Americans possessed but simply that they ignored that knowledge and did not care to take advantage of it. The long hollow bow for which *America* was to become so famous, a design proven and accepted in American waters, was as available to the British as it was to their cousins across the Atlantic. In fact in 1848 a 50-ton cutter, *Mosquito*, was built on this 'wave-line' principle, as it was known – evolved by a Scottish scientist, John Scott Russell – and thrashed all others in her class. Yet British yachtsmen attributed her speed to her iron hull, not

to her design. It was the same, too, with *America*'s sails which were lashed taut to her booms while the canvas of the British – made, as one writer deftly put it, by the sons of tentmakers – were pot-bellied and loose-footed which meant the hull could not be driven as close to the wind. But, as a correspondent in one of the papers of the time pointed out after the race, 'American-cut' sails laced to a yacht's boom had been known and discussed for some years – and derided.

Stevens's confidence was underpinned by the eagerness with which both the designer and builder of the proposed yacht received his idea to cross the Atlantic. The designer, George Steers, was the foremost man for the job at the time, and his keenness soon fired the enthusiasm of his employer, William Brown, a shipbuilder at East River and Twelfth Street, New York. In fact, so enthusiastic did Brown become, he quite seemed to forget he was in business and offered to build *America* for $30,000, saying that if she did not prove to be faster than all the competition the NYYC syndicate could forget the bill! However, the syndicate, who surely must have received Brown's suggestion with incredulity, made a poker-faced reply. 'The price is high,' they wrote, 'but in consideration of the liberal and sportsman-like character of the whole offer ... we have concluded that such a proposal must not be declined.'

It was promised that *America* would be launched on 1 April. This was later extended to 1 May though the syndicate warned that this would be the only extension. One of them, Hamilton Wilkes, had camped on the building site during the winter months to ensure prompt delivery – his death the following year of consumption was attributed to this vigil – and Brown obviously realized the syndicate meant what they said. He actually managed to have *America* in the water on 3 May, though she wasn't fully rigged and ready for her first trial before 17 May. Stevens then tried her out against another of his yachts, *Maria*, a centre-board sloop of phenomenal speed, which though at home in the sheltered waters of New York harbour was reputed unsafe in a seaway. It is not at all surprising that *Maria* was the faster boat and one can only suppose that Brown, in striking his deal, not only forgot his sense of business but his professional acumen as well. *Maria*, with an LOA of 110 feet and a 'monstrous rig', was an all-out smooth-water racing machine, the fastest yacht in American waters, a record she retained throughout her racing career. *America*, on the other hand, was built for a different purpose: not only did she have to cross the Atlantic, but she had to race in the less sheltered waters of the English Channel.

Not unnaturally, *Maria* ran rings – literally – around *America* which enabled the syndicate to go back to the builder and renegotiate. They would, they said, forget the bit about *America* being the fastest yacht afloat and would pay Brown $20,000 for her provided she was 'equipped and ready for sea by 2 June'. Brown accepted. On 18 June the syndicate were in formal possession of *America* and three days later they set sail for Europe. On board were thirteen men. The skipper was Captain Dick Brown, a Sandy Hook pilot. George Steers was on board with his brother James, and his nephew, also named George.

Unlike the hull of *Maria*, and other American racing yachts, *America* was built with a long, fixed keel. Her original lines were never recorded anywhere; though her certificate of registry included the fact that she was a fraction over 170 tons measurement it was not subsequently possible to gauge what her tonnage would have been under the several measurement rules then in force. The one she was measured by for the certificate was the American version of the old Thames reckoning for tonnage. But her length (93 ft 6 ins.), her beam (22 ft 6 ins.) and her sail area (5263 sq. ft) were undisputed as was her draft of 11 feet when under full sail. Her mainmast was 81 feet and her foremast 79 feet 6 inches. She was beautifully built and designed with a sharp bow and her greatest beam aft, making her wedge-shaped in appearance. Below, her saloons were embellished with green velvet, polished American walnut and carved rosewood, and there was even a 'tastefully fitted-up bathroom' below the cockpit.

The syndicate loved her and soon after she arrived at Le Havre, on 11 July, the Stevens brothers joined her from Paris. George Schuyler who had hoped to be with them was detained at home and his place was taken by Colonel Hamilton. Hamilton records that he was begged by several fellow Americans not to proceed with the enterprise as *America* was bound to be thrashed. 'The eyes of the world are on you,' one friend who had just returned from the Great Exhibition said, 'you will be beaten, and the country will be abused, as it has been in connection with the Exhibition.' When Hamilton replied that they were

America's lines

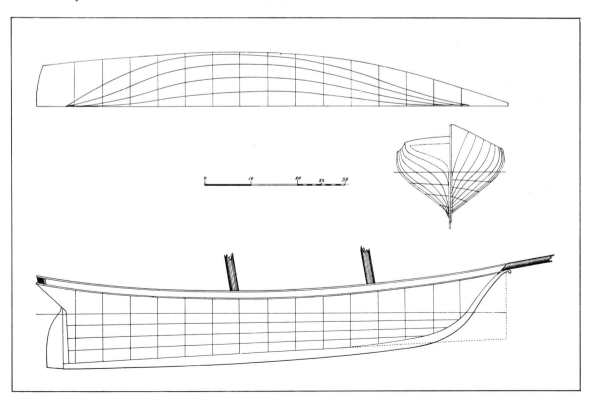

15

committed his friend snapped: 'Well, if you do go, and are beaten, you had better not return to your country.' Undeterred by such outbursts the syndicate had the yacht dry-docked at Le Havre to make her ready for the British. The French helped enthusiastically – but rather slowly – as they were all for aiding the mad Americans beat the British. Eventually on 31 July she set sail but that night had to anchor in the Solent some six miles from Cowes because of fog. There she was found by one of the Britishers' top racing yachts, *Lavrock*, which had come out to find her. The curiosity of the British was intense but it would, perhaps, have been wiser if Stevens had not allowed himself to be provoked, then and there, to test the qualities of his yacht against one of his main rivals if, as he had hoped, he would get good odds when he took wagers on *America*'s racing prowess. Be that as it may, *Lavrock*'s obvious eagerness to have some kind of trial was probably too much for the Americans to resist; they upped their anchor and set their sails, and before long had outrun *Lavrock* – who was towing her dinghy and did not therefore take the informal race perhaps quite as seriously as her adversary – eventually anchoring as much as a third of a mile in front.

Stevens recorded:

During the first five minutes not a sound was heard save, perhaps, the beating of our anxious hearts or the slight ripple of the water upon [*America*'s] sword-like stem. The captain was crouched down upon the floor of the cockpit, his seemingly unconscious hand upon the tiller, with his stern, unaltering gaze upon the vessel ahead. The men were motionless as statues, their eager eyes fastened upon the *Lavrock* with a fixedness and intensity that seemed almost supernatural. . . . It could not, nor did not last long. We worked quickly and surely to windward of her wake. The crisis was past; and some dozen of deep-drawn sighs proved that the agony was over.

It must have done wonders for their morale but it did their pockets no good at all. Despite Stevens offering a challenge for a purse of between 1000 and 10,000 guineas – 'a staggerer' one amazed witness called the larger sum – no one came forward. Then Lord Wilton asked Stevens if he would like to join in a race on the 13th in which vessels of all nations and any rig could partake. Stevens accepted though laying down fairly rigorous stipulations, but then withdrew saying he would prefer to wait upon his challenge against any other single yacht.

Earlier *The Times* had stated that the appearance of *America* at Cowes was like the 'appearance of a

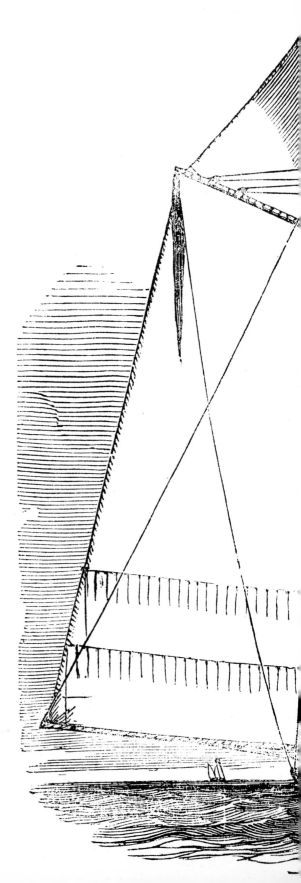

16

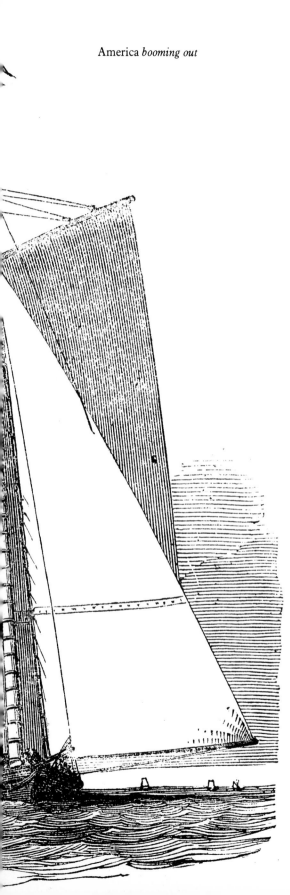

America *booming out*

sparrow-hawk among a flock of woodpigeons or skylarks. . . . The effect produced by her apparition off West Cowes among the yachtsmen seems to have been completely paralysing.'

On the 16th the paper commented tartly on the courage of British yachtsmen, and Cowes boatmen were so open in their contempt for those owners who did not dare take on the American that they offered to rig a boat themselves. One Englishman eventually came forward but the stake was paltry and it was, apparently, only the persuasiveness of Colonel Hamilton that enticed his colleagues to remain and enter a Squadron regatta.

The Squadron's standard trophy for this race, to take place on the 22 August, was an 'ordinary' cup, worth 100 guineas, and Stevens proposed to race for it. The Squadron immediately agreed, and agreed, too, at the American's request to waive the rule that yachts were not allowed to 'boom out', as the extreme rake of *America*'s masts made it essential that she be allowed to do so. The Squadron also accepted that the American yacht could withdraw if the wind did not exceed six knots, and the fact of her ownership by a syndicate, which would normally have barred her from racing in a Squadron regatta. (The Royal Victoria at Ryde had already barred her for this reason.) In fact, *America* raced on her own terms. By this time the reputation of the American yacht had spread far and wide and both the gentry and ordinary folk flocked to the island to watch the race. *The Times* commented:

In the memory of man Cowes never presented such an appearance as upon last Friday. There must have been upwards of 100 yachts lying at anchor in the Roads, the beach was crowded from Egypt [Point?] to the piers, the Esplanade in front of the club thronged with gentlemen and ladies, and the people inland who came over in shoals with wives, sons and daughters for the day. Booths were erected all along the quay, and the roadstead was alive with boats, while from the sea and shore rose an incessant buzz of voices, mingled with the splashing of oars, the flapping of sails, and the hissing of steam from the excursion vessels preparing to accompany the race.

Not all that unlike Newport on a similar occasion perhaps.

Quite unlike Newport, however, and the efficiency of the modern race committee of the N Y Y C, *The Times* correspondent goes on to mention that the cards with the names and colours of the participating yachts described the course as merely being 'round the Isle of Wight', while the printed programme

17

stated that it was to be 'round the Isle of Wight, inside No-man's buoy and Sandhead buoy, and outside the Nab'. In short, there were two sets of racing instructions!

Eighteen yachts entered the race but three dropped out. The remaining fifteen were moored in a double line, 300 yards apart. One row consisted of cutters, the other of seven schooners. It was to be an open race with no time allowances. A preparatory gun was fired at 09.55. Despite the reporter for the *Illustrated London News* recording that *America* hoisted her new jib 'with all alacrity', the visitor was last away. Colonel Hamilton stated in his reminiscences that Stevens gave orders that the sails were not to be hoisted until all the other competitors had got under way. But the most likely explanation of the delay is described by an eye witness on board, George Steers's younger nephew Henry, when he described the start some years later:

The first gun was to prepare, and then you could get up your sails – that is the schooners could hoist their fore and mainsails and the cutters their mainsails. Well, we attempted to hoist ours, and, the wind being to westward, we overran our anchor, and kept slewing around, so we had to lower them again.

Whatever the reason for her tardiness the American yacht was soon in pursuit of the others. *Gypsey Queen* led with *Beatrice* second, and all the way out to No-man's buoy the positions of the yachts changed as the wind increased and then died away. At one point a West India mail steamer got near enough to the yachts to cause an uncomfortable chop, reminding the modern reader that even during this, the first America's Cup race, the competitors were plagued as they have been ever since by spectators. The motion rendered some people aboard the various craft following the race 'ghastly looking and uncomfortable', according to *The Times*, which also recorded that at No-man's buoy only two minutes separated *America* from the leader *Volante*, and lay fifth. Three others followed close behind while the rest, as *The Times* put it, staggered about in the rear. Soon afterwards one of them, *Wyvern* returned to Cowes. *The Times* does not record how *America* managed to run through the rest of the fleet but several other sources – all American – make it clear that the American yacht was not always given free water as she gradually forged her way to the front.

In a pamphlet, 'A Chapter in the History of the Queen's Cup', issued by a Mr W. W. Evans in 1885, in answer to some 'snarlings' on the part of the *Saturday Review* as to the honesty of American yachtsmen, Evans states that 'more than a quarter of a century ago' (i.e. nine years after the race) a relation of his, a Mr John Rutherford, who had been on *America* during the race, told him:

Com. Stevens was standing on the quarter deck talking to a member of the Royal Yacht Squadron, that he carried in compliance with the rules. Chas Brown the sailing master, a New York pilot, was steering. In short time, and when near the No-Man's buoy, the *America* overhauled a large yacht. Brown attempted to pass her to windward, but the course of the yacht was changed and the *America* was headed off. Brown then attempted to pass to leeward, and was again headed off. He then, exasperated by this foul treatment, said to Mr Stevens, 'Commodore, shall I put the bow-sprit in the back of that fellow?'

Stevens said, 'No don't do it,' and turning to the member of the Royal Yacht Squadron, a Captain in the Royal Navy, said, 'Captain L, you may call this fair-play on this side of the ocean, but we, on the other side, would call it ——— foul play.'

The Captain remained mute, what could he say? His blood was probably boiling to think that any of his countrymen would attempt a dirty trick on a grand occasion when the eyes of all the yachting world were upon them.

Not the last time a club representative was to feel uneasy at the tactics of his own side!

The rest of the pamphlet does not lead one to believe particularly in the accuracy of Evans's reporting, which is hearsay anyway – but Henry Steers and another American source mention similar incidents. Whatever the difficulties the Americans may have had in establishing a lead by 11.30 they had done so.

On board *America* was an experienced local pilot called Underwood to guide her who'd been engaged by the American consul at Portsmouth. As warnings had come from several quarters not to trust anybody to pilot the yacht in such treacherous waters Stevens was very glad to receive someone who proved to be entirely reliable. Even so, according to Hamilton, Stevens received dire warnings. 'So strong was the distrust among our countrymen outside,' said Hamilton, 'that, even after the pilot was in charge, the commodore was warned by letter not to trust too much to him and urged to take another pilot to overlook him.... No one now can realize the anxieties of that contest, for we knew the ground was most unfavourable for us.' The pressure of international competition is obviously not a modern phenomenon.

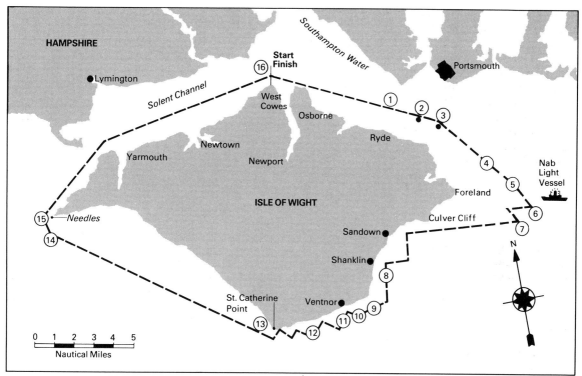

The following description of America's course round the Isle of Wight was compiled mainly from the reports printed in The Illustrated London News and The Times though other sources were used. This course is based on the one printed in Lawson's History of the America's Cup but it has had to be adjusted as the Nab Lightship – as it then was – was shown in the wrong position. The positions of America as indicated are of course very approximate.

The start was off the Royal Yacht Squadron clubhouse, West Cowes, at 1000 hours. The wind was light westerly backing WSW and then SSW variable.

1 Passing Ryde at 1030 Gypsey Queen was in the lead closely followed by America, which in a freshening breeze had passed Constance and Beatrice. Then the wind died and the smaller Volante took the lead which she immediately lost to Gypsey Queen.

2 The Sandhead Buoy was left to starboard so the yachts did not go 'inside Sandhead and Noman's buoy' as the printed programme is alleged to have specified, since the Sandhead marked Ryde Sands. Volante, Gypsey Queen and America all rounded it at 1100.

3 At Noman's buoy the order was as follows:

Volante	1107	Gypsey Queen	1108.45
Freak	1108.20	America	1109
Aurora	1108.30	Beatrice	1109.15

4 Having overtaken the leader, Volante 'off Brading' at 1130 America was now in the lead.

5 At 1137 Arrow, Bacchante, Constance and Gypsey Queen alter course to round the Nab Lightship 4.6 miles off Foreland. The Times said they stood away to the north. But this was impossible as ten minutes later it says that America tacked to the west having rounded the foreland. So the others must have been north of Foreland when they bore away to the south-east.

6 1147 America tacks towards Culver Cliffs. Her nearest rival was now two miles or more astern or to leeward.

7 1158 America tacks twice in ten minutes and runs in towards Sandown.

8 Under Shanklin Chine the tide sets against America.

9 America breaks her jib-boom off Dunnose at 1258. It can be seen what little headway she made against the wind and tide in an hour.

10 At 1500 Arrow ran aground on some rocks in this area. Also, Volante is fouled by Freak and is forced to retire.

11 Off Ventnor America is a mile ahead of Aurora.

12 At 1530 America passes St. Lawrence. Bacchante and Eclipse are 2½ miles to leeward behind her.

13 Wind on America's quarter as she passes Rocken End.

14 America nears the Needles. Aurora, the nearest yacht, was some 7½ miles astern and Freak a further mile behind.

15 At 1750 America rounded the Needles.

16 America finishes at 2037.

Four of the others, however, *Arrow*, *Bacchante*, *Constance* and *Gipsey Queen*, obeyed the other set of instructions and stood away to pass round the Nab, which, as *The Times* pointed out, was certainly the normal course to take. The rest of the fleet followed the inside course. The wind freshened and *America* opened up her lead despite being rather slow in stays when tacking. Then, at 12.58, another incident occurred which was to be repeated time and again during Cup races over the next century or so: one of *America*'s spars – her jib-boom – broke, and away went her flying jib. The skipper, who never had liked using this particular sail when working to windward, just said he was damned glad it was gone but the yacht was delayed by about a quarter of an hour while the wreckage was cleared. As it happened the breakage did not cost the syndicate a penny as Steers had got Ratsey, who had supplied the boom, to bet the cost of it that *Beatrice* would win the race, and the sailmaker to bet the cost of the sail that *America* would lose. The Americans must have been delighted that the cautious Britons had summoned enough sporting spirit to bet something on their ability or lack of it.

The incident did no great harm as her competitors by this time were miles astern – even the small tonnage cutters, *Aurora*, *Freak* and *Volante*, which could have been expected to have some advantage because of the light winds and greater manoeuvrability.

The next incident came at three o'clock when *Arrow* managed to run herself on the rocks. *Alarm* went to her assistance. At this point the wind freshened again and so great was the American yacht's apparent superiority that many of her competitors turned for home. However, three, *Aurora*, *Freak* and *Volante*, hung on, keeping close company as they hugged the coast to avoid the adverse tide while their American adversary stood right off from it. Alas, they kept too close together for *Freak* fouled *Volante* and the latter was forced to retire with her bowsprit carried away, and by 5.40, with *America* close to the Needles, *Aurora* was apparently nearly 8 miles astern with *Freak* a further mile astern of her. The others were hardly in sight. Meanwhile, the royal yacht with the Queen and the Prince Regent on board appeared off the Needles before turning and laying off Alum Bay. Lord Alfred Paget, in the royal yacht's tender, *Fairy*, was sent off round the Needles to see who was in sight while the royal party landed and went for a stroll. They did not stay long however because a wet drizzle drifted in with the wind, which was now blowing faintly from the west-south-west. Lord Paget returned, reported on the position of the American yacht, and was sent off again to see if he could spot any of the others.

The famous exchange of the Queen having been told who was first, asking who was second and being given the reply, after a pregnant pause, that there was no second, must have occurred, if it occurred at all, when Paget returned the second time. It is impossible to know now whether this exchange did occur, but with the wind now light and with only the last of the flood to help her *America* took nearly three more hours to reach the finishing line off Cowes at 8.37, having rounded the Needles at 5.50. Yet *Aurora*, reported seven or eight miles astern before *America* reached the Needles, came in only a matter of minutes later. Certainly, by this time, the weather had deteriorated and this could have made it difficult to identify the yachts. The *Morning Post* described the scene graphically; reading its report now it is easy to understand how confusion could indeed have occurred.

A cutter called the *Wildfire* ran out from Sandown Bay ahead of the *America*, and taking advantage of her favourable position, for some time kept ahead. She carried a colour similar to that of the *Aurora*, and caused a great confusion, as she was mistaken for that vessel.

There was enough going on at the time – with *America* sailing through the large spectator fleet at the Needles and then alongside the royal yacht and raising their hats and cheering and doing all sorts of unrepublican, not to say unseaman-like, actions (considering they were in the middle of a race) – for mistakes in identification to be made. It is certainly difficult to see how such a great distance could have been made up by *Aurora* in such a comparatively short time. On the other hand there seems to be no consensus of opinion as to when *Aurora* finished. One report denies that any yacht came in at all, saying that fireworks were being displayed and it was dark. Stevens himself merely said, 'I could not learn correctly at what time, and in what order, the others arrived,' while the *Illustrated London News* stated that *Aurora* arrived 21 minutes later, and others said 24. But the New York Yacht Club eventually accepted 8 minutes as being correct, and this is what *The Times* said too. *Aurora* has really never been given sufficient credit for her performance but probably if the course had been but a few miles longer the greatest yachting trophy in the world would never have left British shores and there would never have been any America's Cup races to write about. An additional injustice is that *Aurora*'s name is the only one of the vessels which started in the race that does not appear on the famous cup. By some oversight it was not engraved on it with the others.

But, however little she'd won by, the American yacht was first. Of that there was no doubt, though the owner of *Brilliant* did protest at America's short cut inside the Nab, so starting another America's Cup tradition which has been carried on by many challengers – and defenders too. But when the owner was told the facts the protest was withdrawn and Stevens received the Cup and a visit from the Queen, and a *post mortem* was the only thing remaining. This proved rigorous and long lasting, for the race had shaken British yachting circles to its aristocratic core. Letters to the papers signed by 'Matelot', 'Close-hauled', and 'A Constant Reader', demanded to know the full facts. Some compared the new wonder yacht to designs they'd seen in India, others bickered among themselves as to whether *America* had changed her masts on her arrival or merely her sails. Someone wanted to know where it was possible to buy American sailcloth in England. Someone else raised what was to become down the decades a constant complaint of the British: British yachts were built for sailing in, *America* was a mere racing machine (he obviously hadn't heard about the bathroom and the carved walnut).

So it went on for months. The crew of *America* had to bear the brunt of it because everyone, but everyone, wanted to see the yacht and she was besieged by onlookers and curious visitors. One, the Marquis of Anglesey – he who had said of *America*, 'If she's right then we're all wrong' – insisted on climbing out on to the bowsprit to watch the bow wave. After twenty minutes he climbed back on deck and said to Commodore Stevens: 'I've learned one thing, I've been sailing my yacht stern foremost for the last twenty years!' He must have been a game old man because he was eighty-three at the time and had only one leg – he'd lost the other at Waterloo. Others, however, were less ready to admit that the American yacht was superior and a rumour spread that in fact she had a secret propeller, something that the Marquis also felt compelled to investigate with the result that he nearly fell overboard trying to peer under the transom and was grabbed just in time by his host.

1870/1871

On 28 August *America* sailed her last race under the ownership of Stevens and his companions, against *Titania*, won $500, and was then sold to Lord John de Blaquiere for $5000. The Americans returned home, well satisfied with a sailing season that had not only made them a bit of money ($1750 according to Thomas Lawson in his *History of The America's Cup*) but gained them immortal fame – though at the time they could have had no idea that the rather ugly piece of silver they'd won would become one of the most expensively fought for trophies in the world.

America kept racing, however, and on 12 October 1852, beat a Swedish schooner about her own size, *Sverige*, by 26 minutes on a course from Ryde pier to a point 20 miles to leeward of the Nab Light. According to Lawson the Swedes were at that time building the finest schooners in Europe and they, along with just about every other yachtsman in England, decided to build their own version of *America*. In fact, Lawson says she was a copy. Copy or not she was no match for *America*, though Lawson commented that she was badly sailed, possibly because the crew was a mixture of Englishmen and Swedes who probably couldn't understand one another. Sweden were not to re-enter the fray until 1977.

The British did not leave it that long, but it took seventeen years for a challenger from the defeated nation to appear. It was not the loss of the Cup that offended but the fact that a foreign yacht had proved herself so obviously superior at a time when the British were under the delusion that they were the foremost yachting nation, and it must have taken some time to absorb the lessons *America* had taught them. It must be remembered too that the American Civil War occurred during this time.

'We rushed into framing and planking, pulling to pieces and building up again,' wrote *Hunt's Yachting Magazine* in February 1866, in an analysis of what was wrong with contemporary British yachting and why the security of the nation depended on as many people as possible being seafarers, 'putting sterns where bows had been, and almost we might say vice versa'. The magazine also compared the old-fashioned British yacht to a tea-chest alongside her American counterpart. To make matters worse no one seemed to want to race in deep water any more, and the *New York Herald*, taking up the same theme, scathingly commented that 'in British waters the yachts are left entirely to the care of professionals, as a racehorse is entrusted to its jockey', thereby, unwittingly perhaps, putting its finger on one of the recurring reasons why Britain has never regained her Cup.

Hunt's Yachting Magazine, however, bravely commented that once more British yachts were 'nearly approaching to perfection as possible', and at least the British were about to develop a new sail, the spinnaker. It first appeared that year in *Sphinx*, nicknamed 'Spinx' by her crew (thereby showing that the tradition of British professional crews mispronouncing the name of their vessel was already established at that time). They called the new sail a 'Spinxer'. The magazine reminded its readers that 'the ever memorable Cup won by the *America* at Cowes' was up for grabs – and had been for eight years: 'Surely when little Clyde-built cutters of 25 tons can accomplish the voyage to Australia it is not too much to expect that our leading yacht clubs would organize a fleet of powerful schooners to cross the Atlantic and wake up Uncle Sam in the Bay of New York.' The *New York Herald* replied that America was ready and waiting – though their opinion of the Cup was that it was an 'almost forgotten trophy' – and were quite keen in fact 'to undeceive' the British about the superiority they again

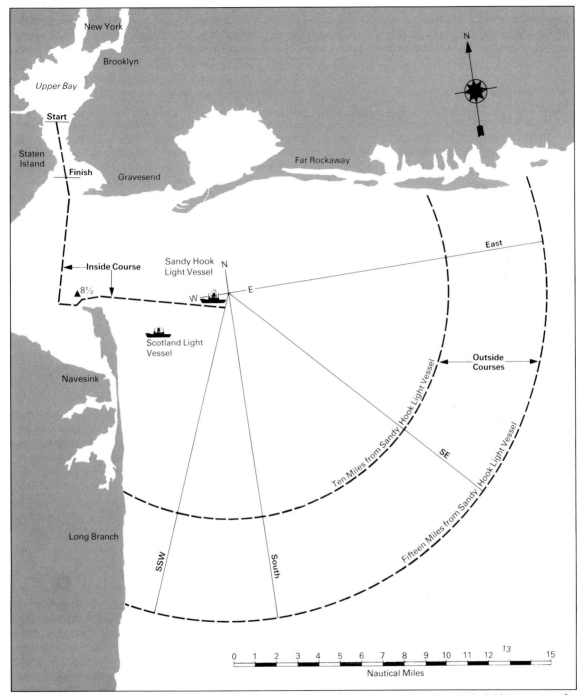

New York

Brooklyn

Upper Bay

Start

Staten
Island

Finish

Gravesend

Far Rockaway

N

East

Inside Course

Sandy Hook
Light Vessel

N

W   E

8½

Outside
Courses

Scotland Light
Vessel

Navesink

Ten Miles from Sandy Hook Light Vessel

SE

Fifteen Miles from Sandy Hook Light Vessel

Long Branch

SSW

South

0   1   2   3   4   5   6   7   8   9   10   11   12   13   15
Nautical Miles

*The courses used for the America's Cup races between
1870 and 1920.*
*Triangular courses could be laid within the extreme points
shown on the ten-mile radius from Sandy Hook Light
Vessel.*

*Windward – Leeward courses could be laid on any one of
the points shown on the fifteen-mile radius.*

*The inside course of the New York Yacht Club, shown on
the left, was last used for cup matches in 1887.*

felt about the design of their yachts. In fact the paper waxed quite belligerent about the prospect and warned the British to be quick.

The New York Yacht Club will furnish a Yankee ship and a Yankee crew to secure and retain the Cup which the *America* won. Let the English yachts come; the sooner the better. If they put off the expedition for another year they may find a fleet of American yachts ready to compete with them on their own waters in 1867. The Paris Exposition will be held in that year, and many Americans will go abroad. Some of them will go in their own yachts, and show the Englishmen not one but a dozen *Americas*.

The *Herald* proposed that besides the usual regattas in the 1866 season there should be a practice match 'for the grand contest that is to decide the relative superiority of America and England' so expressing an attitude which has remained inherent in how the two countries view the Trophy: to the Americans it is an international event of one country against another; in Britain it has always been viewed as a personal match – a British challenger does not represent the United Kingdom but an individual yacht club. Could this attitude have lessened British determination to win back the Cup?

The *Herald*'s article may have prompted the Atlantic race between three American yachts in the winter of that year and certainly the match created interest in Britain. But it was almost certainly the appearance of the American *Sappho* in British waters in 1868 that prompted the first challenger James Ashbury, a businessman and an aspiring Member of Parliament, to begin his protracted correspondence with the New York Yacht Club. His yacht, *Cambria*, was one of four to beat *Sappho* round the Isle of Wight that summer. If he could beat *Sappho*, acknowledged to be the Americans' crack yacht, 'the clipper of them all', why shouldn't he be able to win back the Squadron Cup? It must have crossed Ashbury's mind that if he succeeded it would do his candidature for parliament no harm at all, and could also increase his social standing. Ashbury was obviously a bit of a social climber, something the British abhor. The *Spirit of the Times*, the American equivalent of *Hunt's Yachting Magazine*, reported as follows:

We are sorry to hear that some ill-feeling prevails in England in regard to Mr Ashbury. We are told many English Yachtsmen say that he made the match to render himself prominent and catch popularity, and they hope the *Cambria* will be defeated

– which goes to show that in those days class went before even national pride.

It was perhaps for this reason his correspondence with the NYYC was so protracted – his proposed challenge needed time to catch the eye and imagination of his countrymen. But it is just as likely that it needed a good deal of correspondence to sort out what exactly the challenge implied. Equally likely, Ashbury was a businessman who was going to make damned sure he was going to screw every advantage he possibly could out of his opponents. He therefore proposed that the Americans would choose a champion schooner 'not to exceed 10 per cent of the Thames measurement (188 tons) of the *Cambria*' and send her across the Atlantic to compete in the 1869 season. Ashbury would then race her back across the Atlantic with no time allowance and no restrictions and then race her round Long Island 'on the Royal Thames Yacht Club measurement and their time allowances for the best of three races, this course to decide as to the championship and the final possession of the America's Queen's Cup of 1851'. However, he would not compete if he had to race a yacht built subsequent to his challenge, nor, he said, would he race against a mere shell or racing machine.

The NYYC did not accept his proposal, saying they were only interested in him racing for the Cup and that the challenge must come from a club, not an individual, as stipulated in the Deed of Gift.

Ashbury replied that he hoped to sail under the colours of the Royal Thames Yacht Club and that, if he won the Cup, he'd present it to the Royal Thames so that they could hold it 'as a challenge cup, for other clubs to compete for on a course not less than 300 miles in the channel or any other ocean'. Obviously Ashbury was keen to make sure that the Americans got the message that he wanted to race in open water; apparently receiving no response to this last communication, he cabled: 'Will the *Cambria* be allowed to sail your champion schooner for The America's Cup on basis of my letter of 20 July,' and the Club replied – deviously as it turned out – that 'the necessary preliminaries having been complied with by you upon your arrival here, you have the right, provided no match can be agreed upon, to sail over the annual regatta course of the New York Yacht Club'. While this defined what the club considered a suitable course, it left unanswered Ashbury's obvious demand that the America's Cup should be a match race, i.e. between two vessels only. Why they evaded this crucial issue is not known, but as Lawson remarked, their answer was not distinguished for its directness.

Maybe they automatically assumed that since *America* had had to face a fleet in 1851, any potential challenger must surely know he would have to do the same. However, this is a hard argument to sustain as the original Deed of Gift quite plainly used the word match, and Ashbury had repeatedly mentioned in his correspondence that he proposed racing against one vessel only. Besides, as several writers have pointed out since, it is one thing for a yacht to race with a fleet who are all racing for a cup; it is quite another for one yacht to be opposed by a whole fleet. On the other hand when one remembers that *America* was almost certainly blocked by a number of British yachts working in unison perhaps the Club's eventual decision to allow any of their members to enter the race is very understandable. It was, perhaps, simply a case of tit-for-tat; once they'd demonstrated the conditions under which *America* had won the Cup in the first place, the Club did in fact relent – but only to a degree as will be shown.

Perhaps the NYYC were so keen to get a challenge under way they didn't wish, at an early stage in the negotiations, to put a potential challenger off; perhaps they simply hadn't really decided that issue amongst themselves when replying to Ashbury and had only decided at that point that the race or races should be over their own course – as the original race had been for the English yachts. In any case, by the time all this correspondence had passed back and forth, the 1869 season had passed. And, once completed, Ashbury returned to his writing desk and proposed a match for 1870 – over a triangular course 'from Staten Island 40 miles out to sea and back', though just how he expected to perform that geographical feat he did not explain. (Staten Island is inside New York Harbour, to which there is only one long narrow entrance.) He also maintained, with a sleight of hand that did credit to a budding politician, that as the Cup was won under the rules of the Royal Yacht Squadron, which banned centreboard craft from races, that it followed 'that no centreboard vessel can compete against the *Cambria* in this particular race'.

The NYYC promptly replied that they had no intention of ignoring the terms of the Deed of Gift which stated that 'in case of disagreement' any race for the Cup was to be sailed under the rules of the club which held it. It therefore followed, they said, with the same lack of logic used by the challenger, that they could not exclude any yacht qualified

A ticket to see the first challenge

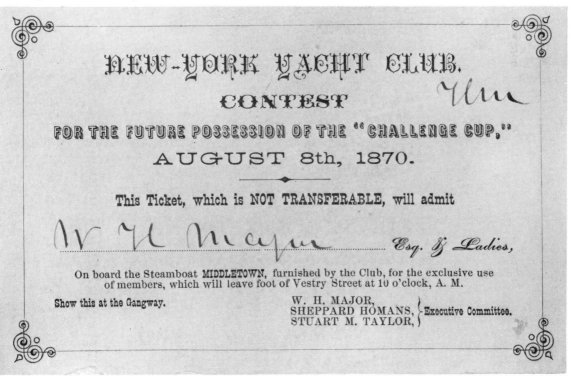

NEW-YORK YACHT CLUB.

CONTEST

FOR THE FUTURE POSSESSION OF THE "CHALLENGE CUP,"

AUGUST 8th, 1870.

This Ticket, which is NOT TRANSFERABLE, will admit

_____ Esq. & Ladies,

On board the Steamboat MIDDLETOWN, furnished by the Club, for the exclusive use of members, which will leave foot of Vestry Street at 10 o'clock, A.M.

Show this at the Gangway.

W. H. MAJOR,
SHEPPARD HOMANS, } Executive Committee.
STUART M. TAYLOR,

under the rules and regulations of the N Y Y C. But as he was coming over anyway, why didn't he discuss the matter further on his arrival?

Ashbury was crossing the Atlantic because another, equally protracted, correspondence – *Hunt's Yachting Magazine* termed it 'so long and so tedious as at one time to make it appear likely to be interminable' – with James Gordon Bennett, the owner of the American prize-winning schooner *Dauntless*, had at last come to a satisfactory conclusion about a proposed transatlantic race from Daunt's Rock, Cork Harbour, to Sandy Hook. *Cambria* won this race, despite taking a longer course, but after twenty-three days the two yachts arrived only 1 hour 43 minutes apart. This result filled the Americans with understandable apprehension. If the British could beat their crack schooner, how safe was the Cup? It is open to conjecture whether it was in the best interests of *Cambria* to win the race: it certainly must have boosted Ashbury's morale – did that *need* boosting? – but it equally certainly put paid to his again-repeated argument that the race for the Cup should be a match race and that centreboarders should be excluded. The N Y Y C voted, eighteen to one, that any or all of the club's fleet could enter. There would be one race only and this would take place over the Club's regular inside course. If Mr Ashbury didn't accept these conditions then there would be no race.

Once faced with this ultimatum it didn't take Ashbury long to make up his mind. The war of words was over. It was now time for action, and he decided he'd better get on with it. It is impossible to re-create the atmosphere in which Ashbury and the N Y Y C had negotiated the terms of the race, but it would probably not be unfair to either side to say that the Americans felt somewhat irritated, even belligerent, with what they regarded as the Britishers' quite unfounded sense of superiority when dealing with their American cousins in the matters of yachting – or anything else too perhaps – while the British possibly thought the Americans too sharp and legalistic. Sailing in their view was a sport, and a gentleman's one at that – and sport was not the place for a legal or verbal wrangle.

The day of the race, 8 August, dawned overcast and gloomy, but by 9 o'clock the clouds had cleared and for the rest of the day the sun shone and the wind blew steadily: 'fresh breeze from south-by-east to south-southeast, with smooth water', the official report stated. The race caused enormous interest and the water was filled with craft of all sorts and

sizes, and on land thousands gathered to watch. There were eighteen entries, including the original *America*, now owned by the United States Navy. The course was from Robbins Reef through the narrows to South-west Spit buoy, around Sandy Hook Lightship and back – a distance of about 35 miles. The start was from a line near the N Y Y C's club-house at Clifton, Staten Island, and was to be from anchor. An American Naval officer, Lt Kelley, writing about the race some fifteen years later in his

The first challenger, Cambria, *heading for the outer mark. The winner,* Magic, *is passing her homeward bound followed by* Idler, Dauntless *and* America

book *American Yachts*, does not report, despite the obvious authenticity of his description of the race, that just before the start the wind shifted. So *Cambria*, who'd been given the courtesy position at the windward end of the line, in fact started to leeward of the fleet. A report in the *Field* presumably by someone who was on board her during the race gives an evocative account:

The wind remained steady up to ten o'clock, when it veered to south, and this veering made the *Cambria's* selected station the leeward one. We directly saw that it was going to be a bad business, and, unless we could set away clear by sheer smartness, there was very little chance of our getting to the front during any part of the match. One thing we considered a matter of congratulation, and that was that the rule of the club was to start with all sail set but head sail. This rule, however, appears to be not a 'standing order', as a member of the committee rowed alongside just as we had got our last pulls on the throat and peak halyards, and informed us that the start was to be with all sails down. Thus vanished our last hope of a successful start, as we knew where the little ones would be by the time we got fairly under way.

The river was already crowded with steamboats, who never seemed tired of steaming around us, with their whistles shrieking by way of salutation, and their crowds of spectators shouting 'hooray' three times three, and 'coming up' with a pure Americanism, the word 'tiger'. There were bands, too, that played 'God Save the Queen' and then 'Yankee Doodle', 'Rule Britannia' and 'Hail Columbia'. This was all very pleasant to the ear; but what concerned us was to know where all these steamboats – some of them huge river boats with 300 people on board – would be when the eighteen yachts were under way beating through the Narrows. Our anxiety on this head was quite premature – the steamboats never molested a single yacht throughout the match, and better management among steamboat captains could not possibly have been. They all declared rather ostentatiously that the 'Britisher should have fair play', and we were more than gratified that their word was a bond.

After a poor start *Cambria* was baulked by some of her opponents. No doubt the Americans had not forgotten the treatment handed out to their yacht nearly twenty years before. The *Field* reported that, among other incidents, *Cambria* was 'jockeyed by the *Fleetwing*, that vessel shaking up to keep her from passing to leeward'.

Kelly reports that *Cambria* lost her foretopmast near the finish but he does not mention what the *Spirit of the Times* subsequently noted:

She also incurred a little delay by being fouled by *Tarolinta* which, being on the starboard tack ought to have kept away from her, by the rules, when she could not go to windward of her. Some think her head gear was a little damaged in this foul, and that the carrying away of her foretopmast (later) was the result of it.

This loss did not affect the race because *Cambria* was nowhere near winning when it happened and, in fact, finished eighth (tenth on time allowance) but it is curious that if Ashbury had suspected a foul he did not protest. By all accounts he was not the sort of man to let such an incident go by without comment – yet he made no mention of it at the time. However, once home the rumour soon spread that *Cambria* had been fouled and no less an authority than Sir George Leach, a vice-president of the Yacht Racing Association, stated some years later that *Cambria* was fouled, 'carrying away a fore-port-shroud, and

foretopmast-backstay, and springing the port arm of her forecross trees', which is a sufficiently comprehensive catalogue of the damage to make an unprejudiced reader feel there must be something in the report. But it could be that a comment by the *Field* some fifteen years after the race revealed the truth behind *Cambria*'s difficulties with her opponents:

Oddly enough the *Cambria* in 1870 was put about by competing yachts when she was on the starboard tack no fewer than six times, and at last came into collision with *Tarolinta*.... We believe this was owing to the fact that many of the owners of the competing yachts had never sailed a match before; at any rate Commodore Stebbins the next day had the rule as to port and starboard tack printed on a slip of paper, and sent on board each yacht. He also had it posted in the club house at Staten Island.

Whatever the truth of it, at the time Ashbury took his defeat in good part and continued racing in American waters for other trophies, while the winner of the race, *Magic*, 'immediately achieved a national reputation'. *America* came fourth which caused everyone disappointment, 'the public prayer being' that *Cambria* be beaten and that best of all it should be *America* which would do it.

During the same month as he raced for the Cup, Ashbury ordered another schooner from the builder of *Cambria*, Michael Ratsey of Cowes, so he must have known even then that he was going to return to have another try. The schooner was called *Livonia*, after a province in Russia where her owner had built a railway, and she was launched on 6 April 1871. Ashbury also consulted lawyers who almost certainly came up with the advice that he should attack the N Y Y C at their weakest point – their interpretation of the word 'match'. Ashbury wrote them in January 1871 saying that if they insisted on maintaining their interpretation of the word he would sail the course alone and claim the Cup. If his claim was rejected it would then be 'for the New York judges to determine upon legal construction of the deed referred to'. In other words Ashbury would take them to court, though he said afterwards; 'I had not thought of being guided by court legal decisions.'

The tone of his letter was far from courteous and indeed the whole tone of his correspondence over his second challenge was, as Lawson succinctly described it, 'notable chiefly for its acrid character'.

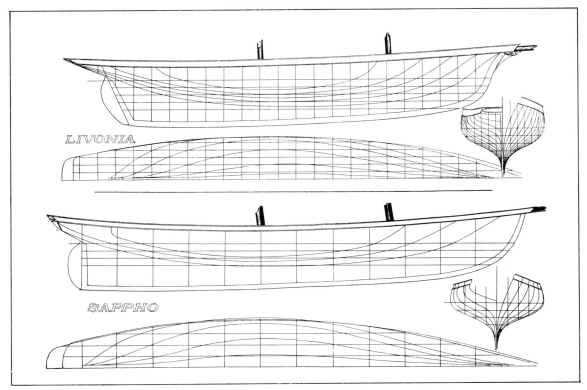

The lines of Livonia *and* Sappho

But, as Lawson also pointed out, Ashbury's stance did, in fact, work at least partly in his favour. It certainly made the N Y Y C wake up to the fact that they could have a very unpleasant situation on their hands. They hurried to consult lawyers, judges, and other sportsmen on their predicament, and in the end they asked the only surviving donor of the Cup, George Schuyler, what he thought. Schuyler, in a letter to the *Spirit of the Times*, wrote that he felt the present conditions as laid down by the N Y Y C made the America's trophy 'useless' as a challenge cup and that in his opinion the word match meant only two contestants. This settled the matter.

Ashbury, hearing of his victory on this vital point, cabled the N Y Y C on 27 May that if they would waive the six months' notice necessary he would sail in September 1871 and race in October. After consultation the Club sent a cable which made quite clear they intended one race against the representative of one yacht club:

The N Y Y C consents to waive the six months' notice, and accepts your challenge as representative of the Royal Harwich Yacht Club – Race for America's Cup next October. Name day in October you desire to race, and answer immediately.

A week passed, however, before Ashbury sent the following extraordinary telegram:

This stipulated notice having been waived, the several clubs will shortly send you necessary certificates for the *Livonia*'s matches some time in October.

This cable must have been received with groans of dismay. What was the wretched man up to now? This latest cable, the Club Committee later wrote, was

so utterly inconsistent with the wording and *our* understanding of the previous correspondence, that a clear conception of its meaning was impossible. What several clubs? Up to this time *we* had heard of but one . . . [the telegram] in fact seemed so entirely irrelevant, to say the least, to the subject matter of the correspondence, as not to require any reply in that connection. Our only proper course was to await further explanation from its writer.

And this is just what they did, but by the time Ashbury's letter of explanation of 12 August arrived it was too late for anyone to write back to tell him not to bother to come.

What he proposed in this letter – 'that he would sail as the representative of twelve clubs in a series of twelve races, one for each club, seven out of twelve to win, and the cup to go to the club under whose colours he sailed in the winning race' – was discussed by Commodore Bennett, and such other members of the Club as could be reached, on board *Dauntless*, and it was decided, in order to make 'all possible concessions', that they would accede to Ashbury's wish for twelve races but that he would have to race them all under the flag of the Royal Harwich. However, they tartly pointed out, the races were not '*the* series of twelve races', as stipulated by Ashbury, but merely 'a series of twelve races', and this was only a recommendation which had to be ratified by the Club, as no formal meeting could be held outside the City of New York. This recommendation, the NYYC pamphlet says, was surely 'sufficiently clear and explicit for even the dullest comprehension'.

However, on his arrival in New York on 1 October aboard *Livonia*, Ashbury once more opened his correspondence with the NYYC demanding first this and then that, the Club replying in equally stiff terms. Despite being convinced that he had the right to sail twelve races under twelve different flags Ashbury eventually agreed to the Club's final proposal to sail the best of seven races, three over the inside club course and four – including the last two – over an outside course. At some point during the interminable wrangle the Club decided to retain the right to field four defenders

Columbia

even though there was only one challenger, a move that historians on both sides of the Atlantic have agreed was less than fair. Be that as it may, in the end Ashbury agreed to race. 'It's becoming cold,' he's reported to have said. 'Let's get it over with.'

The first race took place on the inside course on 16 October. The wind was light and the schooner, *Columbia*, was chosen in preference to *Sappho* – they were both at the starting line. *Columbia* won by over 27 minutes on corrected time. She was chosen again for the second race on the outside course on 18 October and won by just over $10\frac{1}{2}$ minutes on corrected time and established a racing record for 30 miles in doing so, a remarkable performance which showed that even in a strong blow the 'skimming dishes' – so despised by the British as being mere 'racing machines' – were capable of racing in open water.

At the end of this race Ashbury entered a protest on the ground that *Columbia* had rounded the stake-boat incorrectly. Kelley, writing on the incident in his book, said that in England the rule was that, when no instructions were given, all marks were to be left on the starboard hand. *Livonia* received no instructions so carried out a rather dangerous gybing manoeuvre that not only made her stagger to leeward of the mark, thus losing time, but left no doubt in the minds of the spectators that Ashbury thought that he was obliged to leave the mark to starboard. *Columbia* however, slightly astern of *Livonia* at the time but to weather, passed the mark to port and in a wind which was blowing, according to Kelley, a moderate gale, stowed her topsails, reefed her foresail and flew home on a reach. Some commentators have remarked that the incident made little difference to the result but this is to be doubted – and certainly Ashbury doubted it and he demanded the race be given to him. The Sailing Committee, however, promptly replied: 'The sailing regulations for the outside course, a printed copy of which was furnished to you, leaves the matter of turning the stake optional.'

In short, it appeared that Ashbury had not done his homework. If this is true he was not the only challenger to have failed on that score – it could be argued that Sopwith lost the 1934 Challenge for that same reason. However, it was not quite as simple as it seemed. For one thing it had been agreed that the outside course would be 40 miles not 30, which is what it turned out to be, and for another it seems definitely odd that *Columbia*'s afterguard, experienced men who must have known the sailing regulations of the N Y Y C off by heart, nevertheless felt it necessary to ask the committee before the race began which side of the mark they should pass. This is confirmed by one of the yachting authorities of the day, Captain Roland F. Coffin, who sailed on *Columbia* that day:

Previous to the start, when the owner of the *Columbia* brought the written instructions on board, his captain after reading them said, 'There is no direction as to the turning mark, how shall I turn it?'

'I'll go and see,' said Mr Osgood (owner of *Columbia*), and getting into his gig again he went on board the committee boat and returned with the instruction, 'Turn as you please.'

Someone somewhere had made a mistake. The *Spirit of the Times* wrote:

as it was clear that one captain had explicit instructions which the other did not have, Mr Ashbury was perfectly justified in asking for another race, [and] the committee was at fault in not acceding to him.

The press generally were on the side of the challenger and perhaps it was their hostility that flustered the Committee into defending their actions by trying to draw an exact parallel between the present race and that of 1851. Even discounting the controversy of the rounding of the stake-boat there was still the question of the course being some 10 miles less than agreed. The Committee did not exactly

enhance its reputation for efficiency with the third race either – though this time it worked in the challenger's favour. When the day of the race dawned none of the four boats reserved for racing the challenger were fit to cross the start line. Two of them, *Palmer* and *Dauntless*, had torn sails; *Sappho* was in dock; *Columbia* – whose crew had not expected to be called again – had strained rigging, and her sailing master, Nelson Comstock, had hurt his hand and could not take command. This catalogue of damage was doubtless caused by the strong winds of the previous day but with hindsight – always the easiest position from which to criticize – one would have thought it would have been prudent of the Committee to restrain *Dauntless* and *Palmer*, or at least one of them, from shadowing the two competing yachts. By doing so they had laid themselves open to damage and, though *Dauntless*'s sail was mended, one of her stays was fouled by the hawser as she was being towed to the starting line, and was carried away. It was then suggested that *Magic*, the winner of the 1870 race, should sail against the challenger, a proposal Ashbury found quite acceptable. In fact he said he would sail any American schooner provided they found him some kind of adversary. But the Committee, with a punctiliousness that did them credit, decided that they could only elect one of the four previously chosen defenders. Kelley says, after careful research, he was satisfied that Ashbury acted 'with fairness and courtesy, for he waived his undoubted right, both to sail at the hour appointed and to claim as his competitor the yacht which had been previously announced as the American representative for that day'.

Osgood was approached again, and in preference to seeing *Livonia* sail over the course alone he agreed to let *Columbia* race. Hands were lent from *Dauntless* and Nelson Comstock's brother Andrew from *Magic*; the crew was completed with a motley collection of amateurs which included an actor and a magazine editor. Osgood, by all contemporary accounts, was not able to sail, though a later historian says he took the wheel. Wherever he was, he must have been dismayed at how *Columbia* fared and how much damage was done.

Her fore-gafftopsail went first and at the Southwest Spit her flying-jib stay snapped. Without her flying jib she was unbalanced but, instead of reefing the main, the Americans pressed on until eventually, and not surprisingly, the steering gear broke and they had to smash the nickel-bound mahogany wheel box in order to rig up an emergency tiller. The

The second defender, Sappho, *passing through* Livonia's *lee in the fourth race of the second challenge, 23 October 1871.* Livonia *carried 18,153 square feet of canvas, the largest ever borne by a challenger*

next piece of gear to part was the maintopmast-staysail sheet and the staysail thrashed itself to ribbons. At this point, with the emergency steering working badly, the Americans decided that discre-tion was the better part of valour and, lowering their main, finished without further trouble.

With all that happening you would have thought that *Livonia* would have won by about an hour but in fact it was only by 20 minutes (15 min 10 secs corrected time); it would probably have been less if the committee had managed to wait until *Columbia* had at least cast off her tow rope before starting the race.

The reception *Livonia* got from the crowd was, as the *New York Times* put it, 'tolerably good, but we have heard it a little more enthusiastic'. As the same paper reported that when the British yacht had rounded the light ship ahead '*Livonia* was permitted to round and start on her homeward journey in silence' it seems a fair assumption that her win was not a particularly popular one. No one was to know

in those far-off days that to see a challenger win a race was to witness an historic event.

To make up for the error of their ways the Committee had three of the four defenders at the start line for the fourth race which took place two days later, and *Sappho* was eventually chosen to sail the course as the wind was light – though it increased considerably later. *Sappho*, of course, was an old opponent and had beaten *Livonia* twice already that summer on the other side of the Atlantic. She did so again convincingly by over half an hour on elapsed time, and then rounded off the series – at least so far as the Americans were concerned – by winning the fifth by almost as big a margin. It was all over!

It was not, so far as Ashbury was concerned. He still considered he had won the second race so the score was not four to one but three to two; he was, thank you very much, going to be at the start the next day, and if the Committee did not send a defender he would sail the course alone and claim the race. In the event he did not sail alone because he had a private race with *Dauntless* – which thrashed *Livonia* – but he had sailed the course alone so far as the Cup races were concerned. He planned a second private race the next day with *Dauntless*, but the weather was so bad the stake-boat couldn't go out. However, as no defender appeared at the line, Ashbury claimed that race too. That meant he'd won two by default. Add two and two, and that made four, so he'd won back the Cup and he asked for it to be delivered to him. When it wasn't he went home much aggrieved.

Once there he fired off an enormously long letter detailing every grievance that he could lay his hands on. In it he accused the Club of 'unfair and unsportsmanlike proceedings'. Next time, he warned, if there was a next time, he'd ship a lawyer with him. The Club then returned all the cups Ashbury had presented to it. This made Ashbury even more furious and, not content with abusive letters, he issued a pamphlet on the whole affair which in turn drove the Club into writing a letter of protest at the pamphlet's language to the Royal Harwich Yacht Club. Ashbury, they said 'seems to look behind every action for an unworthy motive, and seek in every explanation evidences of concealment and want of candour'. It took years for the furore to die down, and the feeling between yachtsmen of the two countries was so strong that the following year, when *Sappho* was entered for a regatta race at Le Havre, her owner withdrew when he realized he'd be racing against Ashbury.

Canada tries – and fails

3

1876/1881

For a long time after the Ashbury affair the British felt disinclined to challenge again for the America's Cup. The Canadians stepped into the breach, and it is quite possibly they who were responsible for the continuation of the races. Without them they could simply have died a natural death.

When a challenge eventually did arrive, in April 1876, there is little doubt that the New York Yacht Club was glad to receive it, as the Club was in the doldrums, with the membership declining and its finances shaky. In America's centenary year they saw a challenge for the Cup as giving a boost to the sport of yacht racing just when it needed it most. So, even if Ashbury hadn't learnt anything by his policy of confrontation, the Club had, and its attitude to the new challenger was therefore a good deal less intransigent.

The challenge was made by Major Charles Gifford, Vice Commodore of the Royal Canadian Yacht Club of Toronto, head of a syndicate building a schooner specially for the challenge. Her name was *Countess of Dufferin*, in honour of the Governor General's wife, and she was designed and built by a Captain Alexander Cuthbert. Cuthbert, besides being impecunious, was not, according to Lawson, a very original designer and Lawson agrees with the contemporary expert, Captain Coffin, that Cuthbert stole the new challenger's lines from a New Jersey boatbuilder. This builder had designed a sloop for a Canadian yachtsman which turned out to be the fastest on Lake Ontario. Cuthbert swore he would build a yacht to beat her, and did so – she was called *Annie Cuthbert* – by partially copying her lines. In Coffin's opinion Cuthbert thought he 'had only to make an enlarged *Annie Cuthbert*, stick two masts in it and come to New York and capture the Cup'. Certainly American newspapers commented that the challenger had . . .

nothing foreign about her. Her shape is American. Her rig is American. Her steering gear is of New York manufacture. From stem to stern, inside and out, alow and she is simply a Yankee yacht built in Canada.

This comment was not meant to be uncomplimentary; indeed in context it was expressed in a way which implied that 'imitation was the sincerest form of flattery'. The same paper compared the challenger favourably with a British yacht anchored next to her in New York harbour. Kelley, however, states quite bluntly in *American Yachts* that the challenger's 'differences were such as ought to have convinced anybody but a tyro that she was not in rig, equipment, and design of our type'. He quotes at length a detailed analysis of the differences between the challenger and her American counterparts by a writer calling himself 'Devoted Yachtsman'. After reading 'Devoted Yachtsman's' very detailed, and obviously expert, descriptions of the Canadian yacht's lines, build and rigging, and comparing them with a wide variety of American yachts, it is hard to see why Lawson, who must have read 'Devoted Yachtsman's' piece as well as Kelley's comment, ignores it totally.

Whatever her origins, the Canadian challenger was by and large greeted with derision when she arrived in New York. Even the writer of the Annals of the Royal Canadian Yacht Club says that the challenge was 'more courageous than wise'. The Club, having waived the six months' notice that had to be given by a challenger, arranged a series of three races for mid July; this was later postponed a month as the defender *Madeleine* had to take part in the Brooklyn Yacht Club Cruise.

The successful defender of the first Canadian challenge, Madeleine
Countess of Dufferin *ready for launching at Cuthbert's shipyard, Coburg, Ontario*

Negotiations were amicable, the only hint of trouble coming when the Club replied to Major Gifford's query as to whether they proposed to sail one yacht against him, or pick four as they had done with Ashbury, 'or whether it is to be an open race for all the yachts of the New York Yacht Squadron'. The Club replied cryptically, merely saying that 'a yacht would be at the starting point on the morning of each race to sail the match'. Gifford, however, reading between the lines, declined these terms courteously, saying

with the very large number of available yachts in your club, of sizes and rigs, some centreboard, others keel, that you are to have the unmistakeable advantage over me of selecting, on the morning of the race, according to wind and weather, whichever vessel you think the most likely to outsail me. Just nominate one boat.

And this is eventually what the Club did, a significant step forward in the development of the races.

Five yachts seemed likely candidates to defend, *Palmer*, *Columbia*, *Tidal Wave*, *Madeleine* and *Idler*, but when an elimination race was proposed only the last two came to the start line. *Madeleine* won, and she was subsequently chosen to defend. This, the first trial race, showed that the Americans were not latecomers when it came to thorough preparation for a challenge.

On the other hand, everything about the Canadian challenge was hurried. It was a scramble to get *Countess of Dufferin* ready for her departure from Lake Ontario in June as she had only been laid down in February. Many years later Stinson Jarvis, the yachting writer and lawyer who was to declare that the second Deed of Gift was illegal, said that she had only been paid for by the hat being passed round at the Royal Canadian Yacht Club. 'I think,' wrote Jarvis in 1901, 'I still own $5 worth of an American Cup challenger which I am now willing to sell at a reduced price.' He also mentions that the amateurs on board had to pay their own passage. Once the Canadian challengers set sail it was found that her mainsail, which had been made at Kingston, was too large, so she had to stop at Quebec – where Gifford had time to dash off a letter to the papers denying that his yacht was other than of Canadian origin – and have a new mast stepped before proceeding down the St Lawrence and on to New York. Short of training – and indeed experience – as the Canadian crew was, it would have seemed reasonable to assume that they would use the passage for much-

needed training. But a description of the voyage written by someone who was on board, which appeared in *Hunt's Yachting Magazine*, made it sound a relaxed cruise. The yacht was received critically at Halifax, one newspaper reporting that the commander and crew smiled in a 'self-satisfied way' when questioned about their chances but

The general opinion of her was unfavourable. She has been constructed on principles different from those commonly received here, and as she was turned out in a hurry she is in a rough state which can hardly fail to provoke smiles from the New Yorkers. . . . If the strange-looking craft carries off The Queen's Cup there will be a revolution in yachtbuilding in New York.

Nevertheless descriptions of her alleged speed were telegraphed from various points, and the rumour got around quickly in New York yachting circles that the new challenger was a crack yacht and the Cup in danger. How often that was to happen in future years and how often it has been totally without foundation. It was obvious immediately *Countess of Dufferin* arrived that she was going to be no match for the Americans, it was extremely fortunate for her that the races were postponed a month so that she could get herself in some sort of order.

Kelley says that a large number of alterations were made on the Canadian yacht including her booms being lengthened and new canvas being bent on, but a previously unpublished letter now in the possession of the NYYC denies this. Although written many years after the event, the letter has a ring of authenticity about it and throws an interesting light on the help the Canadians needed, and received, from the Americans.

Mr Nicholson Kane   New York Dec. 16 1896

Dear Sir,

I have made enquiries about yacht – *Countess of Dufferin* – and learn that the main boom and gaff were not lengthened.

She was hauled out at Port Richmond near Elenpark, S I, and pot leaded – had a new mainsail and lug foresail and fore and mainsail topsails. Also borrowed Baloon Jib and mainstop stay sail.

Mr Joseph Ellsworth was pilot on 2nd days race – being a friend of one of the owners – He says they had a very poor outfit and very little money. Mr Ellsworth advanced money to pay the crew before they would sail the 2nd days race.

On the race from Sandy Hook Lightship to Brentons reef light and back, Mr Phillip Ellsworth was the Pilot. I saw him two or three days ago and he informed me that this race was sailed with old mainsail – and that the lee rigging had to be slacked up so as to get leach of foresail to stand anywhere.

Mr Philip Ellsworth says he may call to mind some other matters in connection with the races of that date. His place of business is foot West 10th Street.

Respectfully yours

Kim Sawyer

Besides Ellsworth's help, local men augmented the crew and, in the account written for *Hunt's Yachting Magazine* by the gentleman on board *Countess of Dufferin*, the Canadian yacht was also given an extensive overhaul by the Americans. 'Whatever Americans may or may not be good for,' he says, 'on one point I am in a position to speak, and that is that they can put a yacht in fine racing condition.' As on her arrival it was reported that her sails 'set like a purser's shirt on a handspike', her hull was 'as rough as a nutmeg grater' and that she looked what she was, a freshwater boat, it was just as well that there was some expertise on hand.

Just before the races began an enterprising paper, the *Graphic*, ran to ground Mr Ashbury, who happened to be in the country, and asked him his opinion on the forthcoming race. The luckless reporter obviously received short shrift from the Englishman who replied that 'he had taken no interest whatever in the coming contest'; when asked about the origin of the Queen's Cup, Ashbury replied: 'It is not the Queen's Cup. You may call it the King's Cup, or President Grant's Cup, or anything of that sort, you know, but the Cup was given by the Royal Yacht Squadron as an ordinary prize.' From the tone of the interview it could be fairly said that his defeat still rankled with Ashbury. Luckily, however, the antipathy caused by it in England had begun to fade. When *Countess of Dufferin* arrived she dropped her hook next to an English yacht, *Helen*, belonging to the Royal Harwich, which showed that the English were at least on visiting terms once more.

Madeleine, owned by John S. Dickerson, was the very antithesis of her opponent. She was sleek, fast, manned by an expert crew, and was undoubtedly the fastest yacht in the Club having, in a run from Sandy Hook to Cape May the year before, 'showed a clean pair of heels to five of our best schooners'. In the regatta which followed she beat such top racers as *Rambler*, *Resolute*, *Idler*, *Dreadnought*, and *Eva*, then outsailed *Mohawk*, after which, to quote

Kelley, 'whenever the spirit seizes her, she has a way of scampering through the squadron, that keeps her memory green'. She was so good that her then owner, a Mr Voorhis, refused to race because he said her presence prevented others from entering the competitions. Kelley certainly had a very high opinion of her saying, 'The *Madeleine* is, in my belief, one of the fastest yachts ever built.' This is not, he added,

from the possession of any principles of design which can be formulated, for naval architecture is as yet too inexact a science to be employed here, but because her performances have been marvellous; and when least expected, even yet she shows such extraordinary speed, that I can not but consider her an enigma.

It is hardly surprising therefore that the hurriedly built, poorly manned challenger was beaten two–nil by margins in excess of 10 minutes and 27 minutes. The races themselves were of little consequence in the history of the Cup except for the fact that for the first time the yachts started the races under sail, not from anchor. It is also worth recording something else which started with this challenge and has continued ever since: the spectator fleet got in the way. The eye-witness on board *Countess of Dufferin* recorded in *Hunt's Yachting Magazine* that New York Bay was 'literally swarming with craft of all models, rigs, and sizes'. It was, the writer said, 'a beautiful sight', but added a footnote which was echoed over and over for the rest of the century:

It is somewhat singular that small boats seem to have a fascination for being run down; in a crowded roadstead, with large vessels flying about and others at anchor, with barely room to go about in, they invariably seem to get almost under the forefoot; such was our experience and it was enough to stop one's breath to see the hairbreadth escapes some of these small boats had, and it was a relief when the starting gun fired.

What he did not say specifically was that the Canadian challenger's start of the first race was baulked by a brig anchored near the line. It did not make any difference to the result, though the press the next day was a good deal more flattering than perhaps the challenger deserved. 'Splendid sailing of the Canadian, and the result today doubtful,' were the headlines of a paper the next day; it added 'The *Countess of Dufferin* beaten by 11 minutes only' – which will amuse the contemporary Cup competitor who knows only too well that split seconds count and

Scenes and incidents of the second race between Madeleine *and* Countess of Dufferin, *12 August 1876, from the* New York Daily Graphic

1 *At the anchorage*
2 *Passing the forts, the* Madeleine *leading*
3 *The* Countess of Dufferin
4 *The* Wanderer *saluting the* Madeleine
5 *The* Gladwish, *judges' boat*
6 *The* Madeleine *turning Sandy Hook*
7 *The* Madeleine *rounding the lightship*
8 *French man-of-war*
9 *The* Countess *setting her balloon jib*
10 *The* Madeleine *passing the winning line*

one-tenth of a knot advantage is an overwhelming one.

The second race was a disaster, the Canadian yacht being beaten not only by *Madeleine* but by the other yachts, including *America*, which tagged along for the sport. At one point the American pilot Ellsworth took in the *Countess*'s jibstopsail, which made her slump to leeward, and later he hoisted the maintopmast staysail upside down – though the reporter recording the race seems to imply this was a deliberate tactic. Whether it was or not it did her no good and the Canadian challenger finished last, and in darkness.

So decisive a defeat did not, however, reduce Cuthbert's enthusiasm to try again. He would, he said, have work done on *Countess of Dufferin* in New York to improve her hull and rigging, and then challenge the next year. But he and Major Gifford became involved in financial argument. This resulted in the law interceding, and the barring of the yacht from sailing. Cuthbert, obviously a resourceful man, nevertheless managed to regain command of his vessel and was well on his way back to Canada before anyone could prevent him. The wrangle was eventually settled legally; *Countess of Dufferin* was sold to a Chicago businessman, and she had a long and successful racing career, but there was no more talk of her trying again for the Cup.

On 15 August 1876 there appeared in the *Toronto Evening Telegram* a bitter denunciation of the inadequacy of the challenge and of the 'patronizing tone' of the American press to the challenger; blame was laid squarely upon the owners of the yacht, saying that the yacht was not representative of Canadian yachts and that the owners 'represented only Cobourg and themselves'. After remarking – yet again – on all the deficiencies of *Countess of Dufferin*, the paper pointed out:

New York is only a few hours ride from Canada, and it would have been an easy task to know, from observation, just what sails could have been carried in a race for the coveted 'cup', and to have carefully found out all the strong points of the New York yachts. But all this was neglected.... Now that the race is over, and that Cobourg has been beaten, we trust that the original plan of building a truly representative Canadian yacht will be carried out to contest for this trophy.

In fact there was no more talk of anyone challenging for the Cup for several years. Then in January 1881 the *Sun* newspaper in New York reported a note in the *Field* of London that English yachtsmen

were again taking an interest in the cup won at Cowes by the *America* in 1851, and if it were made certain that two or three single-handed matches with the same vessel could be sailed for the cup, some British yachtsman would make a challenge.

However, when another challenge did come, in May 1881, it came again from Canada and from a club that sounded even less representative of that nation, the Bay of Quinte. And they challenged on behalf of no other than Mr Cuthbert.

In the intervening years a change had begun to take place in the design of American yachts. It had become acknowledged, through a series of fatal knock-downs – including *Mohawk* which capsized with the loss of several lives while *Countess of Dufferin* was in New York – that the shallow-draft centreboard hull of the typical American racing yacht of the period had become extreme and was unstable and dangerous. A hull with greater depth, less breadth, and outside lead ballast, was therefore developed, with a centreboard being fitted to work through the yacht's keel. This started the trend of a compromise between the American shallow-draft hull and the deep-keeled British type and brought about an increased interest in the cutter rig. But when the challenge came for a race between two vessels of this rig there were still only five single-masted yachts amongst all the NYYC Squadron, and none stood out as an ideal defender.

David Kirby, the designer of the sloop, *Arrow*, a flyer amongst single-stickers but not belonging to the NYYC, volunteered to build a defender specially for the match. His offer was gladly accepted. *Pocahontas* proved a failure – in fact she sailed so badly during the Cup trials that she was nicknamed 'Pokey' – but she goes down in the history books as being the first yacht built specially to defend the Cup. The eventual defender, *Mischief*, which emerged from the trials as being the best yacht for the purpose, also created a first, for she was built of iron and had been designed on a drawing board instead of from a model by the traditional 'rule-of-thumb' method. She was a real departure from the usual 'skimming dish' and was closer – ironically, when it's remembered how out of fashion they became after *America*'s visit in 1851 – to the traditional English cutter. Even more ironic was the fact that she was owned by an Englishman, Captain J. B. Busk, but the Club could see no reason why this should disbar him.

Mischief winning the first race, 9 November 1881. She was the first centreboard sloop to defend the Cup and was nicknamed 'The Iron Pot' as she was made of iron

39

Curiously she was probably not the fastest yacht in the Squadron. This accolade fell on a yacht called *Gracie*. But *Gracie*, under the rating system then in use, would have had to concede 8 minutes or thereabouts to the new challenger, while *Mischief* conceded less than 3. The owners of *Gracie* did not agree with the Club's choice; the ensuing war of words at least proved that the long-suffering holders of the America's Cup did not just raise the ire of foreign challenging yachtsmen. The Club also managed to infuriate the press on both sides of the line. The *Toronto Globe*, doubtless reflecting the anger Canadians still felt about the earlier challenge, rather jumped the gun by saying that the Club was 'about to resort to the discreditable tactics it has formerly adopted' by refusing to name a single defender; and when it did just that it was attacked with equal fury by some American newspapers which said that it was 'conceding advantages to which no challenging party is entitled'.

The name of the Canadian challenger was *Atalanta*. She was, if anything, less prepared than her predecessor had been and a lot slower in getting launched. In fact, the rumour began to circulate that she was not going to be ready in time, and it was remarked, 'if this much-vaunted yacht is as slow as her owner, she will need a time allowance of hours instead of minutes and seconds'. Cuthbert said that the reason for the delay was other work he had to do and his limited manpower resources.

One American newspaper thought this excuse lame; it went on to quote a scathing local report which doubted Cuthbert's expertise and his motives. 'Who made the model for the *Dufferin* heaven knows. For Cuthbert's sake I hope it was not Cuthbert. And certainly I don't want to injure the reputation of anyone this side of the line by ascribing it to an American.' But bad as her model was she was a trump-card for Cuthbert. She stamped him as the champion yacht-builder of Canada. He came here in her at the expense of his fellow-citizens, had a pleasant junketing excursion and went home triumphant. Major Gifford and the stockholders of the *Countess* were not as well satisfied. In the yacht *Countess of Dufferin* Cuthbert played the Royal Canadian Yacht Club for all it was worth.

Whatever Cuthbert's motives, *Atalanta* certainly did not turn out any better than the first Canadian challenger. Desperately short of time because of launching late, Cuthbert was forced to take his yacht through the Erie Canal. To do this he had to unstep the mast, cant the hull over and have the yacht

The 1881 challenger, Atalanta, was also a centreboard sloop

W. G. WOOD
1902.

dragged through the 8 miles of canal by mules! After this undignified start, she eventually docked at Jersey City on 4 November, and immediately differences of opinion arose about her lines. One old sea salt said she had a sawed-off appearance as though she had bumped her stern against the sides of the canal. The papers too weren't over polite either. 'Rough as a hedge fence' was the headline in one, while another related a probably apocryphal but nonetheless amusing story of the scientific Americans meeting the less sophisticated Canadians – perhaps the first instance of the modern nautical one-upmanship that goes on nowadays before and during an America's Cup series? – 'Some said she was too full forward; others thought that she was not.' The paper reported:

Vice Commodore James D. Smith said: 'She has a long radius to the turn of the bilge, and great perpendicular depth on the topside.' This alarmed a Canadian gentleman, who asked him what he meant.
Capt. Alex Taylor Jr said: 'Her midships section has the least circumscribed length with the greatest amount of area.'
The Canadian looked somewhat reassured and remarked: 'I believe you, my boy.'

The second Canadian challenge was a miserable repeat performance of the first, frantic last-minute alterations being made to *Atalanta* from inadequate funds. Both races were lost by huge margins, and her amateur crew – public opinion insisted that this time they all be Canadians – were quite inadequate. In fact the Canadian yacht was in trouble before she'd even lifted her anchor – which took long enough to do as, for some incredible reason, she had no anchor winch – as she was knocked right down by a fiercesome gust and some thought she would capsize. The second race took place in a high wind, too;

Atalanta lost her spinnaker pole on the way out and was forced to put in a second reef into her mainsail on the beat back. The real race was between *Mischief* and *Gracie*. *Gracie*, though not invited, turned up for both races, and beat *Mischief* to the finishing line on each occasion. 'So, you see!' she is alleged to have signalled to the committee boat, to which the committee merely replied: 'Gate-crasher!'

The *Spirit of the Times* summed up the fourth challenge by saying that *Mischief*

One of the fastest in the world ... fully manned and magnificently handled, distanced the *Atalanta*, a new yacht, hastily built, totally untried, and miserably equipped ... and bungled around the course by an alleged crew, who would have been overmatched in trying to handle a canal-boat anchored in a fog.

The challenge over, Cuthbert again decided to stay on, correct the errors in his yacht and challenge once more the following year. His announcement was received with dismay by the race committee, not because they feared losing the Cup to Cuthbert but because they feared the Cup races would become a farce. Something had to be done.

Three sporting gentlemen

1885/1886/1887

4

What was done was very simple: the Club returned the Cup to the only surviving donor, George L. Schuyler, and asked him to make a new Deed of Gift. The Club resolved on this course of action on 17 December 1881. Schuyler had the Cup back to the Club by 4 January 1882 with a new Deed of Gift which effectively banned Cuthbert from challenging again. Two new clauses were that a challenge had to come from a club

having for its annual regatta an ocean water-course on the sea or on an arm of the sea (or one which combines both)

and

No vessel which has been defeated in a match for this cup can be again selected by any club for its representative until after a contest for it by some other vessel has intervened, or until after the expiration of two years from the time such contest has taken place.

On hearing that, Cuthbert packed his bags and went home. It did not go unnoticed across the Atlantic that the Deed now specifically stated that the match would be between two vessels only and that the latest challenge had taken place between single-masted yachts – for the popular yachts of the day in England were cutters. However, nothing happened until December 1884 when the designer of the two cutters *Genesta* and *Galatea*, J. Beavor-Webb, wrote informally on behalf of their owners, saying they would like to challenge in August and September 1885 respectively.

Between 1881 and this receipt by the Club of notice of another challenge, a curious reversal in the affairs of Anglo-American yachting occurred when there appeared in American waters a Scottish-built cutter, *Madge*. Only 46 feet overall and with a mere 8 feet draught, she was considered too small to cross

J. Beavor-Webb. From Harper's Weekly

the Atlantic on her own bottom and had been carried across on the deck of a steamer. James Coates, from Paisley, in Scotland, was her owner and he raced her with astounding success. Despite having to give time, she won no less than seven of the eight races she entered. 'She was,' says Lawson, 'as wet as a half tide ledge in a sea-way, but speedy and handy, and she made a deep impression here.' So deep was the impression, in fact, that, as in 1851 in England after the visit of *America*, local designers and boatbuilders immediately set about copying her lines. This resulted in much experimentation and no little cost, but what was to emerge over the next decade was an even further compromise between the traditional American sloop and the traditional English cutter, a compromise that had both sides at each other's throats when the next challenger appeared in American waters in 1885 and which indeed caused a lot of friction amongst Americans themselves.

Madge's appearance certainly showed the Americans that the English had developed fast cutters and that the America's Cup was not as safe as perhaps they had first thought it. Some say if *Madge* had not

crossed the Atlantic the America's Cup would have. But the change would almost certainly have come about in any case: the instability of the 'skimming dish' was now recognized; American and British yachts were again regularly competing against one another each summer – and British designers sold their yachts to Americans.

Following Beavor-Webb's letter, the Club accepted the challenge of the Royal Yacht Squadron on behalf of Sir Richard Sutton, the owner of *Genesta*, but suggested that *Galatea*, owned by a retired naval lieutenant, William Henn, should wait until the following year before challenging. This was

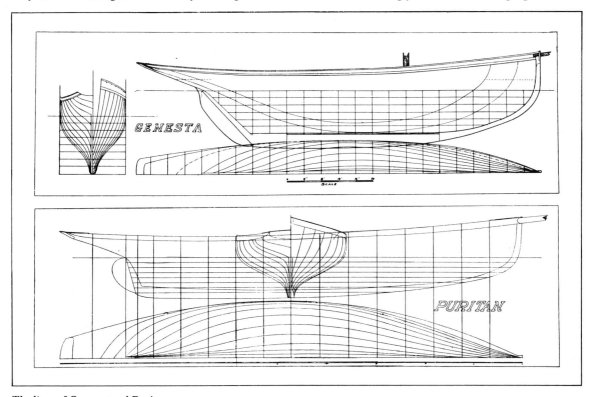

The lines of Genesta *and* Puritan

accepted. After some friendly but futile correspondence from the English requesting a match 'free from tides and shallow waters' and asking the Standard English Time Allowances be used, it was agreed that the match would take place in September 1885. In May of that year the Club issued a circular stating that it was intended to hold trial races in June or July and any 'vessel belonging to any duly organized yacht club in the United States' was eligible to enter provided its length exceeded 60 feet

and it was rigged with a single mast. Four names were put forward for consideration: *Priscilla*, *Gracie*, *Bedouin* and *Puritan*. Of these *Priscilla* and *Puritan* were new. *Puritan* had been laid down some months before by a Boston syndicate in anticipation of contesting for the right to defend; she was designed by a young man, Edward Burgess, who was to become one of the foremost designers in America. Although always a keen yachtsman Burgess was a naturalist for more than fifteen years

General Paine. From Harper's Weekly

after he graduated from Harvard in 1874; he was still secretary of the Boston Society of Natural History while designing America's Cup yachts. In the summer of 1893 he went to England with his family and stayed on the Isle of Wight where he was able to study the English cutter in her home waters, the Solent. On his return he found that his father had met financial disaster which meant Burgess had to find a way of earning his living. Probably more from choice than necessity – he could after all have taught – he set up with his brother Sidney as a yacht-designer, a profession he'd already interested himself in over the years as an amateur. *Puritan* was his first design of any size and he came up with a concept that was amazingly successful. A later observer on yachting matters, the designer William P. Stephens, said of Burgess

he had no interest in mathematics or mechanics, and he lacked the technical training considered essential today for success in designing. . . . His first and greatest effort, *Puritan*, was built on deductions as simple and logical as those which produced the One-Horse Shay.

Lawson describes *Puritan* as

a radical departure from the old-time American sloop, and a type in herself, combining the beam, power and centre-board of the sloop, with some of the depth and the outside lead of an English cutter. In this respect she was the first vessel of her kind, the pioneer in the combination of American and English ideas.

As Burgess, the technical owner of *Puritan*, was not a member of the NYYC the yacht was entered for the trials and the Cup races in the name of General Paine, who was a member.

The other new yacht, *Priscilla*, was built for the Commodore of the NYYC, James Gordon Bennett, and the vice-commodore, W. P. Douglas. They chose the foremost yacht-designer in America, A. Cary Smith, to design her. A conventional centre-board sloop, she was made of iron, and was designed to be an improved *Mischief*. Of the other two contenders, *Bedouin*, says Lawson, 'was the first and only cutter of the English type that contested for the honor of defending the America's Cup'; while *Gracie*, of course, had been an unsuccessful contender to defend the Cup in 1881.

The trials between these four yachts were postponed until after the NYYC cruise, but during the cruise the relative merits of the two new yachts were assessed. It became obvious that *Priscilla* could hold her own in light weather while *Puritan* was superior in a breeze. In one race, for the Goelet cup, the New Englander candidate trounced her New York counterpart by nearly 12 minutes over a 40-mile course, and when the Trials were held *Puritan* beat *Priscilla* by two races to one, the other two contenders not winning once. The third of these races was described by the *New York Times* as 'one of the swiftest and most closely contested and exciting trials of speed ever seen in these waters'. The results to some extent were unexpected as New Yorkers had supposed themselves the leaders of the yachting world in America, an attitude reflected in an article in one New York paper which stated that it was quite in order for Boston to build a Cup candidate – once the trials were finished, she could be used to carry bricks around Boston harbour. This article perhaps set the tone for the war of words that went on before, during and after the 1885 challenge. Compared with earlier challenges public interest was enormous, for the revised Deed of Gift had made it even more plain to every American that the Cup belonged to the nation. It was a matter of national pride to defend it successfully.

This upsurge in interest in the Cup perhaps caused the press to respond to another kind of challenge: the race to get out the Cup news first and to make it readable and different from any competitor's. There is no paucity of reports on the 1885 challenge but the increased number of newspapers makes it difficult to untangle fact from journalistic hyperbole. They also attacked each other – 'one definite and gratifying result was accomplished by yesterday's work,' crowed the *Commercial Advertiser*, 'our contemporary, the *World*, found out that a vessel with a single mast is not a schooner, not even a prairie schooner or a schooner of beer' – and there seemed little love lost between New York and Boston. Altogether press clippings about the 1885 challenge have a modern ring. The tempo has increased over the years but the *Genesta–Puritan* match put the America's Cup on the map so far as the United States as a nation was concerned.

Genesta arrived in New York on 16 July having crossed the Atlantic under jury rig. Lawson says:

Priscilla, a contender for the honour to defend in 1885 and 1886, preparing for a race

She was a typical English cutter of the period, long, narrow, very deep, with low bilges and wall sides, a straight stem, a high overhang aft, long bowsprit, short mast, and tall topmast. . . . Her frame was of steel, and she was planked with oak, being the first yacht of composite build to sail for the cup. Keelson, stringers, and strengthening plates were all of steel.

Genesta was one of England's top racing cutters; in thirty-four races she had won seven first prizes and ten second prizes. She was a direct descendant of the type of cutter that had been designed to evade the English tonnage rule that then governed time allowances. This rule assumed that a boat's depth was double its beam, and any excessive beam was penalized accordingly. By increasing the waterline length and shortening the keel abnormally this penalty could be avoided, producing a vessel of very narrow beam and deep ballast, mostly carried outside on the

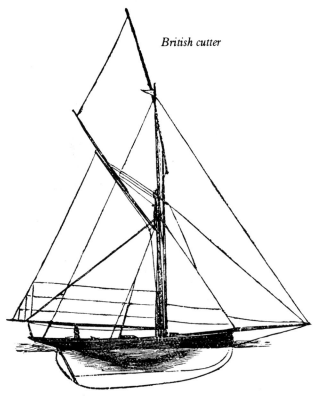

British cutter

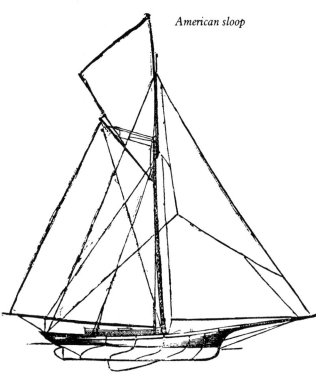

American sloop

keel. As the American rating rule was quite different it is not surprising that the English wanted it done their way. The time allowance eventually granted *Genesta* in the two races, 28 and 31 seconds, proved inequitable.

When *Puritan* arrived in New York there began a protracted correspondence in the *Commercial Advertiser* and other papers about her merits, for her appearance caused as much, if not more, interest than that of the British challenger. 'Devoted Yachtsman' wrote in the *Commercial Advertiser*:

I say that neither the *Puritan* nor the *Priscilla* is an American centreboard yacht and if either one or both beat the *Genesta*, the Englishmen can console themselves that they were beaten by a mongrel racing machine, a cross-breed between a Britisher and a Yankee, and can find comfort in the fact that there was not sufficient yachting brains in all Yankeedom to conceive a Yankee centerboarder, but that we were compelled to pilfer English swadling clothes to wrap the monstrosity in. The *Puritan* and the *Priscilla* are only English babies, born on American soil, and rigged out in English dimity. To complete the outfit, we should get a full crew who drop their *h*s.

The argument swayed back and forth with both sides being governed more by patriotic fervour than scientific accuracy. Beavor-Webb, the designer of *Genesta*, said he would prefer to race *Priscilla* than *Puritan* as he did not regard *Puritan* 'as a type of the American sloop'. She was an English cutter in everything except her proportion of beam to length. Captain Carter, *Puritan*'s skipper, retorted that his boat's lines 'are entirely different from those of the *Genesta*'.

The English did not help to settle matters as they seemed intent on keeping the lines of *Genesta* secret as long as possible – and when *Genesta* was drydocked for her bottom to be cleaned Beavor-Webb at first refused to allow anyone entry to the dock. But after much catcalling from the crowd the watchman allowed them to enter, and it was generally thought that she was 'a beautiful and wicked-looking boat'.

Beavor-Webb obviously did not endear himself to the American newspapers and his pronouncements brought him a bad press. He did not seem to be enjoying himself and one newspaper picked up with

As interest in the America's Cup races increased during the 1880s the newspapers of the day tried to explain to their readers the differences between English and American yachts. They were rarely accurate but this one gives a fair idea of how they looked in the mid 1880s

delight that he had remarked he did 'not like the prospect of racing in these waters' and that the mosquitoes were 'terrible', and a few days later the *New York Times* reported that 'he has of late shown considerable irritability'. His insistence that *Puritan* was basically a British boat was considered a clever business ploy. The *Sun* reported 'a prominent yachtsman' as saying:

It looks very much like an attempt to establish a line of retreat in case of defeat. Of course, if the *Puritan* wins, the demand for cutters on this side of the water at least will fall a good deal below the prospective supply, and the business of English designers will be seriously diminished; but if the American public can be educated to believe that the *Puritan* is a cutter, cutter stock will not suffer so great a depreciation as it would on the theory that she is a sloop, and there would still be a chance for the English designer. It is an adroit and decidedly cheeky move on the part of Mr Beavor-Webb.

Richard Sutton was not very popular at first either – though events were soon to change that – with the ubiquitous 'prominent yachtsman' pronouncing

'*Beans heavier than Beef*' was the caption under this Harper's Weekly *cartoon to celebrate* Puritan's *victory*

the course of Sir Richard Sutton in endeavouring to conceal the qualities of his boat is not calculated to impress American yachtsmen at all favourably. He assumes an air of superiority, as if we had everything to learn from him, while he could not possibly learn anything from us. If he had stood less aloof and shown a disposition to try his boat with some of ours when opportunity offered, he would have awakened a much more cordial feeling. . . . Finding fault with the New York Club course, of which I will venture to say they had pretty accurate knowledge before they came over, and objecting to dry dock the *Genesta* at any place where she can be seen, may accord with English ideas of sportsmanlike conduct, but it looks to the American eye more like querulousness and a purely business propensity to haggle.

'Finding fault with the New York Club course' refers to Sutton's desire for a course 'free from tides and shallow waters'. He obviously kept pursuing the subject even after the arrangements for the challenge had been made and accepted by both sides; Mr Forbes, a member of the *Puritan* syndicate, when asked his opinion of the British claim that there was not enough water for their boat over a part of the course, replied that

it did not indicate the existence with the Englishmen of the spirit which prevails among American yachtsmen. It seemed rather more like a disposition to find fault. In fact,

there was no foundation for the claim, because the *Puritan* with her board down draws 19 feet of water, and she could not therefore go where the *Genesta* could.

He must have said this with his tongue very firmly in his cheek as *Puritan* with her board up drew a mere 8 feet 8 inches while *Genesta* with a fixed keel drew 13 feet 6 inches. Evidence that the Englishman's fears on this point were well founded came swiftly after the first completed race when Captain Joe Ellsworth, who was on board *Puritan*, stated to a newspaper:

I don't think we have any sure thing at all in sailing against that boat – she's a terror. She was not far behind us when we got in to the point of the Hook, but we were able by pulling the centreboard up a little to skin along Flynn's Knoll where she could not go, and so gained on her by working up to buoy no. 8½.

Rounding buoy 8½ *Genesta* was less than 6 minutes behind *Puritan* but finished 16 minutes 19 seconds behind her on corrected time.

However, the second race, over the outside course, shows how closely matched the two boats really were: *Genesta* came in only 2 minutes 9 seconds (1 minute 38 seconds corrected time) behind *Puritan*, and the press were loud in their praise of the match. 'A glorious sea race . . . the liveliest and prettiest race ever seen in these waters,' said the *Sun*, and *Genesta*'s owner, too, according to the paper, was a pretty sight. 'Sir Richard Sutton, in his familiar pink blazer, smoked an inch of cigar as he came forward to touch the peak of his cap in salutation to the people on the tug.' But it wasn't his pink blazer or the cause of being one of 'the liveliest and prettiest races' to be seen off New York that Sir Richard will be remembered for but for the race he gave away.

The first race began on 7 September but the wind was too light and the time limit expired. However, *Puritan* was 2 miles ahead which shows that she was the better light-weather boat. The next day proved better and there was a moderate breeze blowing from the south-south-east. A vast armada of pleasure craft watched the two yachts manoeuvring before the start. Both boats were on the port tack but *Genesta*'s afterguard, finding themselves too far to the westward and too early, went about and headed east putting themselves directly in the course of *Puritan* heading south still on the port tack. *Genesta*, having right of way, resolutely held her course. So did *Puritan* until the last moment when she tried to luff round the British boat's bows. It very nearly worked, but *Genesta*'s huge 36-foot bowsprit just caught the luff of *Puritan*'s mainsail, ripping a 4-foot hole in it. The impact snapped *Genesta*'s bowsprit stays with a sound like gunfire and the bowsprit swung round and fell into the water. Captain Carter, who was at the tiller of the challenger when she hit *Puritan*, remarked afterwards that 'when the man at the wheel on the *Puritan* saw our bowsprit shooting over him he dropped the spokes like hot pennies and ran forward. I think he did quite right; it was a narrow escape.'

After some discussion the race committee decided that the race was Sutton's if he wished to sail the course alone. The American representative on board *Genesta* had asked if they could have time to rig up the spinnaker boom as a bowsprit but while the committee were discussing this point Sir Richard Sutton called over to them: 'We are very much obliged to you, but we don't want it in that way. We want a race; we don't want a walkover,' a pro-

Puritan *leading* Genesta *during the first race, 14 September 1885*

Inset: *By shortening sail as the breeze increased to thirty knots near the finish of the last race,* Puritan *won a narrow victory over the British challenger*

48

nouncement greeted with undisguised pleasure by the Club and by the press. And when it was known that Sir Richard refused any payment for his broken bowsprit he became overnight the most popular man in America. His health 'was copiously drunk' when the N Y Y C held a reception in his honour. They even made him an honorary member. Before she returned to England *Genesta* won no less than three cups and carried them back with her.

No sooner had *Genesta* left America than the N Y Y C sat down and accepted the next challenger *Galatea* under practically the same conditions as laid down for *Genesta*'s challenge. 'Yachting spirit ran high in this country,' Lawson states, 'in view of the showing we had made against *Genesta*, and it was with confidence that plans were made to meet *Galatea*,' and he goes on to say that Boston was again expected to produce the successful defender, 'for the name of Burgess, almost unknown to the general public a year before, was on every tongue when yachting matters were discussed'.

Sure enough General Paine lost no opportunity in placing an order with Burgess for an improved *Puritan*. A syndicate of Atlantic Yacht Club members also joined the fray and commissioned an all-wood sloop called *Atlantic* from the brother of Captain Joe Ellsworth and had her built by John Mumm of Brooklyn. However, she did not prove to be anywhere near fast enough and is mentioned here because she proved the last 'rule-of-thumb' sloop to be built.

The successor to *Puritan* was called *Mayflower*. Like *Puritan*, she was built at George Lawley, a name that was to be closely associated with America's Cup boats over a long period. *Mayflower* had many of the same characteristics as *Puritan* but her bow was longer and finer. She differed from *Puritan* once afloat in not being an instant success. For her first three races against *Puritan* – all of which she lost – her centreboard could not be lowered to its full depth. Additionally her trim was wrong and her sails could not be made to set properly. The watching public and press immediately concluded she was

no good, but they were quickly proved wrong. For once the new candidate's trim and sails had been adjusted it became obvious that she was by far the faster boat. Trial races between *Mayflower*, *Puritan*, *Priscilla* and *Atlantic* were held on 21 and 25 August, *Mayflower* won both easily, beating *Atlantic* by 10 minutes in the first race and *Puritan* by well over 3 minutes in the second. The Club promptly and without ado nominated her to defend the Cup. No one argued.

The British challenger, *Galatea*, had been launched on 1 May 1885, by her builders, John Reid & Sons of Glasgow. She too had not proved an instant success – she sailed in fifteen races that year without winning one – but unlike *Mayflower* she did not improve. It was later found that the lead for her keel had not been properly poured into her, making it full of holes which filled with water. Unfortunately, even when this mistake was rectified, *Galatea* still proved slow off the mark, though she managed two second places in three starts before beginning her Atlantic crossing. This proved leisurely and Henn probably did not press her, for he was really a cruising man by temperament (and a very experienced one), and he had probably only been persuaded to challenge for the Cup by Beavor-Webb who, as a designer, knew the advantages of publicity.

Unique for that day and age Henn had his wife with him and – unique in any age – she had with her several dogs, and a pet monkey called Peggy. Peggy, according to one newspaper, could pull on a halyard like a trained sailor, and she always helped the crew to make and lower sail. She manifested a great interest in the cutter's races. When *Galatea* went ahead, Peggy would run out on the bowsprit and jump up and down. The skipper of *Galatea*, Captain Daniel Bradford, said he believed Peggy exemplified the truth of a theory that the monkey descended from man, not vice versa as Darwin believed. He thought Peggy had descended a few pegs and had then 'hove to'.

For a yacht challenging for what was by then indisputably the world's most famous yachting cup *Galatea* was also curiously furnished, with potted plants in the saloon and leopard skins on the floor. One paper reported:

Galatea's saloon (Beken)

Inset left: *Galatea's motley collection of animals*

Inset right: *Mrs Henn*

Mrs Henn, being the first lady to cross the Atlantic in a racing yacht, affords an opportunity for the fair ones to visit the yacht ... and are rapidly turning the inside of *Galatea* into a flower garden.

Henn, however, proved extremely popular and a man of cheerful disposition. Indeed his whole attitude was so phlegmatic and unhurried that the rumour went round New York that by his behaviour Henn was carefully disguising the true speed of his cutter. Why else would the Britisher tow a dinghy behind him when tuning up, or refuse to hoist anything but working canvas? To see whether he really was hiding anything a massive spectator fleet turned up on the day of the first race. Indeed so huge was it that New York *Town Topics* remarked that

if the popular rage for attending yacht races increases only a little it will soon be impossible to race at all in New York harbour.... The manner in which steamboat pilots crowded on the course was simply outrageous.

It proposed that the yachts should carry cannon to keep the sightseers at a reasonable distance!

Despite the lightness of the wind at the start, both boats got away excellently, *Galatea* just 1 second ahead of the defender. But once under way it became obvious that the American boat was superior when close hauled. 'Whenever the wind was light the *Galatea* seemed to slide off to leeward compared with *Mayflower*,' *Field and Stream* reported, though commenting that the British challenger tacked quicker. Even so *Galatea*, in an effort to overcome her inability to sail to windward as well as *Mayflower*, appeared to be sailing too close to the wind which made her movements slow and sluggish. Her progress wasn't helped by a large schooner anchored in her path. *Mayflower* managed to luff round it but *Galatea* was forced to leeward, and was blanketed. She then continued to lose ground practically all the way and finished nearly 13 minutes behind the American yacht (12 minutes 02 seconds on corrected time).

The next race was planned for two days later. It started but thick fog and a light wind meant it was abandoned. Beavor-Webb, the helmsman that day on *Galatea*, missed the outer mark so it was just as well for the English that the time limit was exceeded. The second race took place eventually on 11 September, but again it was hampered by excessively light winds, *Mayflower* creeping over the finishing line just 11 minutes before the 7 hour time limit expired. She was nearly 30 minutes ahead of the British challenger.

Henn was unable to take personal charge of his yacht during this second race as he was taken ill just before the start. He asked for the course to be

Galatea and Mayflower *at the start of the first race on 7 September 1886.* Galatea *is to windward*

shortened so that he could get to a doctor as soon as possible; the request was refused, as the Committee regretted they did not have the power to alter the race conditions.

The sixth challenge had proved a friendly affair, the only sour note coming from across the Atlantic when it was reported in an English paper that Mr Jamison, owner of the champion yacht *Irex*, had said that he did not wish to challenge for the Cup as he did not think that American yachtsmen, and the American public and press, were impartial and sportsmanlike. He was also alleged to have said that he did not think a fair race was possible in America. When news of this report reached New York it was not well received and Henn was asked his opinion. Henn replied that Jamison was a friend of his and he was sure the report was quite untrue; even if the report was correct the facts were – as he was only too glad to state – that he'd been treated with complete fairness. Even his wife had enjoyed herself. In fact his only grumble was with the weather; when a *New York Herald* reporter asked him if there was any chance of the Royal Yacht Squadron challenging again Henn promptly replied:

Not the slightest on earth. The club hardly thinks the game is worth the hunting. It is a long trip over here in the first place, and then you miss a whole racing season abroad. Then the chances are that you come over here and have virtually no race, for the weather is so calm that it is no real racing.

Despite his disappointment with the weather, Henn laid up *Galatea* on the American side of the Atlantic and raced her in American waters during the 1887 season, though without much success. Just before he and his wife returned to England by steamer for the winter Peggy the monkey died. She was wrapped in a Union Jack and four skippers from near-by yachts acted as pall-bearers. It is not recorded what happened to the dogs.

While Mr Henn, his wife, his dogs and his monkey were so graciously losing the seventh challenge a move to mount the next one was already under way. As a first step in beginning to understand the real problems of winning back the Cup the noted Scott-

Galatea and the spectator fleet

ish designer G. L. Watson set off for New York. He missed the *Galatea–Mayflower* races – a mistake, he readily admitted – but when he arrived he studied closely all the top American yachts and American building techniques. The willingness of Americans to help must have impressed and disarmed the quiet Scot but did not prevent him from shrouding his own creation for the 1887 challenge in the utmost secrecy when she was built. The interviews with him in the press are revealing, for Watson was indisputably the top British yacht designer of the day (the Americans remembered his creation, *Madge*, only too well) and he has been called 'the father of scientific yacht architecture'. One interview pinpointed the differences between British and American yacht design that Watson noticed and which he certainly took account of when designing the next challenger, *Thistle*. American waters, he said, were much smoother than he'd expected. Because of this he felt that the yachts that had been sent from Britain had been undermasted. When a reporter raised the recurring question of whether a British cutter couldn't be designed that would beat an American centreboard sloop, Watson replied tersely that he'd know more about that the following year, but that he would 'put far more sail on the cutter for a race here'.

Watson also raised the question of the terms of the next challenge:

Some of the conditions of the Deed of Gift of the America's Cup are singularly hard on the challengers. Before we can give a certificate of tonnage we must build a boat; then, the boat being built, if the challenge were not accepted the challengers would be left with a boat on their hands.

As no British yacht had been specially built for a challenge for sixteen years it was reasonable, in the light of the advance that had taken place in yacht design and construction since that date, that Watson should find this particular clause onerous. Before he had even been commissioned to build a challenger Watson was highlighting an aspect of the deed which obviously displeased him. He repeated his objections in another interview at the end of that year after he had returned to Scotland.

Another member of the coming Scottish challenge who caught the eye of American papers was Captain John Barr, the skipper-designate. A top racing skipper of the period he already had a distinguished career behind him. His latest success had been racing the 20-ton cutter *Clara* in American waters

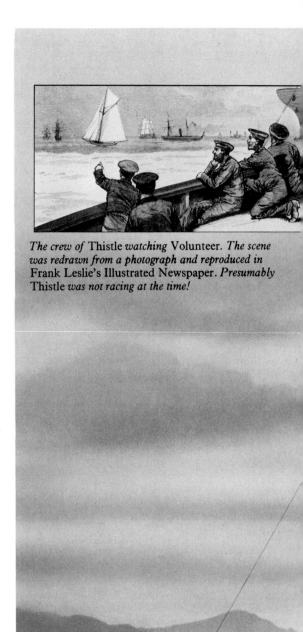

The crew of Thistle *watching* Volunteer. *The scene was redrawn from a photograph and reproduced in* Frank Leslie's Illustrated Newspaper. *Presumably* Thistle *was not racing at the time!*

54

Thistle *on the Clyde in light weather, 1887* (Beken)

for her owner Mr Charles Sweet and achieving the remarkable performance of eleven first prizes out of eleven starts. In his early forties, Barr was a quiet retiring man – when on board *Clara* in America he had not once set foot on another yacht – of middle height and powerful build.

The third person much written about once it was known negotiations were being carried on for another challenge was James Bell, the head of the syndicate for building *Thistle*. A keen yachtsman, Bell was a prominent Glasgow businessman. But unlike Ashbury and Cuthbert before him, or Lipton after him, Bell was more in the mould of Sutton and Henn: he was not challenging for any ulterior motive but because he was a keen follower of the sport.

Bell eventually challenged – eventually because it took both sides many months to agree on what was and what was not an official challenge – through the Royal Clyde Yacht Club, of which he was vice-commodore, and was accepted by the Club on 29 March 1887. The challenge merely said that the challenger's name was *Thistle* and that her waterline length was 85 feet, which did not enlighten the Americans much. Unused to such secrecy, they had for months been trying to find out about the new challenger but all questions had been met with a canny Scots silence. This provoked some American papers to do some sleuthing. The *Boston Herald* somehow managed to get hold of a set of plans purporting to be *Thistle*'s, and published them. *Forest and Stream* then reported that the plans weren't what the *Herald* said they were, and what's more they had a cable from Watson which confirmed this. *Field and Stream* had cabled Watson: 'Plans of *Thistle* in *Boston Herald*, 80 feet waterline, 16 feet beam. Are they authentic?' to which Watson replied: 'Quite impossible that *Herald* can have true plans.' *Field and Stream* published the exchange, and someone else dubbed the *Herald*'s effort at revealing the challenger's dimensions as 'a schoolboy affair'. This made the architect who copied the plans for the *Herald* hot under the collar. He replied:

If one goes through a lot of land, and it is filled with monuments and tombstones, the strong presumption is that it is a graveyard. So my experience in naval architecture forces me to the belief that the drawings in the paper handed me were the working plans of a cutter yacht.... Mr Edward Burgess says the plans are genuine. He has seen them and is forced to this conclusion. He has compared the writing on the plans with letters he received from Mr Watson, and the handwriting is the same.

Burgess indeed did say the plans

represent the *Thistle*, unless she may be changed on account of this publication, which would be extremely unlikely. It is impossible that Mr Watson should have consented to make a deliberate attempt to deceive us as to her size, and I don't see what would be gained by the deception. There is, of course, one other possibility: that this plan was one of several submitted by Mr Watson to the owners, and not selected.

Burgess, commenting on Watson's cable, said that the Scotsman's reply

is an evasive answer. He does not deny in his reply that the *Thistle* is 80 feet long.

The second of Burgess's alternatives seems at first sight the most obvious answer. But there was some point in trying to deceive the Americans as to *Thistle*'s dimensions. Being deceived into thinking the challenger was smaller than she really was could prompt the Americans into building a smaller defender. This could put them at a psychological disadvantage and, depending on a number of factors, at a real disadvantage too. This was especially applicable to the 1887 challenge for at last the old tonnage rating system in England had been abolished, so there was no longer any rating disadvantage in building a beamy boat. So English yachts built for the America's Cup races were bound to be designed more in accord with the American rating system. It was therefore important that the designer of an American defender should know the dimensions of any adversary. It is therefore conceivable that the plans received by the *Herald* were a blind. Some years later, in 1895, the *New York Herald* published an attack on the Scottish designer by an A. G. McVey who states categorically that Watson gave out 'fake' plans. 'He gave, in 1887, to Mr. James Meikle, yachting editor of the *Glasgow Mail*, then the *Boston Herald* correspondent, plans of the *Thistle* which Watson knew to be "faked".'

Only *Volunteer* was built for the 1887 challenge. When it was known that General Paine and Edward Burgess had teamed up again, no one else bothered. Lawson comments:

Compared with *Mayflower*, *Volunteer* had more dead-rise and less beam, and, owing to the fact that ballast could be stowed 2 feet lower in her metal hull, she had greater stability because of the lower centre of gravity. In construction she was very strong, though her outside plating, owing to the haste with which she was built, was somewhat rough.

Rough or not, *Volunteer* soon proved to be a superboat, beating *Mayflower* in the Goelet Cup by no less than 8 minutes 39 seconds, and she then went on to win a whole string of cups. It was thought advisable, even so, for trial races to be held. But only *Mayflower* turned up and in the one race held she was beaten decisively by just over 16 minutes.

In Scotland *Thistle* was launched at the end of April, which gave her a full two months' sailing time over *Volunteer*, and she too proved her worth in early trials. She was completely covered by tarpaulins when launched. One writer has called this secrecy 'a silly business' but Watson's intention (to his eventual detriment, as will be seen) must have been to keep the Americans guessing up to the very last minute – a perfectly acceptable tactic, as any modern challenger will agree. This secrecy was maintained right up to the last minute. One newspaper even went to the trouble of secretly sending down a diver at night, when *Thistle* arrived in New York, to examine her bottom and pass a description of it up to a waiting artist. The result was published and caused great hilarity amongst the afterguard and crew of the challenger as it was totally inaccurate.

Once unveiled, *Thistle* showed herself a 'big, sail-carrying brute' with a clipper bow of the old type and a straight keel with no forefoot, which in future years was to affect the design of all racing yachts. Burgess had *Volunteer* built on almost identical lines, with a clipper bow and a cutaway stem. Close as they were in design *Volunteer* did not turn out longer, though obviously Burgess had intended she should be. The declared waterline length of *Volunteer* was 85 feet 10 inches while *Thistle*'s was 85 feet. But when both yachts were officially measured on 22 September it was found that *Thistle*'s true waterline length was 86.46 feet.

When the race committee pointed out the discrepancy between the declared length of the challenger and the actual length, Bell replied the information was supplied before *Thistle* was launched and therefore absolute accuracy was impossible. In any case, he added cheerfully, he did not know the challengers had to supply the information anyway, implying, perhaps, that if they had known they would have tried to be more accurate. He also admitted that when *Thistle* had been measured after fitting out she had measured 86.4 feet. If he'd read the Deed properly and had supplied the correct waterline length then, as required, he would doubtless have saved himself much anxiety. Watson, when told of his mistake, just shrugged the discrepancy off as an 'overlook' on his part. The committee, however, probably needled by the secret manner of *Thistle*'s building, and made suspicious by the accusations and counter-accusations amongst the newspapers as to the validity of the published lines of *Thistle*, chose to regard the error as serious and questioned whether the Scottish boat was any longer eligible. The committee decided to refer the matter to a referee, even though it was noted that there was no point in trying to conceal *Thistle*'s true length as both

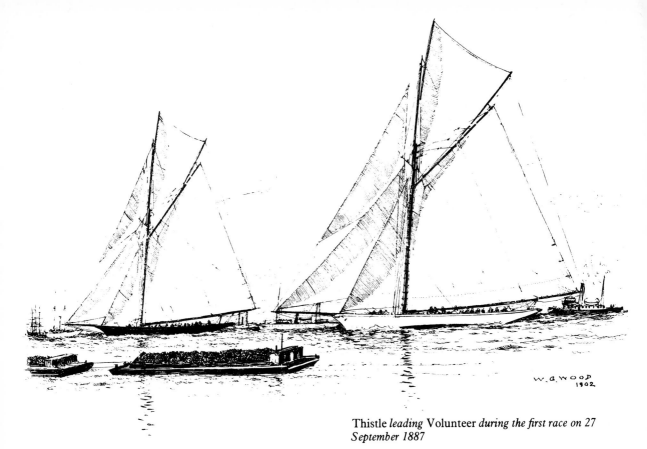

Thistle *leading* Volunteer *during the first race on 27 September 1887*

yachts would be officially measured and handicaps adjusted according to the results of that measurement. George Schuyler was appointed referee. At an all-party conference two questions were put to Schuyler. Did not *Thistle*, Watson asked, as now measured and offered to sail, still correspond with the requirements of the Deed of Gift? The America's Cup Committee asked: was the variation in *Thistle*'s length sufficient to prevent the challenger racing for the Cup with the boat named? Schuyler slept on the problem and the next day presented his decision in a letter to the Committee. In it he quoted Watson's statement, when forwarding his certificate to Mr Bell, that

it was impossible to give *exactly* the water-line length; this, however, is her designed length, and when she is afloat and in racing trim, I have no reason to expect that it will be more than inch or two out either way.

Schuyler commented:

although the variation between the stated and actual load water-line is so large as to be of great disadvantage to the defender of the Cup, still, as Mr Bell could only rely upon

the statement of his designer, he cannot, in this particular case, be held accountable for the remarkably inaccurate information received from him, and I therefore decide that the variation is not sufficient to disqualify him from starting the *Thistle* in the race agreed upon.

The matter of measurement settled, the first race took place on 27 September in very light airs. In fact there seemed more wind in the instruments of the bagpipers who played throughout the first race to encourage the challenger than there was over the course. It was another drifting match with *Volunteer* coming in over 19 minutes ahead of *Thistle* – though part of this time could be accounted for by Barr miscalculating the current and taking an incorrect tack. After the race Bell protested that the inside course was totally inadequate for testing the merits of a keel boat, thereby adding his comments to just about every other challenger to sail over the Club course.

The second race took place three days later and although *Thistle* performed better she lost by nearly 12 minutes, a lamentable performance. After the first race Bell had had his yacht hauled out, so certain was he that her speed had been affected by weed on her bottom. None was found and after the second race, so decisive was *Thistle*'s defeat, there was nothing he could do or say, though in England it was hinted that Barr had deliberately sailed *Thistle* to defeat, having received from certain gentlemen an offer he couldn't refuse. Though Barr subsequently settled in America no one took this slur seriously.

Later Bell remarked: 'Look for us again, and we'll bring our bagpipers too.' He would have challenged again, then and there, if he'd been allowed. Instead he went home and the next year sold *Thistle* to the Kaiser, who renamed her *Meteor*. General Paine and Edward Burgess went home, too, to Boston, and were given a civic reception. Oliver Wendell Holmes sent a cable regretting he could not be present, adding that General Paine was the only general 'I ever heard of whom made himself illustrious by running away from all his competitors'.

Volunteer hung out a 'keep astern' notice in an attempt to keep the spectator fleet at bay

One unsporting nobleman_

5

1893/1895

The next challenge came even more swiftly than had *Thistle*'s – the same day, in fact, as the Scottish boat lost the second race. Hardly had Bell, Barr and their crew stepped off the challenger than Charles Sweet, owner of the cutter *Clara* which Barr had commanded so successfully the previous season in America, sat down at the University Club in New York and penned an informal challenge letter and his resignation from the New York Yacht Club. A Scotsman with strong American business connections, Sweet felt it might be considered 'antagonistic' to remain a member of the Club while challenging. The Club, however, reacted much more strongly to his challenge than to his resignation. The following Monday at a meeting which had been originally called for another purpose a committee was appointed to prepare a new Deed. The Cup was again returned to George Schuyler and the committee, under General Paine, presented a new draft Deed that had been drawn up by the club secretary, John H. Bird. The new Deed and the Cup was officially returned by Schuyler on 24 October. The Deed was signed, sealed and accepted at a meeting on 27 October. The meeting also voted to accept neither Mr Sweet's resignation from the club, nor his challenge, because it was not in accordance with the Deed of Gift that had just been drawn up! This retrospective legislation was then passed on to the Royal Clyde, which was known to be the club challenging on behalf of Charles Sweet.

Embarrassingly – at least, one hopes they found it so – for the Club, the Royal Clyde's official challenge crossed with the Club's letter informing the Clyde of the new Deed of Gift. The Royal Clyde's letter informed the Club that the challenge was 'to sail a match for the America's Cup next season, with a cutter 69 to 70 feet on the waterline', and that Mr Sweet, as he was in New York, would deal with any further formalities that might be required. However, when they received the Club's letter and the new Deed of Gift the Royal Clyde promptly – and politely – withdrew the challenge. The new Deed read, as one writer put it, 'like a mortgage', and Lawson states that

were international yacht-racing not an important branch of a noble sport, it could hardly have survived the period in its history beginning with the changes made in 1887 in the Deed of Gift.

The new conditions laid down by the Club Committee responsible for the drafting of the Deed were tough and uncompromising. Basically a challenger now had to challenge ten months before the races and at that time furnish the club with

the name of the owner and a certificate of the name, rig, and following dimensions of the challenging vessel, namely: length on load waterline, and extreme beam, and draught of water, which dimensions shall not be exceeded

centreboarders or vessels with sliding keels would never be excluded

and no restriction or limitation whatever shall be placed upon the use of such centerboard or sliding keel, nor shall the centerboard nor sliding keel be considered a part of the vessel for any purposes of measurement

and that in future the races must be held

on ocean courses, free from headlands

and these courses shall be

practicable in all parts for vessels of 22 feet draught of water.

A clause also stipulated that the ten months' elapse of time could be waived if mutually satisfactory arrangements were made as to dates, courses, sailing regulations and so on, but this clause did not over-rule the earlier one that the challenger's exact statistics had to be presented to the defending club before making mutually agreeable arrangements. If the parties could not mutually agree on the terms of the match then the best of three races were to be sailed, and there would be no time allowance. To add insult to injury, the final clause stipulated that no club gaining the trophy could in any way alter the Deed as now executed.

Whatever injustices the new Deed was thought to perpetrate at least one good thing had emerged: no longer would a challenger have to sail over the hated inside course. But the Deed now also made it impracticable for either the original course round the Isle of Wight, or the Clyde, to be used should the Cup be relinquished to the British. It also made sure that if such a disaster took place an American-type sloop with a sliding keel could be sent across if necessary.

The new Deed was almost certainly a reaction to the mounting pressure the British were putting on the Club to regain the trophy. From 1871 to 1885 the British had taken no interest in the Cup. Now, in 1887, there had already been three challenges in quick succession and a fourth attempted. It must have seemed only a matter of time before the Cup found its way back to Britain. After all, other prized cups, like the Brenton Reef, won by *Genesta* in 1885, were already in British hands. In 1887 one can be sure that the Cup did not look as secure in New York as it does now!

There's little doubt that the committee drawing up the Deed were also still upset about *Thistle*'s inaccurate measurements, and about the lack of time there had been to build a successful defender. Next time, they must have thought, there might not be the genius of an Edward Burgess or the deep purse of a General Paine to get them out of trouble. To have the measurements – *exact* measurements – of a potential challenger ten months before gave adequate time to assess the danger and meet it.

The Committee were acting, as they thought, in the best interests of yachting and the New York Yacht Club. Its members were all distinguished citizens and experienced yachtsmen, and to look for base motives is absurd. Nevertheless, the wording of the new Deed and the interpretation put on it by the press and other clubs likely to challenge for the trophy did not enhance the Club's reputation for fair play. Indeed the new Deed was savagely attacked on both sides of the Atlantic, by American commentators no less than by foreigners. *Forest and Stream* called it 'an act to prevent yacht racing' and commented

charges were made against the Club, and we still believe correctly, that in assuming the ownership of the America's Cup and making new conditions to govern contests for it, the Club acted illegally and unfairly, having no right to establish any conditions of its own, and having gone further in establishing very unfair ones.

The Yacht Racing Association, to which belonged most major European clubs, perused the new Deed and then wrote to the Club on 22 February 1888, saying 'that the terms of the new Deed of Gift are such that foreign vessels are unable to challenge', and there was a mounting chorus of disapproval and criticism which rumbled on for years. In the appendix of Lawson's book is a letter sent by the lawyer Stinson Jarvis to *Forest and Stream* and printed by them on 7 July 1892. In it Jarvis states, as a lawyer and an authority on yachting matters, that not only was the third Deed of Gift of 1887 illegal but so was the earlier one of 1882. Jarvis argued cogently that the only valid Deed was the one made in 1857 and that the New York Yacht Club were merely the trustees of the Cup:

The only ways in which the New York or any other Yacht club could deal with the Cup were to observe the conditions which should forever attach to it, keep it perpetually open to challenge, and hand it over to the club whose yacht should win.

In the face of this unmistakably clear language in the creation of the trust, the officers of the New York Yacht Club twice handed the Cup over (as is said) to a man who legally had nothing to do with it, and on each occasion took back alleged conveyances from a man who had nothing to convey, because nothing had been conveyed to him. Mr Schuyler, together with the other owners, parted forever with all their title in the Cup in creating a trust in favour of certain institutions. The important benefits passing to the beneficiaries under this trust gift immediately attached as of right to all of them, and could not be revoked or altered by arrangements between Mr Schuyler and the present and merely temporary trustees. Mr Schuyler's former intimacy with the matter, as one of the donors, seems to have blinded everybody's eyes to the fact that after the first conveyance he was, legally, a complete stranger to the Cup; and also that the trusts and conditions first made cannot be interfered with.

Surely it must be clear to all that the New York Yacht Club could not possibly convey to Mr Schuyler an ownership in the Cup which it did not itself possess, and that consequently his alleged conveyances to the Club should never have been made.

This charge was repeated nearly a decade later when the *New York World* called the Club's action 'a preposterous, illegal proceeding', and through the following decades the matter was never satisfactorily settled. However, the club held the cup *de facto* if not *de jure*. After some months it did relent sufficiently to say, in a resolution of May 1888 following a request from the Royal London Yacht Club for an interpretation of the new deed, that, as it was quite satisfied with the terms under which the last three challenges had been held, these same terms would apply to any future challenge provided that any club which might win the Cup held to the new Deed of Gift 'inasmuch as this club believes it to be in the interest of all parties, and the terms of which are distinct, fair, and sportsmanlike'.

At this juncture Australia, for the first time, took an interest in the America's Cup. A syndicate of Sydney yachtsmen sent a yacht designer called Reeks to New York, where he arrived in October 1888 to assess the situation with regard to the new Deed, and to report back on whether a challenge in 1890 was a practical possibility. Reeks inspected *Volunteer* and other American yachts, and had discussions with officials of the N Y Y C. He then went on to London to see if he could get any useful suggestions from the English yachting fraternity. But after he returned to Australia no more was heard of the proposed challenge, and it was not until the early 1960s that Australia reappeared on the scene.

On 19 March 1889 the secretary of the Royal Yacht Squadron challenged on behalf of the Earl of Dunraven. He gave the name of his yacht as *Valkyrie*, and supplied her dimensions. The challenge was accepted on 11 April but withdrawn by the Squadron when it was made clear to them by a specially elected committee of the Club that the Squadron would have to abide by the new Deed of Gift should Dunraven win the Cup. The Secretary of the R Y S wrote:

We would not undertake the responsibility of entering into such a covenant which would make the terms of the new deed of gift binding on any future challenger. We would further point out that the effect of accepting the conditions of the New York Yacht Club would be to compel the Royal Yacht Squadron to insist upon receiving, should it be successful in winning the Cup, more favourable terms from a challenger than those under which it challenged.

In reply the Club pointed out that this was not so if the 'mutual consent' clause were acted upon; it added that, if asked, it would explain too the rest of the Deed, which 'would be found susceptible of easy explanation'. But they found no takers. The matter rested until Mr Busk wrote to Dunraven on 3 April 1890 in an attempt to pinpoint the dislike the British had taken to the new Deed. Dunraven replied the same month with his own reasons for disliking the new Deed, and revealed there was nothing in it with which he *did* agree. He didn't think much of the Deed of 1882 either, 'but I will not trouble you with my personal ideas as to the best possible conditions for arranging and conducting international racing'. The correspondence ceased, and nothing was heard of Dunraven for two and a half years.

Then in September 1892 Dunraven again began negotiations through General Paine and others. The upshot was that a formal challenge from the Royal Yacht Squadron on 25 November of that year. Time had softened attitudes; the conditions under which the challenge was arranged were substantially different to those previously stipulated by the Club, though there had been give and take on both sides. Briefly, it was agreed that length of load waterline was the only dimension required; that any excess above that declared would be penalized when calculating time allowance; and that if the challenging club won the Cup any further challenge would be held under 'precisely similar terms as those contained in this challenge, provided always that such clubs shall not refuse any challenge according to the conditions laid down in the deed of 1887'. The Club formally accepted the challenge on 15 December and, clinging perhaps to the tattered deed of 1887, voted that the races be the best of five, start ten months from 5 December, the date the Squadron's official challenge was received, but adding that 'the date of the match to be subject to alteration for mutual convenience and by mutual consent'. This was not necessary, and the first race took place on 5 October.

While all this politicking was taking place the science of yacht design did not stand still, on either side of the Atlantic, and part of the 1887 Deed of Gift was soon largely outdated. First *Clara* which, with John Barr at the helm, became the leader of the American 53-foot class, and then another British

Nathanael Greene Herreshoff in 1920

cutter, *Minerva*, which, under the command of John's younger brother Charlie Barr, led the American 40-footers for that season, started American designers thinking – particularly one Nathanael Herreshoff.

Herreshoff, unlike Burgess, was given a technical education at the Massachusetts Institute of Technology. Both men were of a similar age, were distantly related and had a long-standing friendship, the rich Burgess family owning several Herreshoff yachts. But while Burgess was successfully designing a new era of America's Cup yachts Nat, after a spell as a mechanical engineer, joined his brother John in his business of building launches and steamers, which led to the creation of the Herreshoff Manufacturing Company. Then, in 1872, they built *Shadow*, the only American yacht to beat *Madge* when she had her successful season in American waters in 1881, but it was not until 1891 that they launched *Gloriana*. Lawson says of her:

A new type had come in, of which the keel 46-footer *Gloriana*, built in 1891 and owned by E. D. Morgan, was

the shining exponent in this country; a type of 'rating cheater', narrower and deeper than our old-time sloops, with overall length in great disparity to their load waterline, a condition much to be desired under the system of measurement whose basis is load water-line and sail area only.

The system of measurement to which Lawson refers was the one which, in 1883, the New York Yacht Club had, along with the Seawanhaka Corinthian Yacht Club, adopted. It was calculated from both waterline length and sail area, and superseded the old method of rating in America by measuring the cubic content of competing yachts. Curiously, the two clubs chose different methods of calculation, but in 1890 the New York Yacht Club adopted the other club's rule ($L + \sqrt{SA}$, where L is waterline length and SA is sail area) and it was under this that *Gloriana* was built. The tax in this rule was on waterline length with no penalty for overall length; *Gloriana* was built to evade it, hence the name for her type, of 'rating cheater'. If a yacht was built with large overhangs more sail could be put on her. This in turn meant greater stability was needed than any centreboard could give. For *Gloriana* – 45 feet on the waterline but 70 feet overall – Herreshoff therefore developed the fin keel which carried a lozenge-shaped lump of lead at its end. During her first season, skippered by Captain John Barr, she was amazingly successful, winning eight first prizes out of eight starts but was succeeded the following year by *Wasp*, also designed by Herreshoff.

This new development in yacht design, however, did not supplant older methods of construction overnight. Indeed, when Dunraven's challenge was accepted each of the four yachts that were specially built as candidates for the defence, while radical departures from the traditional shoal-draft centre-boarders, still contained elements of that well-proven design. Two of them came from Herreshoff: *Vigilant*, a deep-keel centreboarder, ordered by a syndicate representing the New York Yacht Club, was the first America's Cup yacht to be constructed of tobin bronze; and *Colonia*, a fixed-keel yacht designed as an enlarged *Wasp*, was ordered by a syndicate composed of Archibald Rogers, Frederick W. Vanderbilt, William K. Vanderbilt, F. Augustus Schermerhorn, J. Pierpont Morgan, and John E. Brooks. Two Boston boats were also built: John Paine, the son of the general, designed a sloop called *Jubilee* which was built of steel and had a fin keel and two centreboards. She, too, was derived from *Wasp*, though she was more extreme in design than *Colonia*. The other Boston boat, *Pilgrim*, was designed by Burgess's successor in business, Stewart and Binney, as Burgess had died from typhoid in 1891 at the tragically early age of forty-two. *Pilgrim* too was built of steel and had a fin keel; her lines were, as Lawson described them, 'of a graceful canoe'.

Accidents and adverse weather dogged the early encounters of these four contenders and the first trial race had to take place between the two New York yachts as both Boston candidates had been disabled. It produced an extraordinary result. *Colonia* lost by 14 seconds, actual time, but won by 6 seconds after receiving 20 seconds on time allowance. But *Vigilant* was then remeasured, and it was found that she should have only allowed *Colonia* 14 seconds, making the result a dead heat.

The next trial took place two days later in a light breeze with all four yachts participating. *Vigilant* won by 4½ minutes from *Jubilee*, with *Pilgrim* third and *Colonia* last. In this race it was seen that *Colonia*'s design was at fault, for she sagged badly to leeward when close to the wind. The third and last trial was held on 11 September; again *Vigilant* won. Her closest rival *Jubilee* was crippled in this race and finished last.

The performance of the four new craft drew criticism from all sides at first and the newspapers ran headlines like 'Lack of faith in new sloops expressed on all sides ... new types denounced as monstrosities and failures', for it was not thought that the new fin-type keel was suitable for such large yachts, and their overhangs were ridiculed by the critics. 'To the novice,' Lawson comments, 'they had something of the appearance of a person with a receding chin'; he adds that rumour had it that *Colonia*'s poor performance to windward was due to an insufficient depth of keel – because Herreshoff had not wanted the trouble of dredging the water off the slip at the Herreshoff yard!

On the other hand *Pilgrim*'s fin keel was too long and was so flexible that it buckled when she was closehauled. *Jubilee*, *Vigilant*'s nearest rival, never really got tuned properly and her gear aloft kept failing.

Once chosen, faith in *Vigilant* grew, though some old-timers still muttered that *Puritan*, to which the new challenger would probably have had to have given about 18 minutes, should have been chosen instead; certainly *Vigilant* suffered from some serious defects. She steered very badly for one thing, and her 4-ton centreboard gave constant trouble as it continually jammed despite, or perhaps because of, powerful differential lifts to raise and lower it that were mechanical wonders of the time. However, her strengths were numerous. One was her abnormal breadth of deck, which enabled the yacht's manager C. Oliver Iselin, to cram additional crew on board. These additions were used as extra ballast, and she carried no less than seventy men for just that purpose, Iselin having learnt this trick from his days in the old sandbag racers. Up to that time there had been no restrictions on the number of crew on board but thereafter the number was restricted. *Vigilant*'s other great advantage was her polished bronze bottom, far superior to the rough steel of the other American yachts, or the coppered wooden bottom of the British challenger.

The British challenger, after a tough ocean crossing arrived in New York on 22 September, which gave her little time to tune up. She was, however, viewed with respect by the Americans who felt her a dangerous adversary. She was skippered by Captain William Cranfield, described as 'a big-bodied and cleanly built Englishman, with a fair face and blond beard. He has a genial manner and just the faintest suspicion of a twinkle in his left eye,' and he was regarded as one of the best racing skippers England had produced. *Valkyrie II* was of composite build, designed by George Watson and built by Henderson's on the Clyde. She was a powerful boat and at 86.80 feet on the waterline she was just fractionally longer than *Vigilant*. However, despite Watson's already quoted determination to increase the square footage of canvas on future challengers her sail area was only 10,042 square feet against *Vigilant*'s 11,272 square feet.

Valkyrie II's owner, Lord Dunraven, was a man of many parts. Besides being an expert yachtsman (he held a master's certificate), he had written a book on navigation – and on other subjects as well. He was an expert violinist, an ex-diplomat and a one-time war correspondent. He possessed a valuable stud on his Irish estate and he was something of a steeplechaser. In short he was a typical Victorian aristocrat, an all-rounder, a dilettante. Perhaps not typical of his generation were his political views, which were remarkably enlightened for someone of his station and time. His autobiography, a huge two-volume affair, covers his life in minute detail – but it is remarkably reticent about his exploits to retrieve the America's Cup. The following extract shows that he had his problems with his crew but knew how to deal with them effectively.

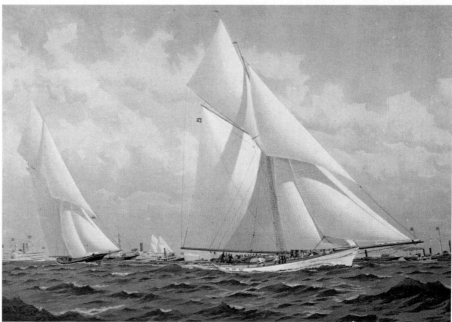

bove: Mischief leading
alanta at the start of the 1881
allenge

ight: Volunteer leading
histle during the first
ce of the 1887 challenge

pposite above: Magic, the
inner in 1870

eft: Columbia leading
ivonia, 1871

Columbia leads *Shamrock I* off Sandy Hook, 1899

Opposite: Defender (Penob-scott
Marine Museum, Maine)

Above: Reliance, the successful defender of the 1903 challenge

Endeavour (Malcolm Henderson Gallery, London)

'Vigilant'

When I got to New York I found my crew in a condition of physical demoralization. They were unaccustomed to the climate. The weather was very hot, and New York can be about as hot a place as I know. . . . Being thorough Britons, and not feeling very well, they naturally deemed more beer and more beef to be indicated, and adopted that method of cure. It did not answer, and I had to put them on a severe diet. That, and a course of Valkyrie cocktails, did them a world of good. Valkyrie cocktails were of a nauseous black-dose description, concocted in large cans, and served out daily.

For the first time since yachts had started from anchor, the one-gun start was employed for the races after a 10-minute warning signal. The earlier method was that the competing yachts were given 2 minutes to cross the line after the starting gun had been fired. Their time was taken from when they each crossed, and any difference in the time of crossing was allowed for when calculating which yacht had won. But on this occasion time for both yachts was taken from the gun – as it is today – so it was vital that both captains crossed the line at the right moment. The new rule produced a spectacular display of tactical sailing which the huge spectator fleet that had assembled to watch the first race loved. *Vigilant* crossed some 28 seconds ahead of the challenger. It was a spinnaker start and *Valkyrie II* surprised everyone by breaking out an extremely light-looking sail. It looked like silk but was unbleached muslin. This first race had to be abandoned through lack of wind, but not before *Valkyne's* lightweight spinnaker had helped her to a 26-minute lead.

65

The British yacht's decisive lead when the time limit expired caused a furore in the press, and the afterguard on the American yacht – C. Oliver Iselin, the skipper Captain William Hansen, Captain Terry (in charge of *Vigilant*'s sails), and the yacht's architect, Herreshoff – were roundly criticized for their performance. However, a friend of Iselin's is quoted as saying tersely: 'I have always noticed how well you can sail other people's boats when you are not on board.'

Despite these doubts *Vigilant* won the first completed race on 7 October with comparative ease (5 minutes 48 seconds on corrected time) in a light wind; and won again, surprisingly easily, in a stronger blow on the 9th, winning by over 10½ minutes to the delight of the huge spectator fleet. The yachts met again on the 11th but there was only a faint southerly air. The committee signalled the competitors asking if they'd consent to a postponement. The Americans agreed but Dunraven did not and the race was started at 1.54. After the yachts had rounded the outer mark in the dark the race was abandoned. At the mark *Vigilant* was near 7 minutes ahead.

On Friday 13th the yachts met for the last time, in one of the great races in the history of the America's Cup. The morning dawned overcast with a strong east wind and a lumpy sea. The first leg of the course was laid right into the eye of the 15-knot wind, which was freshening by the minute. After the start had been delayed, first by the challenger when the sheave of one of the throat-halyard blocks carried away and then by the defender whose centreboard could only be partly lowered, both yachts got away in a fine display of seamanship which put *Valkyrie* over the line a mere 9 seconds ahead of *Vigilant*. 'Every fathom of the course was stubbornly con-

tested,' Lawson wrote, and after 40 minutes *Valkyrie*, though to windward, was only 200 yards ahead. The wind by now had increased to 25 knots or so and both yachts were sailing with lee rails buried.

After two hours' sailing the two yachts rounded the mark with the challenger about a third of a mile ahead, the equivalent of just under 2 minutes. *Vigilant*'s crew then proceeded to cram on all sail and give a remarkable display of seamanship. After rounding the mark her spinnaker went up in stops as was the practice in America (if the British had done the same the result of the race could have been very different), and then her balloon jibtopsail was hoisted in the same manner. But a halyard jammed and the sail would only go half way up the stay; a hand had to be hoisted and then lowered down the stay to free it. The reef in the main was then shaken out by another hand who was secured from the masthead and hauled out along the boom by an outhaul. Two more hands were then sent aloft, one to the topmast head and another to the peak of the gaff to secure the working topsail when the reef was shaken out and the mainsail was then sweated up to its full extent. Once this had been accomplished the no. 2 club-topsail was sent up to windward of the working topsail and the balloon jib-topsail was broken out. 'By this time,' Lawson comments, '*Vigilant* was under a pyramid of rounded and hardened canvas and although her topmast buckled and her stays were as taut as iron nothing parted.'

Valkyrie's crew had not been idle; determined to keep their lead, they set a spinnaker as well as a balloon jib-topsail, but the half-reef was not shaken out so the working topsail was kept aloft. Everyone held their breath as the two yachts raced across the water neck and neck, neither gaining on the other.

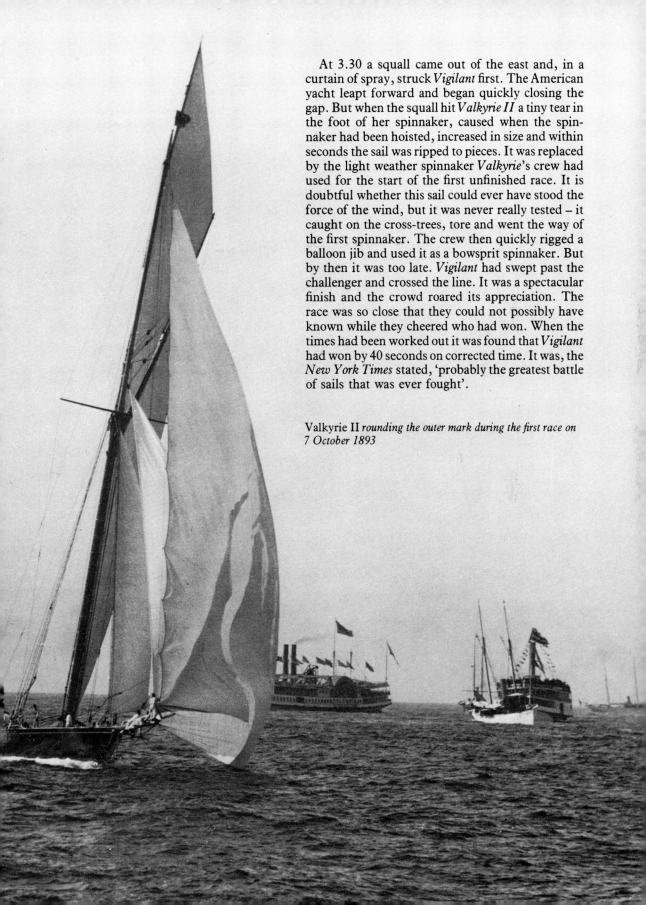

At 3.30 a squall came out of the east and, in a curtain of spray, struck *Vigilant* first. The American yacht leapt forward and began quickly closing the gap. But when the squall hit *Valkyrie II* a tiny tear in the foot of her spinnaker, caused when the spinnaker had been hoisted, increased in size and within seconds the sail was ripped to pieces. It was replaced by the light weather spinnaker *Valkyrie*'s crew had used for the start of the first unfinished race. It is doubtful whether this sail could ever have stood the force of the wind, but it was never really tested – it caught on the cross-trees, tore and went the way of the first spinnaker. The crew then quickly rigged a balloon jib and used it as a bowsprit spinnaker. But by then it was too late. *Vigilant* had swept past the challenger and crossed the line. It was a spectacular finish and the crowd roared its appreciation. The race was so close that they could not possibly have known while they cheered who had won. When the times had been worked out it was found that *Vigilant* had won by 40 seconds on corrected time. It was, the *New York Times* stated, 'probably the greatest battle of sails that was ever fought'.

Valkyrie II *rounding the outer mark during the first race on 7 October 1893*

This great finish was not the only event that made the sailing season of 1893 a memorable one. Apart from the Dunraven challenge, the upsurge in yacht building on both sides of the Atlantic – created in England by the new rating rule and in America by the challenge – produced some exciting racing in both countries. Herreshoff built not only two of the contenders for the defence of the Cup, but *Navahoe* for Mr Phelps Carroll, who crossed the Atlantic specifically in a successful bid to regain the Brenton Reef Cup won by *Genesta* in 1885. On the British side Watson produced *Valkyrie II*, *Satanita* – and *Britannia*, for the Prince of Wales. Just as the new American boats were greeted with scepticism on their side of the Atlantic so their British counterparts were met with open hostility in Britain. 'Hideous machines', they were called, and 'gratuitously ugly' – though later generations were to call *Britannia* one of the most beautiful yachts ever to float. It seemed that whatever was new to yachtsmen was looked at askance, but the new yachts soon proved

their weatherliness and when *Navahoe* arrived in English waters a fine season's racing was had by the big cutters. The following year *Vigilant* crossed the Atlantic to race in the British regattas and also proved a worthy adversary. But neither yacht was able consistently to beat the Royal cutter. *Vigilant* met *Britannia* seventeen times, and won but five, and the skipper of *Vigilant* on his return home remarked: 'We've been to school.'

Success against the Americans proved to the English, if not to anyone else, that it was the local conditions in America that beat them, not American yachts, and British and American designers continued to bring their two types of yachts closer together in design. When Lord Dunraven challenged again for 1895 both designs produced almost identical boats, which made American papers com-

'Defender'

ment that Herreshoff had probably had a bigger impact on English yachting than he had had on American. The *Sun* of 30 June 1895 put it this way:

It is a singular fact that thus far Herreshoff has exercised a more stimulating influence over yacht racing in England than he has here. Here his supremacy has been so pronounced that he has scared off competition. Here he builds a boat for a certain class and she proves so far superior to all others in it that they drop out, and next season she is without a competitor. Here it has been well said that Herreshoff has only been beaten by himself. But in England, in some notable instances they have bettered his instruction. They have turned out racing machines that beat his racing machines.

In America it was decided to build only one defender, and she was called just that. *Defender* was designed by Herreshoff for a NYYC syndicate composed of William K. Vanderbilt, E. D. Morgan and C. Oliver Iselin, and no money was spared in making sure she retained the Cup. Herreshoff employed the lightest materials possible, including aluminium which was lighter than tobin bronze. By doing so it was calculated that Herreshoff saved 17 tons dead weight. But the experimental mixture of metals was not a success; though completely rebuilt in 1899 *Defender* was scrapped a couple of years later as electrolysis, set up through the mixed use of metals, corroded her hull. But in the short term she was a highly successful boat and was the first Cup defender to have a fin keel and no centreboard. Her spars were of steel, her bow canoe-shaped. Many viewed her with scepticism, and rumour had it that she was not structurally sound. So strong was the gossip on this point that Iselin had to issue a statement denying it. The newspapers also pointed out with glee that she ran aground twice, and broke several spars, while her opponents during the trial races, *Vigilant*, *Jubilee* and *Volunteer*, complained bitterly but unvailingly of her violations of the racing rules.

Skippered by Charlie Barr, *Vigilant*, on which $50,000 was lavished by her owner George J. Gould, had several close races with *Defender* and relations between the two boats were far from amicable. During the start for one race Mr Willard, the manager of *Vigilant*, complained that he'd been fouled by *Defender*, and Barr was furious. 'I've been made a fool of,' he said. 'It is unfair that we should have to give way all the time. If these races had been for the cup *Valkyrie* would have held her course each time. I know we were right, and I wish to go on record.'

Willard, however, did not protest officially this time as he had already done so once – though the protest had not yet been heard (it was a Club rule that any yacht twice found wrong under protest would not continue racing). Instead he withdrew *Vigilant*, but later a truce was arranged and *Vigilant* sailed in the official trials. There were three. *Defender* had to withdraw from the first because the steel band round her mast that kept the tension on the stays slipped. However she won the next two easily and was promptly selected to defend the Cup.

Meanwhile, the British challenger, *Valkyrie III*, was not without problems. One account of her said

with a strong breeze, she showed herself a veritable lame duck. . . . Her mainsail was hanging over on the wind, her gaff had fallen out to leeward, and the peak halyards were not enough to set it up. Her jackyard topsail was flying all about, and its clew would not be flattened with the gaff hanging over the yacht.

It was found that she did not have enough ballast and an additional 12 tons had to be added. In the few trial races she entered before leaving for America she lost twice to *Britannia* and won once, but she beat *Ailsa* on the two occasions they raced against each other. She arrived in New York on 18 August a mere three weeks before the races began and had to be fitted out in a great hurry. The steel mast – it would have been the first one ever used in an America's Cup match – that had been built for her did not arrive in time and her wooden one had to be stepped. However, her hexagonal steel boom, 105 feet long and 22 inches in diameter, did arrive and was used. This, too, was an experimental spar and worked very successfully. She was commanded by Captain Cranfield, with Sycamore – the famous 'Siccy', of whom more later – as his assistant.

The negotiations for the ninth challenge were, by America's Cup standards, amicable and the NYYC made a considerable concession when Dunraven asked that he be allowed to substitute another vessel should the original yacht named in the challenge not turn out to be the fastest. However, they rejected his request to hold the races off Marblehead to avoid the crowds of waterborne spectators, and to continue the one-gun start. Dunraven also asked that the yachts be measured with all weights on board, and that their waterlines be then marked. In the light of what was to happen this request is significant.

The Irish Earl, when negotiating his first challenge, had covered and re-covered just about every

'Valkyrie III'

possible aspect of the proposed match, and over an extended – and exhaustive – period of time had levered from the Club conditions which made a challenge possible. It was just as well he did persist for his interest in the Cup sustained it through a very difficult period after the Deed of Gift had been altered in 1887. Everyone else in Britain had come to regard the Cup as impossible to regain when hedged about by so many conditions, and only Dunraven's persistence made the Club see sense. But here, with his next challenge, he brought up an entirely new stipulation, something he had not even mentioned earlier.

The committee replied that they were quite agreeable that the yachts be measured with all weights on board but did not offer an opinion about the waterlines then being marked; apparently Dunra-ven did not pursue this point at that time. Nor did he mention it when he signed the conditions to govern the races on 4 September, the conditions stipulating that the yachts were 'to be measured with all weights on board to be carried in a race, restrictions as to bulkheads, floors, doors, water-tanks and anchor being waived', and an agreement was made that if either yacht increased or decreased her load waterline length or her spar measurement, as taken officially, then she had to be remeasured before the next race. Quite why this agreement was thought necessary or who asked for it is not known. If a yacht's load waterline was to be decreased to take advantage of an increased time allowance that allowance could not be implemented unless she was re-measured by the official measurer. If her load waterline were increased without informing the official measurer then it was surely obvious that the person or persons responsible were cheating. Lawson quotes this agreement in full, but does not comment on it. It does seem probable that Dunraven, concerned about the point raised by him in the negotiations but not commented on by the Committee and not pursued by Dunraven, was anxious to include it in the conditions for the race. If one accepts this explanation it becomes obvious that Dunraven felt that someone might tamper with the American boat's load waterline. Lawson comments that when Dunraven underlined his anxiety on this point in a letter to the Cup Committee two days after signing the conditions of the race he had been listening to gossip among his American friends on board *Valkyrie*'s tender, *City of Bridgeport*, about the manager of the American boat, C. Oliver Iselin. Iselin, apparently, had been allegedly involved in dishonestly ballasting another yacht of which he had been manager, and Iselin's tactic of using extra crew as ballast in *Vigilant* probably did not strike the Irish nobleman as sporting. Certainly Dunraven's uneasiness must have been increased once he arrived in the United States and heard this tittle-tattle which was, as Lawson put it, 'in pretty general circulation at that time among yachtsmen'. But he must certainly have been aware of it before leaving England; otherwise why should he have raised the question of marking the yachts' load waterlines while still on the other side of the Atlantic? It seems probable that this gossip was in general circulation over a period of time – perhaps even when Dunraven had competed against Iselin in 1893 – but was only really brought to the fore on his arrival back in America in 1895.

His anxiety certainly spurred him to write a strange letter to the Cup Committee on the 6th, just the day before the first race was due, asking that the load waterlines be marked after measuring and stating that 'on reflection' he did not consider the matter 'satisfactory'. He pointed out that under present conditions alterations to the load waterline could

be made without the owner's knowledge, and without possibility of detection. It is, of course, impossible to guard absolutely against such an occurrence. But these contests cannot be compared with ordinary races; and in the interest of the public, and of the owners who have to do their best to see that rules are obeyed, it is surely right and necessary that the Cup committee should take every precaution to insure that the vessels sail on their measured load waterline length.

The Club received the letter the same day. It immediately sent down a special committee of two of

Mr and Mrs C. Oliver Iselin. Behind Mrs Iselin is Woodbury Kane, a member of Iselin's afterguard since 1893

its members to Erie Basin where the yachts were being measured for the race the next day with the object of complying with Dunraven's request; Iselin had immediately agreed to it. Dunraven, quixotically, could not implement his own proposition because the challenger had left the basin and could not get back in because of the tide! In short, Dunraven was already behaving erratically. But worse was to come.

As any restrictions on bulkheads, doors, floors and water tanks had been waived, *Defender*'s crew quickly divested her of these and extra lead was added to compensate. (*Valkyrie III* had already been stripped before crossing the Atlantic, which is why this special clause was inserted in the conditions for the race.) The lead added to *Defender* was insufficient to sink her to her original load waterline so additional lead was added while she was in the Erie Basin and stored temporarily on the cabin floor, and she was then officially measured for the first race. Later it was found that to store the additional lead below *Defender*'s floor it was necessary to cut the twenty-one pigs in half. This was done on *Defender*'s tender, *Hattie Palmer*, which lay alongside the American yacht. At the same time a party of riggers arrived to fix new wire bridles on to the mainsheet block and work continued on this until about three o'clock in the morning. This work did not go unnoticed by the British contingent on board their tender. The next morning Dunraven, just before the race, told the American representative, Latham Fish, who was to sail on *Valkyrie III*, that he thought

some mistake had been made, and that all the weight put into *Defender* after measurement had not been taken out before the race; that I was positively certain that she was sailing at least a foot beyond her proper length, and I requested him to take the earliest opportunity of mentioning the matter to the Committee.

Latham Fish, doubtless somewhat amazed, asked Dunraven if he had any suggestions as to what should be done. Dunraven later stated

I replied to the effect that I wished the Committee to put one of the members, or some reliable representative, on board of each yacht immediately after the race, and to have both vessels remeasured, if possible, that evening. If that were impossible, then that the members of the Committee, or their representatives, should stay on board in charge of the vessels until they were measured.

Nothing more was said or done until the first race had been started and the outer mark had been turned. The subject was then raised again. Mr Fish was given a notepad by Dunraven's representative in America, a man called Kersey, and Fish and Dunraven went below. Fish then made notes of Dunraven's request for remeasurement and read them back to him. According to Fish, Dunraven added three words (italicized) to the note which, in full, read:

Lord Dunraven believes from *his own and* observation of those on *Valkyrie III* and *City of Bridgeport*, that *Defender* sailed to-day's race three (3) or four (4) inches deeper than when measured. Bobstay. Pipe. D. Captain of B. Pilot, Glennie. Ratsey. Kersey.

Fish's shorthand meant this: Dunraven maintained that not only was *Defender*'s bobstay bolt nearer the

water, which might have been the result of alteration of trim, but a pipe previously flush with the water was not to be seen. This evidence was seen not only by Dunraven (D) but by the Captain of the *City of Bridgeport* (B) and by three other reliable witnesses. Fish was put on board the Committee boat immediately after the race and reported to the Cup and Regatta committees. A remeasurement of both yachts was called for the next day, and the load waterlines marked. The difference on *Defender*'s waterline was found to be one-eighth of an inch, and on *Valkyrie*'s one-sixteenth. As far as the Cup Committee were concerned this ended the matter. 'Lord Dunraven stated,' they said later, 'that he believed the change had been made without the knowledge of *Defender*'s owners, but that it must be corrected or he would discontinue racing.' In a manner of speaking it had been corrected because the remeasurement showed no fraud had taken place. When Dunraven pointed out that remeasuring the yachts next day proved nothing, the Committee revealed their attitude to Dunraven's charge when it had been first put before them by Fish:

The accuser had neglected his opportunity to protest before the race, and so secure a remeasurement that day, and in view of such neglect the onus of taking up the charge of fraud did not rest on the Committee, and *a fortiori*, they were not bound to have recourse to methods unprecedented in the history of American yacht-racing. The charge involved the transference of 20,000 to 30,000 pounds of weight, and the connivance of the whole crew of the American yacht and her tender, and was considered by the Committee absurd and preposterous. The Committee decided to treat the complaint simply as a call for remeasurement, and to disregard all imputations of fraud; and by so doing to force upon the accuser the issue either to support his charge and protest against his treatment by the Committee, or to drop the subject and go on with the match. . . . We maintain that the Committee were entitled to regard his action in continuing the contest after his complaint as tantamount to a withdrawal of his charges, and an acknowledgement that he no longer had grounds of complaint, and that he was also in honor bound to so regard it.

But Dunraven did not see it that way. 'I was reluctant,' he stated later, 'to make a formal complaint to the Cup Committee on the matter which it was, of course, impossible for me to verify; and in any case nothing could be done before the races started,' and his cross examination at the subsequent enquiry held by the Club shows that though he still felt he had behaved properly by continuing to race his attitude, in the light of some sharp questioning by Iselin's lawyer, was irrational and muddled. But he did continue to race and at the time neither Dunraven nor the Club said anything. Naturally, the whole matter was kept under wraps and neither the public nor the press had an inkling of what had occurred when the two yachts headed for the start line for the second race, the first having been won in mostly light winds by *Defender* by 8 minutes 20 seconds elapsed time.

Apart from his accusation of fraud, Dunraven had also protested to the Committee about the interference caused by the enormous spectator fleet – before the first race it was reckoned to contain something like 60,000 people aboard over 200 steamers and other craft. Now, before the second race began, events proved that Dunraven was right about one thing at least: a large excursion steamer blundered right across the course of the two yachts as they headed for the line. *Valkyrie III* managed to cross the steamer's bow but *Defender* had to go under her stern. Once clear of the obstruction it was obvious to all who were watching that the two yachts were on collision course. *Defender*, to leeward of *Valkyrie* and therefore with the right of way, was travelling faster and just as she got under the latter's lee, the British yacht bore off and then luffed sharply. It would have been a good manoeuvre on the part of Captain Cranfield's assistant, Captain Sycamore, who was at the helm, if it had worked – for the British yacht would have blanketed *Defender*. The result, however, was disaster. The end of *Valkyrie*'s main boom caught in the American's starboard topmast-shroud, springing it out of the spreader and causing the topmast to bend precariously. *Defender* immediately ran up a protest flag, which was acknowledged by the Committee boat. To everyone's amazement the British yacht kept going, forcing *Defender* to follow her which she very pluckily managed to do only 1 minute and 15 seconds later after carrying out emergency work and lowering her jibtopsail before the topmast broke.

Despite this handicap – alleviated somewhat on the run home because she was on the other tack and could therefore set whatever sails were necessary – *Defender* finished only 2 minutes 18 seconds behind, a mere 47 seconds after her time allowance was applied. There seems little doubt that if the race had been a mile or two longer she would have won. Iselin promptly sent in a letter of protest saying, 'I shaped my course for the line, (which, course, according to my orders, was not altered in the slightest degree), on the starboard tack, with sheets trimmed down, when *Valkyrie* bore down on us with wide sheets.' Dunraven, despite photographic evidence to the contrary, said that *Defender* luffed into *Valkyrie III* after establishing an overlap and that he only had just enough room to clear the Committee boat. He then went on to say that he did not see the protest flag or he would have protested himself and what was more Mr Henderson, his representative on *Defender*, did not see it either!

Iselin's protest was sustained. Some thought it would teach Dunraven a lesson in manners if the Committee had ruled, as it had a right to do, that the race be resailed, but this the Committee reporting on the incident refused to recommend. However they were quite agreeable to sanctioning an offer from Mr Iselin to resail. 'There were not a few members of the N Y Y C itself, and hosts of other yachtsmen,' Lawson comments wryly, 'who thought this a fine distinction.' Nevertheless, the offer was made by Iselin but declined by Dunraven, who said that as the Committee had already ruled he was in the wrong there was nothing more to be done.

The same day the second race finished, and before he knew the result of the protest against him, Dunraven wrote the Cup Committee that unless he had a clear course for the third race he would not sail. He said it was impossible to decide the merit of two competing vessels under such crowded conditions and that 'to attempt to start two such large vessels in a very confined space, and among moving steamers and tugboats, is, in my opinion, exceedingly dangerous, and I will not further risk the lives of my men or the ship'. Dunraven felt strongly on this score, and with good reason, for the year before he had been at the helm of his previous challenger *Valkyrie II* when she was sunk by *Satanita* while trying to avoid a spectator boat before the start of the race for big cutters on the Clyde. It must have been a traumatic incident and although everyone escaped from the wreck alive, one seaman later died of his injuries.

The next day the Club sent a special Committee to confer with Dunraven. At 11.30 that night he wrote to the Cup Committee saying that although the special Committee could not guarantee him a clear course he would race, provided the Cup Committee agreed to declare it void if the competing vessels were obstructed by the spectator fleet. By the time the Cup Committee received the letter, however, it was too late to do anything and later it was stated they had no authority to agree to such conditions anyway. When interviewed the day after the race the Chairman of the America's Cup Committee said:

Lord Dunraven's demands were absurd, unbusinesslike and utterly impossible to comply with. Now, supposing the *Valkyrie* had been a mile and a half ahead and we declared the race off, because some boat interfered with the *Defender*, what would people say? Why, the country would be too hot to hold us. Lord Dunraven makes a point of it that the Committee did not answer his letter. How could we? We did not receive it until eight o'clock Thursday morning. . . . When they [the Special Committee] left him Wednesday night he said he would start the *Valkyrie*. In his second letter, which was received on the morning of the race, he left it in doubt whether he would cover the course or not.

The race was in fact delayed so that steamers could be cleared from around the start line but Dunraven did not consider this complying with his request. He had obviously hoped the races would be postponed for the day so that further discussion of his latest letter could take place. However, as the Committee said in a special report, it seemed to them 'useless and undignified to delay the start for further parley with a challenger who in the middle of a contest had seen fit to advance new conditions in the form of an ultimatum, under a threat to withdraw'. They added that the start was quite clear so there was no reason for Dunraven to complain, at least until interference had definitely taken place. As it was the British challenger, as soon as she appeared that morning, made it quite evident to the spectators that she had no intention of racing. When the starting gun fired she did cross the line – so that Dunraven kept to the letter of his promise of the previous evening if not to the spirit of it – but then immediately recrossed it and dropped her racing flag. She then ran up the burgee of the N Y Y C as, according to Dunraven, 'a gesture of friendship and courtesy', showing that sublime Irish ability to accomplish two completely contrary acts without in any way finding them contradictory.

Dunraven's withdrawal caused as much disgust in England as it did in America; he was roundly castigated as being a quitter and no sportsman. It was bad enough that the challenge should end on such a dismal note, but worse was to follow. On 9 November Dunraven reiterated his charges of fraud in an article published in the *Field*. Iselin reacted strongly and asked the Club to clear his name. This the Club did by appointing a committee of enquiry which wrote to the Royal Yacht Squadron enquiring whether the charges levelled by Dunraven had been laid before the Squadron, as they were given to understand that the article in the *Field* was based on a report Dunraven had sent to the Squadron secretary.

The Yacht Squadron had already been in dispute with the Club that year as they had implied during the negotiations for the match that they might not be willing to accept the Cup on the conditions laid down under the 1887 Deed of Gift should Dunraven win it. 'Squadron will not demand Cup, failing satisfactory agreement as to receipt' they said in a cable to the Club, which promptly replied that the Squadron would not have the right to reject custody of the Cup. The Squadron then capitulated, agreeing to accept the Cup under the conditions of the 1887 Deed of Gift and the modifications added to it by the Club, but doubtless they were none too pleased to imply they agreed with the terms laid down by the latest Deed of Gift. It, no doubt, did not take them long to compose their reply to this latest communication. 'The Squadron,' wrote the secretary, 'has taken no action in the matter'; as the Club had ignored Dunraven's request for immediate re-measurement, or for both vessels to come under the supervision of the Cup Committee until the measurement had been completed, the Squadron felt no redress was now possible and that it was purely a matter between Lord Dunraven and the Club. In other words, the Squadron agreed with Dunraven and proposed to have nothing further to do with the matter. The committee of enquiry was promptly set up. Dunraven agreed to appear before it, and three days after its appointment reiterated his charges in a speech in Wales. If his charge was now called an insult, he said – and it certainly was in America – why·was it not called that at the time? Some accused him of making the charge from the safety of his own country, yet he felt he would have been better able to stand up for himself if 'this violent hurricane of indignation' had broken when he originally made the complaint as he would have been on the spot. 'I confess it seems a little out of date now.'

His explanation to the committee of enquiry as to why he published the article in the *Field* was simple: he had asked through his American representative, Mr Kersey, that the Club not reveal to the public the dispute over *Defender*'s waterline, and the Squadron had also been cabled to his effect. Nevertheless the subject found its way into the New York papers and

Defender in 1899, with Uriah Rhodes at the wheel

appeared on 25 October under the banner headline 'Dunraven Cried Fraud'. Dunraven then felt he had to defend his actions by publishing his account. The responsibility for making the whole business public lay with the Club.

Up to this point Dunraven's actions and attitude are at least understandable. Anyone can make mistakes. That astute modern observer of the yachting scene, Douglas Phillips-Birt, points out in *The History of Yachting* when describing the atmosphere in which Dunraven judged *Defender* to be above her measured length:

The air that morning must have been electric with pre-race tension, nerves strung with anticipation, the steadiness of judgement rocked by unremitting blasts of pepped-up publicity . . . by nature imaginative and now made suspicious, after living for weeks in a hot-house world, the observations of that morning were enough to convince Dunraven that he was being cheated. The atmosphere and the urgency of the moment could do nothing to cast a saner light revealing the moral preposterousness of his idea or its practical absurdity.

Absurd Dunraven's charges were soon understood to be, but less understood by anyone reading the evidence is the Earl's implacable adherence to them at the committee of enquiry, and afterwards. How can anyone in their right minds suppose that thirteen *tons* of lead could be taken out of *Defender* – for that was the amount needed to affect her load waterline by the three or four inches observed by Dunraven – before she was officially measured, and then the lead put back again that night! To add to the wildness of Dunraven's accusations, Latham Fish denied that Dunraven had ever asked that members of the Cup Committee be put on both yachts after the race until remeasurement could take place. He still had the note which he had read back to Dunra-

Lord Dunraven

ven during the first race and it did not mention this fact. Dunraven could only reply that he only vaguely remembered Latham Fish making notes, that they weren't read out to him and that he made no alterations to them, but insisted that he had asked Latham Fish that the boats he put in charge of Committee members. Dunraven's observation of the bobstay bolt and the discharge hole was easily discounted by expert evidence which proved that the one was caused by the crew moving forward to their sleeping quarters and that the other by the main boom being inclined to starboard.

There was no case to answer, as opinion on both sides of the Atlantic accepted completely. The Committee said in its report, rather mildly under the circumstances, that had Dunraven remained throughout the investigation there was little doubt that he would have withdrawn the charge. Dunraven however did not remain but returned to England

after the first day of the four-day hearing, and he did not apologize when he heard the findings. The Club then voted to withdraw his honorary membership; this was done with great acclaim. In the meantime Dunraven had resigned from the Club. Phillips-Birt comments:

Essentially, I believe, it was Dunraven's vivid imagination, his lack of judgement in small, immediate matters, fired by a temper always easily rushed to the boil, that managed to overcome his native Irish charm and even his very keen sense of humour and led him to behave with some absurdity for several months in 1895, when he became a spider in the middle of a web of what can only seem most unpleasant gamesmanship.

W. P. Stephens, however, was rather more blunt in summing up Lord Dunraven's character. In his book, *American Yachting*:

If report be true, his withdrawal from international racing was but a repetition of his previous leave-taking of journalism and later of politics.

Diplomatic relations between the two nations during 1895 were not at their best, and the Cup races did not improve matters. It was therefore just as well that someone showed a sense of humour: a cable was sent to the New York Stock Exchange saying that it was hoped that, when war was declared, excursion steamers would not get in the way of the British fleet. The New York Stock Exchange replied that in the interests of a fair fight they hoped British warships were better than their yachts. 'All very funny,' Dunraven commented years later in his autobiography, 'but not funny to me.'

One of the more amazing aspects of this amazing affair is that *Defender*'s crew, albeit unwittingly, had after all disqualified their yacht from the second race not because she was carrying excess lead but because they were probably still loading it after 9 p.m. – a technical violation of the rules. Brooke Heckstall-Smith, a British yachting expert of a later period, is quite explicit on this point in *All Hands on the Mainsheet*:

If the *Defender* shipped ballast after nine p.m. the day before the race she was disqualified by the fact of having done so. I believe it was admitted that a small amount of ballast was replaced as late as ten p.m. No doubt there was no intentional unfairness, as the same amount was decided to have been put back as had been taken out. That was not the question. The point was merely whether a rule was infringed.

So if Dunraven had been less suspicious and susceptible to gossip and had read his rules properly he might have won at least one race.

On the face of it Dunraven behaved disgracefully. Yet it is impossible, at this distance in time and reviewing all the available evidence, not to think there was far more to the whole affair than meets the eye. It therefore seems fair to end this unfortunate chapter in the history of the America's Cup with a quote from Sherman Hoyt, a brilliant yachtsman and a much-respected man, who says in his memoirs that he had conceived 'a certain childhood prejudice' against Iselin for whom he felt dislike and he 'had an insight into much that went on behind the scenes' as Dunraven's American representative, Maitland Kersey, was a frequent visitor to his home. 'I had, prior to the actual races, become aware of the strained feelings existing between Dunraven and Iselin and of the former's conviction – whether well found or not is of little moment at this day – that the latter might resort to sharp practices,' Hoyt wrote, concluding: 'I never could become quite as bitter as most Americans at Lord Dunraven and his peculiarly unfortunate and ill-judged conduct.'

The Lipton era

1899/1901/1903/1920

6

When Dunraven withdrew from the third race of 1895 the general opinion was that it would be a long time before anyone else would challenge. Yet hardly had two weeks passed after the fiasco of that last race when the New York Yacht Club received another challenge, by the Royal Victoria Yacht Club on behalf of *Satanita*'s new owner, Mr Charles D. Rose. He intended building a 'cutter yacht *Distant Shore*, load waterline 89 feet', and would challenge in 1896. This letter must have given heart – if they needed any – to the Club to know that whatever Dunraven thought there were still Englishmen happy to challenge under the existing conditions. What is more, the *New York Daily Tribune* reported that Rose was not the only person interested: 'now comes the news from London that Mr Herbert Moir, a well-known colonial yachtsman, is anxious to compete for the America's Cup, and has secured pledges of £30,000 for the building of a yacht for that purpose', and *Yachting World* announced that Moir was 'astounded' at the response to his appeal for funds for building a new challenger. No one records Mr Moir's nationality but as his yacht was to be called *Westralia* he was probably Australian.

Happy though the Americans may have been at this continued interest – Rose's challenge was quickly accepted by the Club on 15 October and the chairman of the Cup Committee declared the challenge a vote of confidence in himself – the British yachting establishment in general and Dunraven in particular were definitely not, for Rose's challenge was 'unconditional', in the sense that he made no attempt to negotiate the terms of the match. It was thought by such an authoritative magazine as the *Field* to be an 'off-hand' challenge calculated to offend the sensibilities of British yachtsmen, and would be construed as supporting the behaviour of the N Y Y C. Worse, it was thought that the Prince of

IT'S NAILED FAST!
Sir Thomas—I've come to lift the Cup.

With this cartoon the New York Tribune *predicted that Lipton was going to have a hard time 'lifting the auld mug' as he termed his efforts to win the America's Cup. It was right*

Wales was involved in the challenge and was backing Rose (because Rose's father had been the Prince's financial agent), and the Prince in some influential circles was not a popular man at that time. This rumour was quickly denied by Rose in a letter to *The Times*. But this did not placate the feelings of the yachting establishment that the challenge was ill-judged and gave comfort to the enemy – a treasonable offence in war-time, and who was to say that America and Britain, already at loggerheads politically over the question of the frontiers of Venezuela, would not soon be involved in hostilities? Politically each country was suspicious of the other's motives anyway: and if Britain had once gone to war over someone's ear being cut off, why not over the America's Cup?

The correspondence columns of both British and American journals and papers, and the bitter editorials, reflect the depths of feelings on both sides. One letter, to *Yachting World*, came from an English reader newly arrived in France from the United States and shows how seriously the Dunraven affair had affected the relationship of the two countries. Perhaps, but perhaps not, it exaggerates the seriousness of the situation but the comparative sobriety of its tone compared with some of the hysterical – and ignorant – comments printed makes it worth quoting:

We cannot take the risk of further antagonizing the Yankees, for they seem already too much inclined for a serious conflict, and evidently you do not know their numerical strength and resources. I do not doubt, that at the outset we would get the best of them, but I am equally positive in the end we would be so badly used up, and receive such a thrashing that we may never again be the strong Empire we now are. We are having enough trouble in the Transvaal and Turkey without your sheet trying to foment more discord.

Even four years later, when tempers had cooled, the *New York Journal* wrote in martial terms about the new challenge from Sir Thomas Lipton:

Victories won with American battleships are becoming commonplace [a reference to America's war with Mexico]. We therefore gladly welcome the new challenger for the America's Cup and cheerfully demonstrate that Yankees can sail yacht races as successfully as they can fight naval battles.

But what almost certainly killed Rose's challenge – he hurriedly withdrew it a week after it was accepted – was not the feeling of belligerence between the two nations but the origins of the new challenger. Dunraven, in an alleged interview with Dixon Kemp of the *Field* which was fed to United Press, not only remarked that the challenge was 'offensive to me for the reason that the American people have been

assured by [their] press that the challenge is intended as a mark of censure upon me and a vindication of the action of the Cup Committee' but that the new challenger was 'an American' and not British at all. It turned out that Rose was in fact Canadian born and educated (though his father was English) and as one American paper expressed it

many in the old land still rate all 'colonial' subjects a little lower than themselves ... the coming of a colonial to the rescue soon after Dunraven's failure to bring home the coveted cup is especially galling to a certain contingent of English yachtsmen.

Nothing more was ever heard of Mr Rose or of Mr Moir.

For the next thirty years or so challenges for the America's Cup were dominated by one man: Sir Thomas Lipton. He brought in a new era of harmony backed by astute publicity and carried it through till the 1930s when the Cup matches were taken over by a new generation led by T. O. M. Sopwith in England and Harold S. Vanderbilt in America. Though novelist Alec Waugh wrote a complete biography of him, Lipton, a life-time bachelor, is really a man of mystery: next to nothing is known about his early childhood and youth. And what is known is only what he chose to reveal in his press interviews and his autobiography. Nothing really reveals the inner man, though, unlike Nathanael Herreshoff, he was always willing to talk to the press – there are enormous files in Glasgow and New York filled with press clippings based on interviews with him. In fact he was only too ready to be interviewed, quoted and misquoted. It was all part of the game of publicity to bring him into the limelight, and there must be somewhere sales graphs of the increase of Lipton tea sales in the United States once Lipton started competing for the America's Cup. To this cynical assessment it should be added that without doubt it was Lipton who saved the Cup from gathering dust on the shelf. Doubtless someone else eventually would have challenged but whether they would have carried off the campaign with quite such tact and aplomb is doubtful. Lipton was the right man in the right place at the right time. He knew this and exploited it for all he was worth, not only for the sake of his business and his own esteem but for the good of the sport.

Lipton was born in 1850 in Glasgow of poor parents of Irish extraction. He apparently did not fight his way out of grinding poverty, motivated by

Lipton with some of his 1920 America's Cup crew. He always challenged through the Royal Ulster Yacht Club

the injustices of the world and the desire to distance himself from his background. On the contrary his childhood was, according to Waugh, 'extremely happy. He was proud of his home and of his family . . . He was proud, too, of the provision shop that his father was to open.' He worked in this grocery store, scraped an elementary education, and formed with a gang of young friends a 'yacht club' based on a local pond where each member floated his own wooden boat whittled out of the lids of boxes. Lipton, aware of his Irish ancestry, called his *Shamrock*. He spent much of his time at the docks watching the comings and goings of steamers and merchant ships, and eventually, aged thirteen, became cabin boy on a steamer that crossed to Belfast and back every night. Two years later he set out across the Atlantic in search of fame and fortune. He found the second first. Fame came later when he became a millionaire

friend of the Prince of Wales (who liked, it was said, his women friends to be beautiful and amusing, and his men friends rich and amusing). Then, in 1898, Lipton challenged for the America's Cup.

His friendship with the Prince and his challenge were not entirely disconnected. His Royal Highness was a greater lover of yachting and had been much disturbed by the Dunraven affair, in which he had been closely involved as chairman of the Royal Squadron's Cup committee in 1895; there is little doubt that he encouraged Lipton to put the situation to rights. But Lipton did not challenge as a whim of the moment or to please his royal patron. He had been thinking about doing so for many years. When he first challenged in 1898 it was revealed that ten years previously he had offered, through the then MP for Cork, W. J. Lane, to put up the money for a challenger provided the yacht was designed, built, and manned by Irishmen. His offer was regretfully rejected because no Irishman had been capable of designing a potential challenger.

80

Gretel nearest the camera
closing *Weatherly* near
the finish of the fourth
race, 1962 (*Darling*)

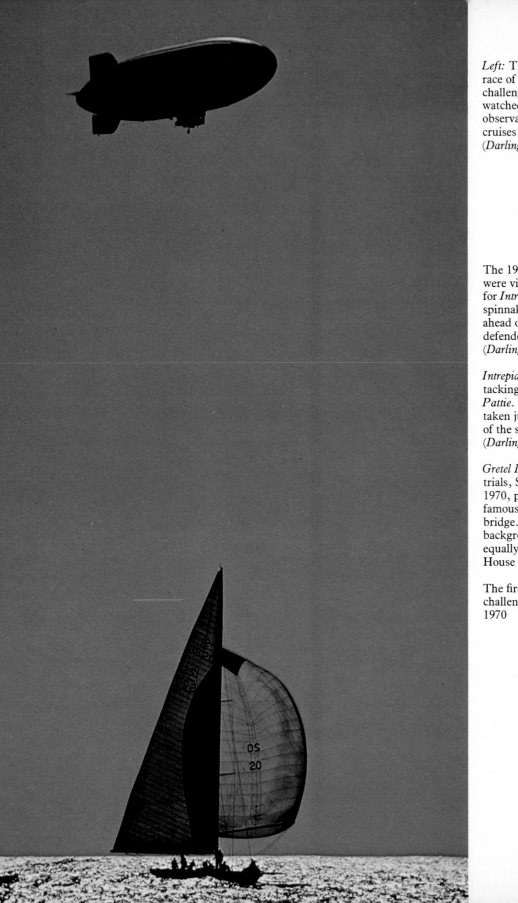

Left: The fourth and last race of the 1964 challenge: *Constellation*, watched by the observation balloon, cruises to an easy victory (*Darling*)

The 1967 Cup Trials were virtually a walkover for *Intrepid*. Here, under spinnaker, she strides ahead of the 1958 defender, *Columbia* (*Darling*)

Intrepid engaged in a tacking duel with *Dame Pattie*. This shot was taken just after the start of the second race (*Darling*)

Gretel II during her trials, Sydney Harbour 1970, passing under the famous Sydney Harbour bridge. In the background is the equally famous Opera House

The first French challenger, *France I*, 1970

Above: Courageous leads *Southern Cross* around the first mark, race one, 1974 challenge (*Darling*)

Right: The Swedish challenger, *Sverige*, trailing *Australia* in the third race of the final elimination trials for the 1977 challenge (*Darling*)

Opposite left: A spectacular aerial shot of *Intrepid* during the 1970 Observation Trials (*Darling*)

Above: On the final leg of the second race *Australia* matches *Courageous* tack-for-tack but cannot close the American defender (*Darling*)

Left: Victory! Ted Turner and crew after fourth and final race (*Darling*)

Columbia *in dry dock, 1899*

When the challenge was sent it was unconditional, Lipton leaving all conditions for the match in the hands of the N Y Y C. He still planned that the yacht at least be built in Ireland and manned by Irishmen, though his designer William Fife Jr was Scottish. However, when the proposed builders, Harland and Wolff, saw Fife's plans they felt they did not have the necessary experience of yacht construction, and the work was passed to Thornycroft's, of Millwall, in London.

Any pretence at following the construction of a traditional English cutter was abandoned by Fife. He designed an out-and-out racer that conformed to the rule still in force in America which only took account of the load waterline and the sail area. His yacht had a long overhang (39 feet), a flat hull and a deep narrow keel with a lot of outside ballast. She had manganese-bronze bottom plating and topsides of aluminium.

Lipton's idea of having an Irish crew did not materialize, and *Shamrock I*, as the new challenger

was called, was skippered by an able Scottish captain, Archie Hogarth, with a Captain Robert Wringe as his assistant. The crew was drawn mostly from the Clyde and the West of Scotland and from the traditional villages of the Colne, with half a dozen from Exmouth and Southampton.

Once the challenge had been established J. Pierpont Morgan promptly commissioned from Herreshoff a new cup defender to be called *Columbia*, with C. Oliver Iselin (who had a share in her) as the boat's managing owner, and it was decided to refit *Defender* to act as a trial horse for the new yacht. This, too, was underwritten by Pierpont Morgan, and Butler Duncan was her manager. Charlie Barr was named to skipper *Columbia*, with a crew made up of Deer Island men, while *Defender* had a Scandinavian crew with Captain Uriah Rhodes named as skipper.

Both sides kept their designs under wraps, causing much speculation in the press and bitter asides from commentators. Lawson, for instance, writing only a short time after the event, remarks on the impossibility of giving an accurate description of the new defender, as the Herreshoff Manufacturing Company 'considers itself under no obligation to yachtsmen or the sport of yachting which should lead it to make public any facts concerning vessels turned out at its shops'. Herreshoff, as usual, was obviously keeping mum, as were the British when they arrived in New York.

Unfortunately, Lipton's first challenge gives the impression of hasty improvisation, and Fife came in for some criticism after the races were over, John Spears of the *New York World* saying

Shamrock would have been better off if Mr Fife had remained at home. It was because of Mr Fife's over confidence that *Shamrock* was not thoroughly tested for defects in advance of the race. And for that reason too the crew of *Shamrock* were not trained to work together as they might have done. Further than that additional trials would have shown how to place the ballast to the best advantage.

But it was not just Fife's attitude that evoked sarcastic comment about Lipton's first challenge. Two years later, when discussing the merits of taking *Shamrock I* across the Atlantic as a trial horse for *Shamrock II*, Stinson Jarvis, the American correspondent of *Yachting World*, remarked

we want her with all faults, just as she was, otherwise her use as a gauge on the new boat will be nil. We want the same bending boom that drew a hard spot down across the mainsail and left a hole 7 feet deep behind it in the sail. Perhaps it will not be possible to get the rigging quite as bad as it was in the last race, when everything was over the side and the canvas shaped for ten-point tacking. Wringe knows what the boat wants, and, even if forbidden any cutting of rig, will naturally have the boat somewhat better. And he steers too well to make the boat perform as she did in Hogarth's hands. Still, he might do everything the same way if he tried, or he might give the vessel over to the cook.

In England *Shamrock I* was launched on 24 June clad, as the *Yachtsman* described the scene, 'in petticoats' to prevent her lines being displayed; 'it is a little difficult,' the magazine added, 'for the ordinary mind to grasp the object of Mr Fife's extreme solicitude in guarding the secrets of his design. Even if a highly satisfactory photograph of the vessel on the ways could be obtained, there is hardly time now

for Messrs Herreshoff to build a new vessel.' It is indeed difficult to understand now why so much secrecy was enforced. Neither designer needed nor desired publicity, nor could they very well be influenced by one another's work as it was being carried on simultaneously. Watson had started it all off with *Thistle* but he had a motive, and the habit was doubtless continued by Herreshoff for temperamental more than for any other reason. Why Fife indulged in it no one knows. But he was not to be the last.

Construction problems had delayed *Shamrock*'s launching and only two hurried trials were held, with *Britannia*. *Shamrock I* won the first easily and *Britannia* gave up during the second as the Prince of Wales, who was on board, had a previous appointment. Compared with the thorough, if unexciting, races *Columbia* was sailing at the same time with *Defender* it was an unsatisfactory tuning-up period, which did not go unnoticed in America. W. P. Stephens commented in *Forest and Stream* that *Shamrock*'s trial races against *Britannia*, a smaller yacht, were useless. Lipton should have carried through his intention of buying *Valkyrie III* as a trial horse. Failing that the German Emperor's *Meteor* should have been used. 'There seems little use,' he said, 'in bringing to this country an untried and undeveloped boat to meet a yacht chosen after such a series of trial races as are now going on between the *Columbia* and the *Defender*.'

Permission was granted by the NYYC for the challenger to be towed across the Atlantic and she arrived in this manner on 18 August. Lipton came by passenger liner and was greeted enthusiastically.

He already knew America well, of course, and was known by many. Those who did not know him or of him knew his tea. Newspapemen – and women – besieged him, crowds pressed in on him, the curious tried to inveigle their way on board *Shamrock I* and his steam yacht, *Erin*. Lipton took it all with good humour, a broad smile, and tactful comments about the sporting attitude of the NYYC. He was not to be drawn on the secrets of the challenger but in other matters he was expansive. To one lady journalist he opened his heart about his love life.

'Was I ever in love? Never!' Sir Thomas's blue eyes twinkled with not so much as the shadow of a disappointment in them.

'Come, now, there must have been one—'

'Bless you, one? A hundred!' cried he. 'I tell you I'm daft on them. Blonde, brunette, redhead – there's a special charm in every one.'

While working up against Defender on 2 August 1899 off Point Judith Columbia *was dismasted. This was the first accident involving a steel mast, and it caused a lot of adverse comment. But no one was hurt*

The problem with Shamrock I *was that her spars were too light and this defect lost her the second race. Earlier, as can be seen here, her steel gaff buckled and then collapsed while she was tuning up off Sandy Hook*

Immediately she arrived *Shamrock I* was put into racing order and sent out into New York Bay for trials. She proved a fast yacht in light airs, and on 24 September the best-known American yachting correspondent of the time, Thomas Fleming Day, editor of *Rudder* magazine, reported:

The *Shamrock* yesterday gave a complete and remarkable performance, and showed herself to be, on one point of sailing, a wonder. In a breeze varying strength, but at no time exceeding 15 miles, she covered a course of 30 sea miles in 2 hours, 20 minutes and 20 seconds. There is no known record of any yacht ever having equalled this performance. . . . She is without doubt the fastest reaching vessel ever built.

Three days later Lipton and Iselin met and agreed on the final arrangements for the races. Iselin suggested that each boat should have a representative from the other boat on board when official measurements were taking place; and that 'each yacht shall stand by the consequences of any accident happening to her, and the uninjured vessel shall sail out the race' as 'the America's cup races are no less a test of the strength of construction of the competing vessels, than of their sailing qualities'. Obviously Mr Iselin still had Lord Dunraven very much in mind. But, whatever the backwash from the unfortunate challenge in 1895, one aspect of that particular match would not recur, for on 19 May 1896, a special Act of Congress had amended the American navigation laws to give the Coast Guard powers to keep the course clear.

For the 1899 challenge six revenue cutters and six torpedo boats were used. Through the willingness of the captains of the excursion steamers, or possibly through the presence of the torpedo boats, the course was kept completely clear and neither yacht was in the least troubled by the spectator fleet. What they were troubled by, however, was the weather. The day of the first race was set for 3 October, but it was not until 16 October that the first race was successfully completed, light airs and fog preventing a finished race before that date. The yachts started on the 3rd, 5th and 7th but did not finish within the time limit, and they were prevented from starting at all on the 10th, 12th, 13th and 14th because of fog.

These delays frayed nerves and made for edginess, which affected not only the competitors but the newspapermen as well, and on 11 October the *New York Journal* let forth a blast to blow Mr Iselin out of the water. Everyone in the American camp was getting extremely nervous, for in the three

unfinished races of the 3rd, 5th and 7th *Shamrock I* had shown herself faster in very light airs. Twice the races had been abandoned with the British boat ahead (though only just), and on the third occasion only 100 feet separated the two yachts.

The first completed race, on the 16th, was in a 10-knot breeze that eased slightly during the middle of the race. It was hazy and there was a slight swell. *Columbia* won by 10 minutes, 8 seconds after allowing *Shamrock* 6 seconds.

The next day the yachts met again. A good breeze was blowing and everyone on *Shamrock* was hopeful of a win, but the weakness of her spars betrayed her, and her topmast, carrying her biggest club-topsail, collapsed. *Columbia*, which had been ahead, sailed on. There was another inconclusive race the next day, but when the time expired *Columbia* was 1¼ miles ahead.

The final race, on the 20th, was, according to Lawson, 'one of a very few of the kind in the annals of the sport', to be compared with the last race between *Genesta* and *Puritan*. A 20-knot breeze from a northerly direction put fire into it, and the start was magnificent with *Shamrock* crossing the line just 34 seconds after the gun sounded. A stern chase followed with both yachts using spinnakers that proved hard to control but slowly *Columbia* overtook the challenger and rounded the mark 17 seconds ahead. It was, said Lawson, 'the finest 15 mile run in international yachting history'. On the return beat *Columbia*'s ability to point higher and ride the waves more easily was apparent, and the leech of *Shamrock*'s mainsail was flapping badly. *Columbia* won by 6 minutes 34 seconds, and that night Lipton announced that he was going to challenge again.

Lipton's next challenge, in 1901, is really dominated by a row – not between the opposing sides this time but between Boston and New York, between a New Englander, Thomas W. Lawson, and the New York Yacht Club. Rivalry between the two places has already been remarked upon. It had not lessened with time, and ever since Edward Burgess had died Boston no doubt wanted to re-enter the field. By 1901, however, the New York Yacht Club had gained long experience in defending the Cup and was not at all keen on the idea of an outsider entering the fray on their behalf. In any case the Deed of Gift specifically stated the Cup should be defended by the club holding it, and this, by inference, meant members of the Club had to sail the defender. The earlier defenders from Boston or their representatives had always been members of the New York Yacht Club, and the defender could fly the burgee of the New York Yacht Club. Lawson, however, had no intention of joining the New York Yacht Club. There followed a long and bitter wrangle between the Club and Lawson as to the right of Lawson's *Independence* to enter the Trials and, if the fastest boat, to defend the Cup. The correspondence was courteous but the newspaper campaign mounted by both sides – or indirectly by their sympathizers – was anything but polite. (There is an interesting change in tone and style of Lawson's *History of the America's Cup* at this point: Lawson's collaborator in the project, the noted yachting journalist Winfield M. Thompson, provided most of the text, but Lawson alone wrote of his battle with the Club and of his opinion of the men who ran it.)

Mr Lawson did not like the gentlemen who ran the New York Yacht Club or their interpretation of the first deed of gift. He set out, at vast expense, to make them admit that 'no American other than a member of the New York Yacht Club is possessed of a right to take any part in the America's Cup defence'. The Club felt themselves not only the holders of the Cup but the trustees of it, and their duty to uphold not only the letter of the Deed but its spirit. The original Deed stated quite specifically that the match was to be made with 'the club in possession' of it. It followed that only members of the defending club were eligible to defend, as only they were bound by the rules and regulations of the club. Lawson, the Club said, could either join the Club or could charter his yacht to a member as by the Club rules this made a yacht eligible to fly the Club burgee. Lawson replied that he would charter the yacht to the Club but not to an individual, and so on and so forth.

While Lawson was arguing with the Club his yacht *Independence* was nearing completion. Designed by a young Bostonian, Bowdoin B. Crowninshield, initially for a syndicate but eventually for Lawson alone, *Independence* was really an enormous scow. This type of craft was of light displacement and designed to take advantage of the vessel's lines when heeled to increase the load waterline and therefore speed. The scow type of yacht had been used very successfully by the Canadians in defending the Seawanhaka Cup and was in use in several parts of the United States, but a yacht the size of *Independence* had never before been built on the principle. It

was also Crowninshield's first attempt at a 90-footer. These factors, and that she was built by a company who had never constructed a craft at all resembling her, and riveted by men who'd never done similar work, made *Independence* a miserable failure.

Her early trials in Massachusetts Bay showed that she was badly out of balance but phenomenally fast on certain points of sailing. What she badly needed were trial races and plenty of them, but she was banned by the N Y Y C from entering their trial races with the other contenders for that year, *Columbia* and the new Herreshoff-designed *Constitution*, until Lawson agreed to the Club's terms. There seemed little prospect of the Boston yacht getting properly tuned. *Defender* was provisionally purchased as a trial horse but found fit only for the junk-heap. General Paine offered *Jubilee*, but she too was not in a condition to race. Lawson managed to find two trial horses but neither were really in the class of *Independence*.

During these initial trials her steering gear was found inadequate and this necessitated changing her rudder. As no private dock large enough was available the yacht was towed to a naval dockyard north of Cape Cod. Hard weather hit her on the way and she very nearly sank as her all-too delicate hull was badly strained. The newly formed Newport Racing Association had contrived a series of races for her in which the other two cup contenders were participating. Haff, *Independence*'s skipper, reported to Lawson by telephone that the repairs would take weeks but was told by Lawson to get the yacht to the starting line at Newport even if she sank before crossing it. Work on the damage went on day and night, and Haff did indeed manage to get *Independence* to the line. She did not sink but she was defeated so humiliatingly that it may have been better had she done so. She moved, someone reported, 'like a sleep-walker'. At the outer mark she was so far in the rear that the committee had packed up and gone home by the time she eventually crossed the finishing line in darkness. The reason for her sluggishness was not hard to find: she was still leaking. In fact she sailed that trial race with her fin full of water. In the subsequent races she shipped a pump and did better, but not nearly well enough to convince anyone that she was a serious Cup contender. In her last race her stern had worked so badly, making her rudder-head bind at the deck, that three men were required to steer her. Three months after she was launched *Independence* was scrapped, much to Lawson's disgust and, no doubt, to the relief of

The freak Independence, *owned by Thomas Lawson of Boston, was built as a contender for the 1901 defence of the Cup. Lawson had a book written after the 1901 races to which he contributed in order to argue publicly that he'd been right to challenge the New York Yacht Club's rule that only a yacht owned by a member, or chartered by a member, could defend the Cup. Even if he had won the argument with the Club* Independence *could never have defended anything as she leaked like a sieve*

the NYYC. Yet despite the briefness of her racing life she made her mark, for Herreshoff had noted that her scow form gave a phenomenal turn of speed under certain conditions. He used this information to build an entirely new concept for the 1903 challenge by *Shamrock III*.

With *Independence* crippled, the field lay clear for the new contender, *Constitution*, to fight it out with the old *Columbia*. During their trials both yachts

were dismasted. There rose the cry that the types were too extreme, that the Cup bred unseaworthy yachts, and that the American Rules must be adjusted to encourage a more wholesome model. Though it was by then too late to influence events for the 1903 challenge, the authorities did take note. By the time of the next challenge, the Universal rule had come into existence which made for a less extreme type of vessel.

Much to everyone's surprise *Columbia* showed herself the superior yacht – and certainly more reliable; after some early defeats by the new boat she was finally chosen in preference to *Constitution*, though the number of races won, nine each, was not conclusive evidence of her superiority. There was probably not much difference between the two

Constitution, *another unsuccessful contender in 1901*

86

Columbia *was chosen to defend again in 1901. Notice the two men at the helm*

yachts but the handling of *Columbia* was, by all accounts, superior. The trials were not held in particularly amicable circumstances, Barr on *Columbia* being accused of foul tactics on several occasions. Indeed *Columbia* was disqualified from one race for bearing away at the start and the *Rudder* magazine commented that 'Barr violated all rules of civilized warfare'.

The behaviour of *Constitution* puzzled observers. She was fast one day, and did not go at all the next. However, there seemed to be a consensus that her sails were not right. While *Columbia* sailed with the same mainsail as in 1899, a fortune was spent on *Constitution*'s sails, each set seeming worse than the last. After the second day of defeat with one new set the skipper, Uriah Rhodes, suggested they be thrown overboard, and when the yacht's manager, Duncan, asked why Rhodes replied: 'I don't know why, the cussedness of sails is that no one knows why.'

There was gossip that *Constitution*, under the Herreshoff contract, had to have Herreshoff sails but that the company, which had provided the cloth for

Shamrock II was dismasted in the Solent before crossing the Atlantic. King Edward VII, a friend of Lipton's was on board at the time

Columbia's sails, refused to supply any for *Constitution*, and inferior cloth had to be obtained elsewhere. Rumour had it that the company refused because 10 per cent had been docked from bills for canvas previously supplied at contract net prices! On such small stumbling blocks have great enterprises foundered.

Columbia, on the other hand, was a proven boat with a first-class crew, and Charlie Barr later remarked

Mr Morgan and I defended the cup that year for a few thousand dollars, while before that it had sometimes cost some two hundred thousand, and since then much more. You see I had laid *Columbia* up carefully in 1899 and when she was put in commission again she was in good shape.

Nat Herreshoff's son, L. Francis Herreshoff, added his opinion that *Columbia*'s success was also due to the fact that Barr by 1901 was

Shamrock II in the Erie Basin having her mast stepped prior to the 1901 challenge

so used to *Columbia* that he could handle her like a knock-about, and he knew just what he could do with her under all conditions. . . . He could handle *Columbia* like a top and scared the afterguard of *Constitution* almost to death.

In England, Lipton had this time turned to his old friend, Watson, to produce a 'Cup-lifter' for him and the Scottish designer had, somewhat reluctantly, agreed to help. *Shamrock II* was built by William Denny at Dumbarton and was launched much earlier than her predecessor, on 20 April, in order that she could compete in extensive trials with *Shamrock I*. Two accidents in quick succession raised doubts, as in America, about the sturdiness of a modern racing yacht's rigging and its general seaworthiness. On 9 May the challenger's steel gaff collapsed, Lipton only just escaping injury by a falling block. Then, less than a fortnight later, with King Edward VII on board, the mast went over the side after the bowsprit had carried away. The quick action of Sycamore, who was at the helm, prevented the disaster having fatal consequences but the races, already nearly cancelled because of the death of Queen Victoria, had to be postponed a month while the damage was repaired. This accident marred the prospects of the new challenger being tuned properly, but what races there were seemed to prove that *Shamrock II* had little in the way of speed over her predecessor despite the scientific tank testing Watson had carried out.

After a disagreement with some of the crew of *Shamrock I*, who refused to ship on the new challenger because of an inadequate bounty payment, *Shamrock II* sailed from Gourock for New York on 27 July and arrived on 11 August. On 14 August she was docked, and Americans were then able to express their opinion of her and compare her to the American Cup candidates. The consensus was, Lawson wrote,

her body-lines appeared similar to those of *Columbia* and *Constitution*, although her ends were longer, her counter and stern finer, and her bow lower, with the fulness carried farther forward, and with more of a 'snub' in the turn of the stem. Her lateral plane seemed not to be cut away so much as that of the Herreshoff yachts, while her bilge was somewhat fuller. In profile forward she appeared to favour the 'scow' type, but from other points of view she was more like the so-called normal type of modern bronze yacht, with fair, full body, and very fine fore-and-aft lines. The shape of the bow was her most striking feature. While one visual expert saw all the qualities of speed in her others said she had too many curves to prove a winner.

It could have been the curves or the fact that Sycamore was just not the equal of Barr, or any number of reasons in between, but when the races were sailed after being postponed again, this time because, on 6 September, President McKinley was shot, *Columbia* won three in a row once more – though this time by much smaller margins. Indeed in the last race *Shamrock II* crossed the line first but lost by 41 seconds when her time allowance was applied. It was later acknowledged by most yachting authorities that *Shamrock II* was a very fast boat indeed.

Lipton faced his defeat equally and announced he was not ready to give up, though the cost of keeping his fleet of boats during the races amounted to $2000 a day. 'Next time for sure,' he said. 'After all, the shamrock has three leaves!' and he reminded doubters that

The British boat was freely admitted to be the best and swiftest challenger ever sent over. . . . My boat lost to the American defender by an aggregate of only 3 minutes, 27 seconds actual time [over a] total distance of 90 miles.

He suggested that a match be held the next year, but the Club declined and were fiercely criticized for doing so. But Lipton was still determined. 'I'm still out to lift that mug,' he said, 'unless someone else does it first.' But by now challenging for the America's Cup had really become 'Lipton's Business' in England and no one else was sufficiently interested. In fact racing the largest cutters had by 1901 almost become defunct in England, and the way was clear for Lipton to challenge for a match in 1903. This he duly did, despite protests from his shareholders, who for some reason felt his efforts were damaging the business.

For the design of *Shamrock III* Lipton returned to William Fife, Watson almost certainly having refused to try again though he co-operated with Fife on the new boat. Fife, at a disadvantage through not having been on board his earlier creation during the Cup races – he was ill at the time – and therefore unable to gain invaluable information, and to make useful comparisons, nevertheless came up with 'an exceedingly lively vessel and quite the most beautiful that ever raced for the Cup', as John Scott Hughes described her in *Famous Yachts*, while another commentator pronounced that

the outstanding feature of *Shamrock III* is the manner in which the hull is filled out and drawn down to the fin, with

By 1901 America's Cup candidates were always built in the greatest secrecy – though no one quite knew why – and the press, as here, made rather a joke of it. 'Is anybody looking, Butler?' Herreshoff asks. 'Not a soul in sight, Nat; let her go!' replies Duncan.

a suggestion of more of the full-bodied British racing cutter than of the flat-floored type which we have adopted from the American centreboard boats.

However, it was really her bottom and her steering wheel that drew most attention, her bottom because at last designers had overcome the problem of the roughness of steel plating and her steering wheel because quite simply one had never been used before in a British challenger. This is a remarkable fact when one considers that American yachts had been steered by wheels for years and the difficulties encountered by a helmsman steering a large yacht with a tiller.

Shamrock III's trials were marred by losing her mast at Weymouth just where *Shamrock II* had lost hers. This time the accident had fatal consequences; one man was knocked overboard and drowned, and several others suffered serious injury.

In America Herreshoff produced *Reliance*, which was a radical departure from his earlier designs and took in the best features of *Independence*. *Reliance* was the biggest yacht ever built to defend the America's Cup, 144 feet long overall, and her sail spread was over 16,000 square feet, some 2000 square feet more than *Shamrock III* and twice the area of *Puritan* and *Mayflower* combined. With her club topsail aloft – it alone equalled the entire sail plan of a 12-metre – she towered 196 feet into the air. On deck she was covered with winches while all her sheets and backstays were trimmed from below. She was a formidable racing machine and she showed it during the trials by beating both *Constitution* and *Columbia* with ease.

When *Shamrock III* docked in America it was evident to the knowledgeable that she followed the same path of development as *Shamrock II*, *Columbia* and *Constitution* had trodden. Interest centred on

how this 'traditional' type of design would fare against the radical one of Herreshoff. When the races were over W. P. Stephens commented in the *Yachtsman* that

It is safe to say that while a win for *Shamrock* would have done much to turn back the wheels of progress in yacht-designing, and to promote safer and abler yachts of all classes, the actual result of the races will be to produce more extreme forms in the larger classes, both cruising and racing.

This coming from a yachting authority of such eminence, shows the tremendous influence wielded by the Cup races on ordinary yacht design. As it turned out the races were a disappointment – again. Wringe, who had replaced Sycamore at the wheel of the challenger, was no match for Barr, and in the third race the British yacht got lost in the fog and

failed to finish. She lost the first race by 9 minutes – bad sail handling accounted for some of this time – and the second by 3 minutes 16 seconds, both elapsed times. In the postmortems after *Shamrock III*'s failure, several interesting facts showed that despite all the care and attention and money Lipton had put into his challenge the British still lacked the professional and thorough attitude of the Americans to the races. *Shamrock III* had raced so well in England because she was immersed below her measured length and her poor performance in the races was in part due to the fact that a good deal of ballast had to be removed to bring her down to 90 feet. 'Fife,' said an American paper, 'produced a very fast 92-footer but an indifferent 90-footer.' It also became clear afterwards that Lipton had been wrongly advised as to which yacht to use as trial

Shamrock III *leading* Reliance *just after the start of the final race on 3 September 1903. The British yacht got lost in fog and failed to finish*

Captain Charlie Barr at the helm of Reliance *during one of the races against* Shamrock III *in 1903*

horse. 'The man who counselled Sir Thomas to use *Shamrock I* as a testing machine,' wrote Stinson Jarvis, 'was either an enthusiast, a lunatic, or a fraud. The boat was outclassed years ago.' After the races, Lipton commented to Jarvis that he had been measuring by the wrong yardstick. 'I was led to believe,' he said to him, 'that *Shamrock I* was really a better boat than *Shamrock II*. The whole of my calculation has been based on that mistake, and it has gone to pieces.'

Lipton's adviser was reported to be Fife, who believed his first creation to be the faster of the first two *Shamrocks*. Possibly this belief, coupled with the fact that *Shamrock II*, still lying in the Erie Basin, did not look in first-class order, led Lipton to ignore the Watson-designed yacht. *Shamrock II* was soon broken up and, some say, the N Y Y C breathed a sigh of relief when she was gone for the rumour had it they believed her to be the most dangerous challenger that had yet crossed the Atlantic and Barr admitted that on five separate occasions in the 1901 challenge *Shamrock II* had had the upper hand.

Lipton did not hide his disappointment of the result of the 1903 challenge. Though he said he would challenge again in 1905 it must have been hard for him to convince others, much less himself, that he stood much chance. *Shamrock III* losing was, he said, 'the greatest disappointment of my life. What can I do? I have tried my best.' He had indeed and the Americans appreciated his sportsmanship with tokens of esteem and farewell banquets. But it was to be a long, long time before they saw another *Shamrock*. It was not that Lipton gave up trying to retrieve the Cup, but after 1903 circumstances seemed to be against him. Big-Class yachting was in the doldrums and on both sides of the Atlantic strenuous efforts were at last being made to implement new rating rules which would produce a healthier type of boat, but which put in doubt for some time in which direction big-class yachting – including the America's Cup – would develop. In America the New York Yacht Club adopted – though not for the

America's Cup – the Universal rule where, at last, displacement was taken into account and excessive sail area penalized. In Europe thirteen nations got together in the summer of 1906, and in January 1907, and devised what became the International Rule of Yacht Measurement, or simply the international rule, from which developed the modern 12-metre used for America's Cup races today. As with all rating rules it was a complicated formula but Brooke Heckstall-Smith, the conference secretary, Britain's leading yachting journalist and a great technical expert, explained that the new rule aimed: firstly, to tax overhangs or full pram-bows; secondly, to ease the penalty upon draught which had been introduced in 1887 to compensate for the then excessive draught of British cutters; and thirdly, to insist that all yachts be classed at Lloyd's. The Americans did not attend, though they had been invited, and it was not until the 12-metre era that the yachting community in the United States had the same rating rule as the rest of the world (the international rule in America was accepted up to $14\frac{1}{2}$ metres in 1929, but this still left out the largest class, the Js in America and the 23-metre class in England. This in turn led to the America's Cup races in the 1930s being raced under the Universal rule and the Big Class in England adapting themselves to this rule in order to race with the English J-boats being built to compete for the Cup.)

After the 1903 challenge there were rumours of a Canadian challenge and of a Scots syndicate building no less than three yachts to race against each other, the winner to challenge, but nothing materialized. In 1907, after it seemed probable that the NYYC would be guided by the Universal rule for America's Cup challenges, Lipton issued a challenge conditional on the Club abiding by the Universal rule and that the waterline length of the defender would not be more than the challenger's. The challenge, however, was not acceptable as the Club saw no reason to deviate from the Deed of Gift and felt they should be allowed to build any type of yacht they liked. This did not make sense to Lipton but as there seemed no common ground on which to organize a challenge, he withdrew and built himself another *Shamrock*, built in accordance with the new International Rule. The 23-metre *Shamrock* – 'I'm reserving number IV for Sandy Hook,' Lipton remarked – was a great success and won many prizes. But this only whetted Lipton's appetite the more for bringing back 'the auld mug', as he called the Cup. He put out feelers again in 1912, but again the Club rejected

Caulking the deck of Defiance, *one of the Cup candidates for 1914. The First World War prevented the races taking place until 1920 but* Defiance *did not then take part in any of the trial races*

him. Finally, and doubtless impatient, Lipton asked for an unconditional match 'just for the fun of it'. The Club, unhurriedly, agreed. They agreed, too, at last to abide by the Universal rule but reserved the right to build a defender any length they wanted, up to the maximum length allowed under the rule of 90 feet. This the challenging club, the Royal Ulster, declared 'highly unsatisfactory' as they, rightly, deemed it a waste of everybody's time if the match were between two yachts of unequal size. However, it wasn't until Lipton had declared the proposed length of *Shamrock IV* – 75 feet – and had signed the set of conditions for the races that the Club declared the length of the proposed defender – 75 feet! After this remarkable display of one-upmanship (which seems to have irritated Cup historians far more than it ever did Lipton), both sides settled down for the thirteenth challenge.

In England Lipton turned to a brilliant new designer, Charles Nicholson, for *Shamrock IV*. In America three syndicates ordered boats: one, headed by Cornelius Vanderbilt, went to Herreshoff, who built them *Resolute*; Alexander Cochran, heading another group, commissioned William Gardner, the designer of the famous schooner *Atlantic*, to build *Vanitie*, one of the most beautiful yachts ever raced; and George Owen of Boston was commissioned by a third syndicate to build *Defiance*. The last two designers were new to building Cup defenders, so it was not surprising that during the four early trials – of which *Resolute* won three and got lost in a fog during the fourth – it seemed *Resolute* would be chosen. But before the final trials could be held war was declared in Europe and the races abandoned. *Shamrock IV*, in mid-Atlantic at the time, hurriedly made for Bermuda. She then managed to get to New York, where she was laid up. She had not been particularly well received on the other side of the Atlantic where, of course, the English were not used to seeing yachts designed to a different rule. Her designer called her an 'ugly duckling' while other experts thought her 'a powerful scow' and 'a hammerhead shark'. Alfred Loomis, later one of America's best-known yachtsmen, described her as looking 'something like a cross between a tortoise and an armoured cruiser'. Douglas Phillips-Birt, in *The History of Yachting*, called her 'Graceless snub-ended, hog-sheered', and thought that Nicholson 'had contrived to force an immense scow type of hull through the terms of the American Universal rule'. But though Phillips-Birt is undoubtably correct in his description it is doubtful whether Nicholson in fact knew enough about the rule to take advantage of it. Nicholson is quoted in the *Rudder* as saying: 'I have no data to go by, the designers of the American defenders have eight years experience to base their plans upon.' When the races were eventually held, in July 1920, it was obvious that while Herreshoff had managed to evade the rule he himself had helped to formulate – or, at least, use it to his own advantage – Nicholson had ignored its implications completely. When the yachts were measured the challenger had the incredibly high time penalty of 7 minutes 1 second (reduced to 6 minutes 40 seconds when *Shamrock IV* used a smaller topsail). On paper at least this is what lost her the Cup, for in three out of the five races she crossed the line first.

But statistics, of course, never tell the real story. It is a curious fact that though *Shamrock IV* came closer to winning the Cup than any previous challenger there seemed no doubt in the mind of anyone involved that the defender was the superior boat. It just was that – for a change – lady luck worked the other way. Instead of the gear of the challenger failing it was that of the defender; instead of the puffs of light airs working in favour of the defender it was the challenger that ghosted over in front.

In the first race, when *Resolute* was ahead, her throat halyard broke and she retired from the race. *Shamrock IV* was also in trouble – both yachts had sailed through a particularly vicious squall – but her crew managed to nurse her over the course and to the finishing line. According to Sherman Hoyt, the N Y Y C representative on board *Shamrock IV*, there was some discussion amongst the afterguard of the British boat as to whether they should continue, as it seemed unsporting to claim a race over a crippled opponent. But when Hoyt pointed out that the races were as much a test of a boat's seaworthiness as her speed the scruples of the British afterguard were overcome. Lipton immediately offered to have the race re-run but the Club, used by now to such gentlemanly protestations, refused to allow it. Lipton, according to all accounts, was not excited by the result. Winning in such a manner was not Tom Lipton's way. However, when the second race, too, was won by the British yacht, he became, quite naturally, tremendously excited. At long last the 'auld mug' seemed within his grasp.

But though luck for once was on Lipton's side and *Shamrock IV*, although not superior to her adversary could certainly foot faster, that third vital ingredient, the human element, worked consistently against him. Either by chance or design both contestants, for the first time, had amateurs at the helm. In *Resolute* was Charles Francis Adams, later secretary to the Navy, and in *Shamrock IV* was Britain's top amateur helmsman, William (later Sir William) Burton. But while Adams and his afterguard had a supremely efficient crew under the experienced eye of a professional skipper, Chris Christensen, those on *Shamrock IV* were divided and mutinous. To make things worse the British afterguard, which included Burton's wife, bickered continuously amongst themselves. Although the back-biting was less in the third race than in the others the general effect on morale and efficiency is not hard to calculate.

Shamrock IV crossed the line 19 seconds ahead of *Resolute* in the third race. Had the race been a mile or so longer the defender would not have been able to save her time, as *Shamrock IV* was drawing ahead steadily. As it was *Resolute* won, and went on to win the next two races as well. It was a bitter blow to Lipton but he took defeat with his usual grace. His edginess at the closeness of the contest got the better of him only once, when both yachts decided not to race because of fierce wind. When it was put to him that the lives of his crew could have been endangered, he replied, '*Shamrock* had much worse weather than this coming over,' but Sherman Hoyt had little doubt that the right decision had been made. Even if *Shamrock*'s afterguard had decided to race it seems doubtful that they'd have got the best from their crew as Sherman Hoyt's notes show:

8.45 – Boarded *Shamrock* at moorings. Clear hard southwester about 30 knots. *Shamrock* has single reefed mainsail and working topsail up in stops. Mrs Burton, pilot and Nicholson not on board, replaced by other huskies. Crew grouchy. One remarked to me, 'She will never hold together to get around.' Other remarks of following nature overheard, ''ell of a note, three skippers,' 'Never again,' 'Thank God this will be the last day' and many others of like nature. *Resolute* has full mainsail, and topmast bridle again for peak halyard which J. Parkinson is much worried about, 'Ich auch,' wish they had left it down. 9.15 – *Shamrock* under way. 9.25 S Breaks out rag of a working topsail and R. Leaves moorings. 10.00 Heavy short sea and blowing like hell. S evidently would be glad if race called off. 10.15 Diaper has just created a near panic. Came aft, demanded that Burton should turn *Shamrock* around and get back under lee of land before she breaks up. Shouting this so that most of crew overheard and got their wind up. Hell of a yellow performance! Burton asks me to accompany him below to make inspection. Find little wrong. While much loose water forward, shipped through fore hatch and deck leads, was splashing plenty in heavy pounding we were taking while crossing the bar, little had worked aft and the well was nearly dry. Told Burton he had no grounds to ask for postponement to repair damage. Crew appear divided about sticking it out. She sure is pounding like hell and the mast is all over the shop. We are eased to all possible extent but she is chucking spray from one end to the other. Burton makes good speech, bucks up crew and will continue in spite of Diaper.

Hoyt's memoirs give a vivid first-hand picture of what it was like to be on board a yacht racing for the

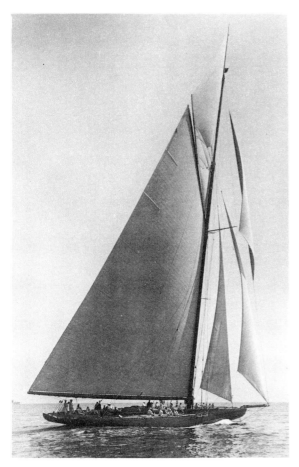

Shamrock IV

Burton at the helm of Shamrock IV

America's Cup – the confusion caused by a race committee ignorant of its own rules, the arguments, the tensions, and the pressures, and there's no doubt that they show that the challenger had more than her share of problems, each perhaps unimportant in itself but with a cumulative effect on the yacht's efficiency. The boat was so stripped of all inessential furnishings that the crew could not even make hot tea, and this infuriated them; Mrs Burton was on board as timekeeper and the crew didn't like that either; the afterguard bickered; and the yacht's rig obviously caused concern throughout the contest.

In short the wonder of the thirteenth challenge is not that the challenger won two races in succession but that she won any at all.

The J-class

7

1930/1934/1937

The 1920s were a time of change in the world of yachting as well as socially and economically. The decade began with the feeling that, after the holocaust of war, the old order would be restored and nothing would really change. The Wall Street crash that ended it occurred too late to affect the massive campaign mounted to defend the Cup in 1930 – no less than four defence candidates were built, one alone costing in the region of a million dollars.

During this time the Bermudan rig superseded the gaff. The complicated staying required to keep up the taller masts gave them the appearance of Marconi wireless stations, hence the initial appellation, 'Marconi' rigging. A higher sail plan developed, meaning the boom became shorter. This enabled a permanent backstay to be rigged, which in turn meant easier handling and therefore a smaller crew. The application of modern technology to yachting created unemployment just as it did, and does, in other fields: no longer were crews of forty and fifty required.

After the 1920 races there were rumours that the Canadians were going to challenge again. Plans were made for a public subscription to pay for the challenger – to be called *Maple Leaf* – but the scheme came to nothing. At the end of 1921 a group of yachtsmen in New Zealand declared their desire to build a challenger, but again nothing came of it. Interest was really still focused on Sir Thomas Lipton. Wherever he went he was asked the one question: 'When are you trying again?' But Lipton was in no hurry to challenge. Waiting served his purpose. The longer he waited the more the New York Yacht Club would realize that unless conditions were made more favourable to the challenger there just would not be any more races for the Cup, though after the 1920 challenge one point had at last been decided in

favour of any future challenger: in future the races would take place off Newport – where they are held today. But it was not until 1925 that there came any discernible shift of attitudes in America. In that year the North American Yacht Racing Union (NAYRU) was founded, creating for the first time a central authority which could unify the racing and measurement rules in Canada and the United States and could act on behalf of the sport internationally. This led to the setting up in 1927 of a committee of members of NAYRU and the International Yacht Racing Union (IYRU) which resulted in NAYRU adopting the International rule of measurement for yachts up to $14\frac{1}{2}$ metres. It also accepted that large yachts had to conform to Lloyd's scantling rules. This was the breakthrough that Lipton was waiting for as a challenger could now be built that was strong enough to cross the Atlantic without fear of meeting an adversary with no such restrictions placed on her. Both defender and challenger would be built to the same rule. What remained to be settled was which rule. Although Britain in 1928 had opted for the International Rule for big yachts (over $14\frac{1}{2}$ metres), it was agreed, when Lipton finally challenged once more in the autumn of 1929, that the yachts would be built to the American Universal rule.

As the America's Cup had always been raced for with yachts of the largest class – and as both *Resolute* and *Vanitie* had, in 1928, been converted from schooner to cutter rig of the J-Class of the American Universal rule – it was agreed by both parties that the competing yachts would be built to the J-class (which led to Britain's abandoning building her large yachts over $14\frac{1}{2}$ metres to the International Rule). The NYYC's racing fleet had always traditionally been classified by letter. Schooners and ketches were A to H, A being over 100 feet, H not over 31 feet, while sloops and yawls had the letters I

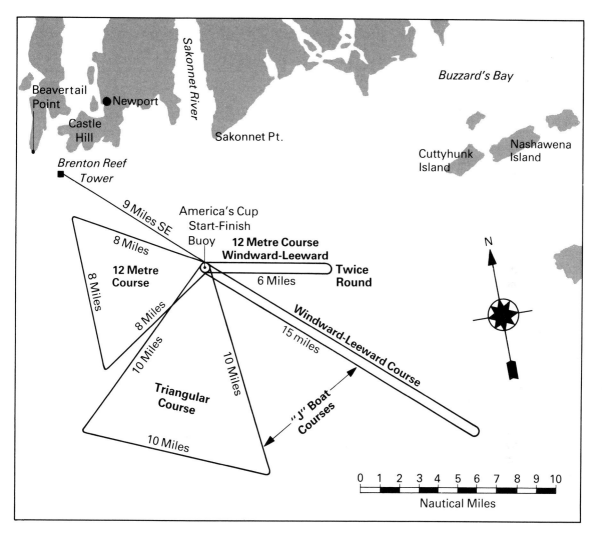

The following labels appear on the map:

Beavertail Point

Newport

Castle Hill

Sakonnet River

Buzzard's Bay

Sakonnet Pt.

Cuttyhunk Island

Nashawena Island

Brenton Reef Tower

9 Miles SE

8 Miles

8 Miles

8 Miles

America's Cup Start-Finish Buoy

12 Metre Course Windward-Leeward

12 Metre Course

6 Miles

Twice Round

N

10 Miles

10 Miles

10 Miles

15 miles

Windward-Leeward Course

Triangular Course

"J" Boat Courses

10 Miles

0 1 2 3 4 5 6 7 8 9 10

Nautical Miles

to Q, I being over 88 feet, Q not over 30 feet but not less than 25 feet. The J-class of 76 rating varied between 76 feet and 87 feet on the waterline. The rating of 76 had nothing to do with the length of a yacht but was the fixed answer in an equation made up of a yacht's load waterline length, displacement and sail area, a minimum displacement, calculated by another formula, being allotted to each yacht according to its load waterline length.

The Universal rule differed from the International in that it allowed considerable flexibility in length without taxing sail area – which by the formula was almost constant – so long as displacement was likewise increased. This encouraged sail plans of a high aspect ratio which maximized the sail area available to drive the greatest possible displacement

The courses used for the America's Cup races at Newport between 1930 and 1962.

through the water. The problem was, as Heckstall-Smith pointed out, 'curiously complex and exceedingly scientific', for any designer to tackle. When Lipton came to him for *Shamrock V*, Nicholson knew he only had one chance at getting the formula right while the Americans, accustomed anyway to the rule, had four, creating the biggest boom in yachtbuilding since the Dunraven challenge of 1893. This quartet of cup candidates – *Enterprise*, *Weetamoe*, *Yankee* and *Whirlwind* – were all built to different lengths, making the best possible chance of finding the best possible answer to the restrictions imposed by the formula of the Universal rule.

The 1930 Cup candidates. Left to right: Whirlwind,
Weetamoe, Yankee, Enterprise

Curiously, the smallest, *Enterprise*, at 80 feet, won
the honour to defend, but as we have seen many
factors have to be taken into account with an
America's Cup candidate, and the fastest boat is not
necessarily the best. It was acknowledged afterwards by most people that *Weetamoe* was faster than
Enterprise, but *Enterprise* alone had two secret
weapons: an extraordinarily light mast and a quite
extraordinary manager called Harold S. Vanderbilt,
Mike to his friends. Vanderbilt took the management of a large yacht into the modern era. He was
tough, determined, knew how to pick the top team
and understood with almost uncanny perception the
tantamount importance of total dedication to the
task at hand and of delegating responsibility in a way
which had never been previously conceived of on a
Cup boat. He made the British look, during the
three challenges of the 1930s, what they were:
talented amateurs.

Professionalism was one of *Enterprise*'s secret
weapons. Another was her duralumin mast. She had
started the season with a normal hollow mast probably weighing in the region of 6000 lb. It rose, as did
those of all the Js, some 150 feet above deck. She did
not do well in her early races but her designer Starling Burgess, son of Edward and an accomplished
aircraft designer and a published poet, had a card up
his sleeve. He had asked his brother Charles to
design a lightweight metal mast. Charles had for
twelve years been in the airship design section of the
Navy department and was well qualified to apply the
elaborate mathematical theories developed for
designing metal aircraft structures. His mast was
twelve-sided and composed of two shells of duralumin held together by no fewer than 80,000 rivets. It
weighed only 4000 pounds, provoking the remark
from one magazine that though there were now
scantlings for yachts' hulls there were none for their
masts. To give it sufficient play it was stepped in a

Inset above: *Below decks on* Enterprise

A dramatic shot from the masthead of Enterprise *showing
the width of the Park Avenue boom*

Inset below: Enterprise's *miracle mast, made of
duralumin. 80,000 rivets held it together*

steel tube filled with a liquid resembling quicksilver. Clinton Crane, the designer of *Weetamoe*, commented, with a hint of justifiable envy, that the mast was a miracle 'and that it was a miracle it stayed in the boat!' But stay in it did (the distribution of the load on the shrouds that kept it there was analysed by a fascinating-sounding mathematical method known as 'the principle of least work') – and *Enterprise* began to win races.

She was helped by another extraordinary device, the Park Avenue boom, which many people thought evaded the rules. This triangular-shaped spar enabled the foot of the mainsail to be altered, by a series of tracks of holes with pegs in them, so the wind flow was used to maximum efficiency. This ungainly but useful piece of equipment was so wide that two men could quite comfortably link arms and walk down it side by side – hence the name, Park Avenue. Each of the tracks of holes was specially coloured so that those altering the curve of the sail would have a guideline to follow. These eventually came to be called after the coloured lines on the map of the New York Subway System: Seventh Avenue, Times Square Shuttle, and Lexington Avenue; and when the British adopted the Park Avenue boom in 1934 they used the same colours and called them after lines on the London underground!

To add to her efficient rigging and modern spars *Enterprise* had a great many winches, so many that Sherman Hoyt, who was a member of the afterguard, called them 'our "57 and one varieties"' and, when comparing them with the number on board *Shamrock V*, agreed with Nicholson 'that if we had too many, he had far too few'. But it was not just her equipment that got *Enterprise* names like 'the mechanical ship', 'robust robot' and 'box of clockwork', for her crew, too, were trained to a pitch of perfection that made them appear more like automatons than men. Each had his allotted station to perform a specific task. To this station Vanderbilt gave a number, which appeared on a crew member's sweater. Orders were given by number not by name. If a crew member was required to swap stations with another then they swapped sweaters too. In 1930 many of the winches were below decks, which were completely gutted, and seventeen of the twenty-six-man crew worked permanently below. They were known as the black gang.

The afterguard were organized with equal efficiency. *Enterprise*, truly a team boat, was in marked contrast to the challenger – which came over with a professional skipper, a discontented crew, and an afterguard of amateur gentlemen who ignored all advice and sailed to a four-nil defeat – and was considerably advanced in managerial methods over her three rivals to defend the Cup. George Nichols, for instance, was a brilliant helmsman and his handling of *Weetamoe* could hardly be faulted but his handling of his crew failed him, as Clinton Crane pointed out: 'The one weakness that George had was that he did not find it easy to rely on his afterguard.' The other two candidates, *Yankee* and *Whirlwind*, did not perform as well but both of them were interesting yachts. *Yankee*, commissioned by a Boston syndicate including Charles Francis Adams, later developed into a remarkably fast yacht. *Whirlwind*, a double-ender designed by Nat Herreshoff's son, Francis, could have been fast but she never really worked. She was the only one of the five J boats involved in the 1930 challenge which started the season with a double-headed rig, something all the Js adopted for the later challenges, but she was never tuned properly and suffered from the same problem that had bugged earlier Cup candidates: she was almost impossible to steer. On one occasion the man at the helm was pitched right over her wheel while struggling to keep control.

Probably none of the Js in 1930 were as good as they could have been in theory. Nat Herreshoff commented on *Weetamoe* and *Enterprise* that they were 'about as different as two boats could be, but there doesn't seem to be much difference in their speed, so I guess they're both wrong'.

As the four American yachts fought for the honour to defend the Cup, the challenger, *Shamrock V*, was racing on the British regatta circuit. She had been launched on the day that grand old man of professional skippers, Captain Sycamore, died. It was, in a way, the end of an era and the dawn of a new one, as old 'Syccy' was the last of the great old-time professionals, for progressively during the 1930s the Big Boats, the Js and the 23-metres, were sailed by their amateur owners. Despite his sarcasm – 'If you gentlemen will come up to windward', he was once heard to say to some guests on the 23-metre *Shamrock*, 'you will be in the sunshine, altogether more comfortable, *and out of the way of my main boom*' – and his willingness to flout the racing rules if he thought he could get away with it, Sycamore was an immensely popular figure. Lipton, now in his eighties, must have been greatly saddened by his death. 'Burly, sturdy but straight-backed', was how John Scott Hughes described him. 'Gold bearded, boyish-eyed Sycamore when I sailed with him appeared in the prime of life. But he was then seventy-four years of age.'

Shamrock V proved a fast yacht and British confidence was high. But *Enterprise* won four races in a row, with ease, and after the last Lipton wryly commended the afterguard of his yacht for keeping their opponent in sight all day. Summing up the fourteenth challenge in his book *Enterprise*, Vanderbilt wrote that he beat *Shamrock V* because

the luff of *Enterprise*'s headsails, owing to shorter headstays and greater tension thereon, sagged off to leeward much less than *Shamrock V*'s and that *Enterprise*'s lighter mast – 4000 lb against the 6350 lb of *Shamrock*'s – and Park Avenue boom proved superior to *Shamrock*'s spars.

He added that when sailing free, *Enterprise* used better sail combinations and had a greater variety to draw on, and that her afterguard 'had a greater appreciation of the value of tacking to leeward'.

Shamrock V in the Solent, May 1930 (Beken)

Lipton accepted defeat in his usual sportsmanlike way, and it is perhaps doubtful whether he any longer really cared whether he won or lost. Challenging for the Cup had become such a way of life with him that, as he noted in his autobiography, it 'has been my principal recreation for over thirty years. It has kept me young, eager, buoyant, and hopeful. It has brought me health and splendid friends.' He returned home vowing to try again and he was at long last elected to the membership of the Royal Yacht Squadron. However, he seems never to have visited the place. In October 1931, with his challenge with *Shamrock VI* delayed because of the economic crisis, he died. The job of challenging for the Cup passed on to the next, and very different, generation of yachtsmen who had grown up in Britain in the decade following the war; a new breed of men who were not content to stand by and watch their yachts being raced for them but were eager and competent enough to take the helm themselves. One of these men was an aircraft manufacturer, T. O. M.

Sopwith whose First World War aeroplanes had made him a millionaire. His knowledge, and that of his professional colleagues and advisers, like Frank Murdoch, of the new technology of aerodynamics and metallurgy stood him in good stead when building a J boat. To start with Sopwith, who had graduated, like many of his big-boat rivals in Britain at that time, from 12 metre racing, bought *Shamrock V* and raced her for two seasons before deciding in 1933 to build a J and challenge for the Cup through the Royal Yacht Squadron.

At first King George V, the commodore, had doubts about the wisdom of the challenge because 'with industrial conditions as they are in America and elsewhere . . . this was not the opportune time'. However, Sopwith argued that if the Royal Yacht Squadron did not issue the challenge there were three other yachtsmen whose clubs would do so on their behalf; eventually he won the day. The challenge was made and accepted, and the British challenger *Endeavour* was built.

The King, however, had a point. Unlike 1930, when the Wall Street Crash and the subsequent depression had not yet begun to bite, 1933, when the next challenge was made, was a bad year for the economies of both defending and challenging countries. To spend enormous sums on a handful of yachts, sailed in order to keep or take back a near-worthless cup, was at odds with the tenor of the times although it would have meant employment for many skilled workers out of a job. So, on the American side the 1934 challenge was done on the cheap compared with the massively expensive defence of 1930. Only one new yacht was built, *Rainbow*, so named by her owner, Vanderbilt, as an augury of emergence from the Great Depression. It was only decided to commission her because Vanderbilt's 1930 J, *Enterprise*, could not possibly have been converted to comply with the new regulations and rating formulae – the *New York Times* described these as 'worse than a Chinese puzzle or Professor Einstein's theory of relativity' which had been agreed between the two countries in the intervening years. Even so *Rainbow* nearly did not appear because no one would put up the money to pay for her. In the end Vanderbilt and three of his family had to underwrite much of the expense and there were eighteen names in the *Rainbow* syndicate.

Endeavour (K4) tuning up with Velsheda *in the Solent, 1934*

Inset: Mrs Sopwith at the wheel of Endeavour, *1934*

To cut costs Vanderbilt made good use of equipment from *Enterprise*, and borrowed some expensive sails. The total cost for building and equipping her probably did not exceed $400,000. Two other contenders for the defence of the Cup were also put into the water that year; *Weetamoe*, who had come so near to becoming the defender in 1930, and *Yankee*, the Boston boat which, with *Whirlwind*, had been eliminated early on in the 1930 trials. In 1934, however, the roles of these two yachts were reversed. Both had extensive alterations made to their hulls and rigging but it was *Yankee*, this time, which nearly snatched the honour of defending from Vanderbilt and his syndicate. Of the first eleven races, between *Rainbow* and *Yankee*, *Rainbow* won only one and it was not until Vanderbilt increased his yacht's waterline length by adding ballast that *Rainbow* managed to begin winning against the Boston boat. In the end she was selected after she won the last of a five-race series by 1 second. The selection was fair: not only did *Rainbow* prove marginally faster, but she had fewer mishaps and gear failure – a record she was not wholly to continue during the Cup races themselves. However, many Bostonians thought the selection precipitate, not the first time New Englanders had disagreed with the judgement of their New York colleagues. Vanderbilt is on record as saying that the trials were the hardest-fought series of races he had ever competed in, and when *Rainbow* lost the first race in the final series, her navigator, Zenas Bliss, wrote in his notebook. 'This will come near to finishing our hash.' As had often happened in the past – and was to happen again in the future – the Trials looked as if they were going to be more thrilling than the Cup races themselves. What makes the fifteenth challenge so different is that this did not turn out to be the case.

As the American boats tuned up against each other, like against like racing under identical conditions to those of the Cup races, *Endeavour*, for her tuning up, entered the time-honoured British regatta racing circuit. This began every year at Harwich on the east coast, worked its way round to the Solent, then up to Scotland – and sometimes Northern Ireland – before coming south again for Cowes Week and the big West Country regattas. By comparison with the exhaustive thoroughness of the American trials the British regatta circuit was a leisurely affair and, certainly so far as the big classes were concerned, geared primarily to entertaining both the King and his millionaire sailing opponents and the British public, who used to turn out in their

Rainbow, *lee rail under* (Beken)

thousands at the various holiday resorts to watch the big cutters racing. So important was the spectator aspect of the Regatta circuit that courses for the Big Boats were laid for the convenience of those watching, not for those racing – and certainly not for any potential challenger for the America's Cup. Sopwith was certainly aware of this deficiency and tried to rectify it by organizing a series of trials with *Velsheda* (the only other J racing in British waters besides *Shamrock V*), but these proved abortive as *Velsheda* was simply not sufficiently geared to such competitive racing, setting the wrong headsails at the start of one race and then taking no less than 8 minutes to set her spinnaker. Sopwith needed sterner competition but unfortunately there was no one around to provide it; in the twelve races she entered before crossing the Atlantic, *Endeavour* won eight and came second in three. What those races did prove, however, was that she was a very fast boat indeed; so long as the by now superbly trained crew worked together, and the afterguard didn't make any really

appalling errors, then here was the best chance Britain had ever had to bring back the Cup.

Unfortunately, neither requirement was met. The professional crew struck for higher wages eight days before *Endeavour* was due to leave and most of them had to be replaced by hurriedly recruited amateurs; and *Endeavour*'s afterguard presented at least one race to *Rainbow* 'wrapped up in cellophane and handed to her on a silver platter with Sopwith's compliments', as one American observer put it.

But *Rainbow* had her troubles too. She was completed in a record 100 days because of the delay in deciding to build her at all; then she had to face not only the tough series of trials but a strike of her crew as well. The crew wrote down their claims and grievances and then signed their names in a circle in true 'round-robin' fashion. However, unlike the British crew's strike the differences of opinion between the American crew and management were amicably settled and the new terms were accepted by the crew who this time signed, not in a circle, but in a square. 'Now you see we are on the square!' was added to the note of acceptance by one crew member, suggesting that man management in the United States was far more advanced and enlightened than in Britain where the behaviour of *Endeavour*'s crew was regarded by many more as a mutiny than a strike.

The management and crews of the two competing yachts were, of course, of tantamount importance but so too were the yachts themselves, and there were many changes in their rigging and design. Some occurred because they were a natural improvement on the earlier Js, and developed out of experience, while others followed changes in the rules governing the J class and the America's Cup competition itself. Many of the rules – like the one changing the aspect ratio of the forestay which resulted in the triple headsails being replaced with double headsails – are either too minor or too technical to mention here. Two of the more important ones must be described, if only because they caused dissension when the British saw how the Americans had interpreted them. As was the custom, when *Endeavour* arrived at Newport the two yachts were inspected by each other's afterguard and club representatives. No one had any criticism of *Endeavour* but when the British inspected the American yacht they found that all *Rainbow*'s cabin fittings had been stripped out to save weight. This was not, definitely not, playing the game and the British protested. Sopwith's bathtub was still in place so why had Vanderbilt's been removed, they demanded to know. The protest caused some ill-feeling amongst the American yachting fraternity but the Race Committee eventually acceded that the British had a point, and they were allowed to remove their owner's bathtub along with all her furniture and a large part of her cabin fittings.

The battle of the bathtubs had hardly subsided when one of Britain's top yachting journalists, Brooke Heckstall-Smith, reported that not only was *Rainbow* just a racing machine with rough board partitions instead of proper cabins but that an 'enormous and powerful winch', used for trimming the genoa, contravened the new rules – which stated that no standing rigging except for the fore- and headstays was to be worked from below the upper deck – because the winch's gear was below deck though it was worked from above. The Americans dug their toes in over this dispute and it remained unsettled – and unsettling.

Besides new rules and new boats there were new sails, and these last, whatever might be said about the other two, were a big step forward in increasing the speed and efficiency of the Js. The American crew – American-based Scandinavians mostly recruited from Deer Island – had names for the two most effective ones. The new spinnakers, the parachute type, were christened 'Mae Wests' because of their curves, and the quadrilateral jibs became known as 'Greta Garbos', perhaps because the development of this sail had been conducted in such a secretive manner. That it originated in Britain no one disputes but there are several claimants for inventing it. Sir Thomas Sopwith, in a recent interview, states that the idea was his:

I was talking to Charlie Nicholson one day. He was always extremely anxious to pick up anything new. We were looking for some way to crowd on a bit more canvas and he suggested two jib topsails, one over the other, so I said, 'If you're going to do that why not fill in the open space between the two clews.' Hence the quadrilateral.

Whoever invented it certainly didn't keep this phenomenally successful sail secret long enough; no sooner had it been hoisted for the first time in the Solent than it was broken out at Newport. Both sides have always had their spies at work before an America's Cup challenge and 1934 was no exception. Indeed Sherman Hoyt averred that he knew there was going to be a strike on *Endeavour* before Sopwith did!

Even before the races began it became evident there was not much to choose between the two boats. Sopwith says that 'we were slightly better to windward, we were slightly better downwind, and *Rainbow* would always outreach us', and Sherman Hoyt qualifies this only by saying he thought *Rainbow* had the edge over *Endeavour* close hauled when the weather was very light. With the boats so evenly matched it was really up to the afterguard and crew, and it was here that the British more than met their match.

The first mishap for the British occurred before the first completed race even began on 17 September (the first race was abandoned through lack of wind) when the mastheadman on *Endeavour* knocked himself out while attaching the head of the British yacht's mainsail to the hook at the top of the mast, an innovation which helped to relieve the enormous compression on the mast. Luckily for Sopwith the Race Committee postponed the start, something they were under no obligation to do. Their action considerably annoyed the afterguard and crew of the defender, though on reflection they decided they would have hated to have sailed round the course alone. If they had done so they knew Vanderbilt would have become overnight the most unpopular man in America! However, once begun the British yacht won the first race by 2 minutes after *Rainbow* ran into spinnaker gear trouble – no doubt reinforcing Sherman Hoyt's opinion of this sail as an 'abomination and dangerous curse of modern yacht racing'.

The second race was also won by the British, Sopwith again winning the start and retaining his lead throughout in a race sailed over the 30-mile triangular course in a freshish north-westerly breeze. It was the fastest race ever sailed over an America's Cup triangular course and *Endeavour* won by 51 seconds.

With the British two-nil up Vanderbilt must have wondered what had hit him. Halfway round the course during the third race, with *Endeavour* over 6 minutes ahead, he must have known that only a miracle could save him from being the first American ever to lose the America's Cup. Half in disgust, half in despair, 10 minutes after rounding the last mark, he told Hoyt to take the helm with the remark that perhaps Hoyt 'could make the darned thing go', and went below 'to drown my sorrow in coffee and sandwiches'. What happened next could not perhaps be called a miracle but to the crew of *Rainbow* it did not fall far short of being one. Hoyt, who had often sailed against Sopwith in England, knew the only possible chance of avoiding defeat was to bluff his opponent. He knew that Sopwith always covered a rival yacht regardless of where the mark was. It was a hazy day and no one could see the finishing line but *Rainbow*'s navigator, Zenas Bliss, knew where it was and the crew knew they were fetching it. Hoyt's bluff was to luff up, guessing that the challenger would follow suit so as to keep between the defender and the line. *Endeavour* did just that, ran into a calm patch, went about only just crossing *Rainbow*'s bows, tacked again and then twice more, and lost the race. Sopwith maintains that he was forced to tack, and it could well be that he did not realize the subtlety of Hoyt's manoeuvre, but the truth probably is that in those hazy conditions his navigator did not know for certain where the finish was while *Rainbow*'s, a professor of mathematics, knew precisely. So, instead of being three down the Americans were only one down – with four more to sail if necessary.

Losing the third race obviously rattled the British. Losing the fourth, which they did in a welter of protests and acrimony, unnerved them completely, and they lost the last two without regaining their confidence. However, even these two races were by no means a walkover; indeed it was only by sheer chance that *Rainbow* was not obliged to forfeit the fifth race to her opponent as one of her quartermasters was knocked overboard during a gybe. As the rules state that a competing yacht must finish with the same number of crew she started with there was no question of leaving the unfortunate man to be picked up by the spectator fleet, and Vanderbilt would have had no alternative but to come about and affect a rescue. Luckily for him, however, and for the quartermaster, the latter had the presence of mind to grab the loose backstay he had been in charge of which was trailing in the water, and managed to hang on until pulled aboard. Later the other members of the crew read him one of the owner's most rigid rules: no swimming off the boat during a race!

The incident had hardly caused any loss of time at all and despite splitting a spinnaker *Rainbow* won this fifth race by the handsome margin of 4 minutes 1 second.

The sixth race was a heart-stopper and both yachts went over the start line with protest flags hoisted after a luffing incident. Then began a tacking duel which *Rainbow* looked as if she was winning. But then, on a fetch to the second mark which would have put her about 3 minutes ahead, she set the wrong spinnaker 'a miserable sail loaned by *Weetamoe*', as Hoyt described it. By the time the leg was half over *Endeavour* was abreast and beginning to take *Rainbow*'s wind. Hoyt wrote:

It looked all over for us. Vanderbilt, highly nervous, suddenly departing from our usual procedure, asked me to relieve Parkinson at the helm and went below leaving me in charge. Once again I gambled upon my knowledge of Sopwith's tendency to try and keep an opponent covered regardless of course. Zene Bliss gave me the compass bearing of the finish, then about 5 miles away. I asked him for the compass course for a point 1 mile to leeward of the finish and put *Rainbow* on it. To my intense gratification *Endeavour* followed suit parallel to our course. Both yachts were now sailing considerably by the lee. Sopwith, instead of heading straight for the finish, bore off in an attempt to again cut our wind. To do so he had to sail even more by the lee than we and promptly slowed up. He did not dare jibe in order to really cover us, knowing that we would probably sharpen up and force him to make a second jibe back. We slowly commenced to pull away as he foolishly persisted in his efforts to take our wind which would, due to our sailing by the lee, require him to get on our theoretical lee quarter. He could not do so and when about a mile or more away from the finish, I sharpened *Rainbow* up and due to our leeward position, better angle and a slight favourable shift in the wind to what had been our lee quarter, was able to pull ahead to win by a bit less than a minute.

Enthralling as the fifth and sixth races were, it was the fourth on which the fifteenth challenge hinged. Its result caused more controversy and bitterness than any America's Cup race since the days of Dunraven. In retrospect, the shades of the litigious Earl probably caused a lot of the problems because the Race Committee were as anxious as anyone not to cause controversy – Vanderbilt was told not to protest if he could possibly avoid doing so – but their means of doing so almost certainly created the very situation they were striving to avoid. Briefly, the two yachts were involved in a luffing match before the start which nearly resulted in a collision. Vanderbilt, heeding the Race Committee's strictures about protesting, did not hoist his protest flag and neither did Sopwith, though each thought the other in the wrong. Though 23 seconds behind the defender at the start because of this incident, Sopwith sailed his yacht superbly and on rounding the first mark was some 24 seconds ahead. At this point the second incident occurred. Just after Vanderbilt rounded the mark to the weather of *Endeavour* Sopwith luffed him. Under the rules the yacht being luffed would have to be hit forward of the rigging to be forced to bear up. Though Hoyt, sitting on the spinnaker boom at the time, tactfully does not mention this in his memoirs, several eyewitnesses, including Sopwith himself, heard him shout to Vanderbilt, 'For Christ's sake luff, Mike,' but his advice was ignored by Vanderbilt who maintained his course and afterwards averred that Sopwith luffed too late. Vanderbilt says *Endeavour* was 30 feet away when she bore off, but everyone else says she was a lot closer than that and Sopwith maintains that it was just 10 feet.

Sopwith consulted with the American representative on board, 'Bubbles' Havemeyer, about hoisting his protest flag. Havemeyer thought it would be quite in order to hoist it when the Committee boat was nearer, and Sopwith followed his advice. But the rule actually says that the flag shall be displayed 'at the earliest possible moment, and when next passing the Committee boat'. Unfortunately for Sopwith the custom outside America was to ignore the vital comma and the 'and': in Britain it was sufficient to display the flag 'when next passing the Committee boat'. Havemeyer did not know about this difference in semantics, and the upshot was that

the Race Committee refused to allow Sopwith's protest because he had not hoisted the protest flag 'promptly'. There was an immediate furore on both sides of the Atlantic with headlines such as 'Britannia rules the waves but America waives the rules' being freely bandied about.

In fact the Race Committee had acted on the very best of motives, for Sopwith had, unwisely, not only protested against *Rainbow*'s failure to respond to his luff but on the much more doubtful issue as to who was to fault for the incident before the race began. This first incident had taken place right under the noses of the Race Committee who were in no doubt that *Endeavour* was in the wrong. It followed that if her first protest was disallowed she was disqualified anyway, making the second protest of no consequence. The most tactful line for the Race Committee was to find an excuse not to hear Sopwith's protest at all, and this is just what they did. Unfortunately, it did not look that way to the world's press, or to the afterguard and crew of the challenging yacht. To them not only had justice not been done but it had not even been seen not to be done, and nearly half a century later Sopwith still thinks that he did not get 'quite a square deal'. At the time he stated he would never race for the America's Cup again. He wasn't the first to have said that – nor the first to change his mind.

Disturbed by the depth of bad feeling aroused by the 1934 challenge Gerard Lambert, the owner of *Vanitie*, bought *Yankee* and took her across the Atlantic in 1935 to race in Britain on the regatta circuit. The visit was a great success and much of the bad feeling between the two yachting communities was dissipated; in the autumn of that year Sopwith ordered *Endeavour II* from Nicholson with the idea of challenging again for races in 1936. His carefully laid plans were, however, nearly thwarted when Richard Fairey (like Sopwith an aeroplane manufacturer and a keen yachtsman), now the owner of *Shamrock V* renamed simply *Shamrock*, announced that he was proposing to build a yacht named *Windflower* and would challenge for the Cup. The challenge via Fairey's club the Royal London was duly delivered by hand by Dr Reggie Bennett, one of Britain's top amateur helmsmen and now a leading British MP, and the fat was in the fire. British sporting instincts were outraged and Lipton's highly respected yachting adviser, Colonel Duncan Neill, expressed them strongly. 'There is an unwritten custom,' he announced, 'that a defeated owner in a cup challenge should have the first chance of getting his revenge.'

As it happened the NYYC were not too pleased either, as Fairey had decided not to challenge with a J-class yacht but with a boat built to the top of the K-class, i.e. 75 feet long on the waterline. Opinion was divided on both these aspects of the unexpected challenge but Fairey's initiative was well judged in some respects because many people felt the J-class were not seaworthy, their rigs being too delicate. Js were also enormously expensive to build and race, and the economic and political climate in Britain did not take kindly to such costly toys of the wealthy. The NYYC, better versed in diplomacy than their predecessors, did not exactly decline Fairey's challenge but Fairey soon heard that it was not being viewed favourably and he promptly withdrew it. *Windflower* was never built, and the way seemed clear for Sopwith. But when *he* let it be known he wanted to challenge he was warned off by an NYYC member as 1936 was presidential election year; to hold an America's Cup series at that time was not deemed politically acceptable. So the challenge was postponed till 1937 and this gave Sopwith plenty of time to get his new J properly tuned.

Nicholson built just about the biggest boat the rules allowed and when the owner went to see her at Camper and Nicholson's before her launching he exclaimed, 'Good Lord, Charlie, she's like a ruddy great pantechnicon.' Nicholson, however, had watched the performance of *Yankee* the previous summer and he was convinced that, like any other class of yacht, the longer the boat the faster she was. He knew also that the improved headsails of the Js made it possible for the larger hull to be driven through the water with the allotted sail area and he was not inhibited on this score, as had been the designers of the earlier Js.

Starling Burgess, this time teamed up with the young designer Olin Stephens, also decided to build to the maximum length of 87 feet, but while Nicholson again judged the design of *Endeavour II* by instinct and experience Burgess and Stephens, though of course drawing on their experience, went to the testing tank to find the answers. Tank testing was not new but had never been particularly favoured. 'It is said that G. L. Watson designed *Shamrock II* after testing her model against others,' Olin Stephens wrote in *Yachting*, 'and that, following her defeat by *Columbia* in 1901, he expressed the wish that Nat Herreshoff might also have had a towing tank'; Stephens went on to say that although

Aboard Ranger, 1937. Harold Vanderbilt is at the helm. Among his afterguard that year were two brothers, Rod (pictured here) and Olin Stephens, who both became major figures during the 12-metre era. Rod's speciality has always been masts and rigging (Rosenfeld)

model tests were used in the design of other America's Cup boats, among them *Vanitie*, Watson's expression was typical of the general opinion among designers of towing tank tests. However, Professor Kenneth Davidson of the Stevens Institute of Technology had developed tank testing much further and, by using smaller models, made the operation much less expensive – 3 foot models cost only $50 or so, according to designer Clinton Crane, as opposed to many thousands. Davidson had developed a technique which enabled the lateral force of the wind to be applied to a model in addition to the normal forward thrust resulting from it at differing degrees of heel. His experiments showed that this lateral thrust had never been properly calculated before and when the models of *Endeavour* – the lines of which had been generously supplied by Nicholson after the previous series – *Rainbow* and

Ranger finished 18 minutes ahead in the second race. A small foresail has been set inside her huge silk quadrilateral

Weetamoe were tested the results corresponded very closely with the designers' observations of these three boats, and this encouraged Burgess and Stephens to put their faith in the new tank testing method. Four models were tested and one, 77-C, was chosen. Despite many statements to the contrary – including one from Vanderbilt himself in the 1950s – 77-C was a Burgess model, but if the model was Burgess's the lower stern afterbody profile of 77-C belonged to Stephens, who had been using similar lines in his 6 metre designs.

Having chosen the model, the two designers tried to improve on it but could not do so (it was not so much the speed of the model the designers were trying to improve but its looks). 'The model selected,' Burgess commented, 'was so unusual that I do not think any one of us would have dared to pick her had we not had the tank's results and Kenneth Davidson's analysis to back her.' Model 77-C was something of an ugly duckling, but when it eventually became *Ranger* it was probably her bulbous stem and flattened stern that were responsible for her remarkable speed on the wind. Whatever the cause *Ranger* was a remarkable boat, and when Nicholson saw her in dry dock he announced her the most revolutionary advance in design for fifty years.

Before they even began the races *Ranger* lost her mast once and *Endeavour II* lost hers twice. But by now everyone was quite used to the Js being dismasted. (A yachting magazine printed an unkind couplet that ran: 'When the winds of July and August blow, The masts of most of the J-class go.')

At Sopwith's request the races were held early – in July and August – and, also at his request, he was not obliged to declare the name of the challenger until immediately before the beginning of the first race. He then persuaded his business partner Fred Sigrist to charter *Endeavour I* from her new owner Herman Andreae and to take her across the Atlantic with Sopwith's new *Endeavour II*. This meant that extensive trials could be carried out; if the old *Endeavour* proved to be faster then she would challenge again. However, this did not prove to be the case and it was *Endeavour II* which came to the line for the first race on 31 July.

After their thorough tuning up and careful preparations the spirits of the British contingent were high. But they were soon dashed when *Ranger* took the first race by the phenomenally large time of 17 minutes 5 seconds. The other three races were processions too, though when the winds blew more steadily during the last two the British challenger

performed better. Sopwith won the first two starts and Vanderbilt the second two. Sherman Hoyt, however, was doubtful whether Sopwith could really be credited properly with winning the first two; apparently Vanderbilt had been strongly cautioned by the race Committee against getting into any kind of situation which could recreate the unfortunate circumstances of the 1934 series. But Vanderbilt, according to Hoyt, got so annoyed by the praise heaped on the Englishman for winning the start twice that he reverted to his normal tactics and won the last two starts.

The 1937 challenge did not have the tensions and frustrations of the 1934 series for the Americans, as it was so obvious right from the beginning that *Ranger* was the superior boat. That the American afterguard were supremely confident and efficient is well described by Sir Fisher Dilke, the British observer on *Ranger* during the races, who wrote in his book *Observer on Ranger*:

Harold Vanderbilt, who seems to be universally known as 'Mike' in America starts the boat and sails her to the windward mark, where he hands the wheel to Olin Stephens.

Vanderbilt very rarely indeed looks at anything but his compass, and sails the boat by a combination of that, the feel of the helm, which can be very delicately adjusted by the centre-plate, and the suggestions (orders is nearer the proper word) of his afterguard. I saw him look at *Endeavour* only a very few times and then just a quick turn of the head was enough. If he wants to know where the enemy is he asks and gets the answer, 'Two points on our weather quarter, range 450 yards', or whatever it may be. The bearing by compass from Olin or Rod, the range by stadimeter, as they call the range-finder, from Bliss.

Olin Stephens, as everyone knows, has designed the winners of many ocean and smooth-water races before he is thirty, and sailed them himself too. He also designed *Ranger* and is generally a notable young man. But his job here, besides sailing the boat off the wind, is to study the tactical position and give advice to the helmsman. When asked a question he waits four seconds and then says, 'I don't think so, Mike', or 'We should tack now'. Nothing more.

Younger brother Rod is in charge of all the sails and gear and is responsible for having things ready when wanted. Also he deals with all trouble, which means trips to the masthead or boom-end, at very awkward moments. He generally sees the turning marks before anyone else, as he

Fourth and final race, 5 August 1937. From ten minutes until two and a half minutes before the start both yachts sailed in circles, Ranger *always on* Endeavour II's *stern*

This Certifies That

ARTHUR KNAPP Jr

Was one of the RANGER BOYS, crew of the 1937 America's Cup Defender "Ranger," and that his services were first class in every respect.

Geo. H. Monsell MASTER.

Everyone, even the afterguard, was given one of these certificates after Ranger *had won. This one belongs to Arthur Knapp Jr, one of America's best small-boat sailors, who was at the helm of 12-metre Cup candidate* Weatherly *in 1958*

carries glasses round his neck to see if anything is foul aloft. A pretty fine seaman.

Zenas Bliss, who isn't my idea of a university professor though his hair is greying a little, does the navigation and leads a hard life at it, as he has to say just where we are when no one can know very exactly.

And sometimes we aren't there and things are said. . . .

Arthur Knapp trims the headsails, and the 'Ranger's song' says he oils the squeaks, but I don't know when, as I never saw him anywhere but holding on to the lee rigging with head in the air saying 'No Higher' or 'All full' in answer to the helmsman's 'Coming up' or 'Going away'. Yachting papers say he is a goodish small-boat sailor.

Mrs Vanderbilt's only remarks on deck in a cup race are said slowly in a clear, distinct voice. 'Endeavour – is – going – to – tack. They – are – setting – something – on – the – forestay.'

She sits on the deck just aft of the observer, who is himself only just not having his hands trodden on by her husband at the wheel. They both like her a great deal.

A vivid portrait of a winning combination, and there's no doubt that Vanderbilt is one of the great names in the history of the America's Cup.

Britain tries twice – and fails 8

1958/1964

The Second World War and its aftermath caused a twenty-year hiatus in races for the America's Cup; it was not until May 1957 that a formal challenge for 1958 was received by the New York Yacht Club from the Royal Yacht Squadron on behalf of a syndicate of British yachtsmen headed by Hugh Goodson.

The history of the cup is characterized by long inactive periods – 1851 to 1870, 1903 to 1920, and 1920 to 1930, to name the longest – punctuated by ones of frenzied activity. But what makes the 1937 to 1958 gap so different is not so much the length of time but the social, technological and economic change that took place in the west during those two decades. The super-rich became merely wealthy, and the wealthy had to earn their living to stay that way. But the rest of us found there was more money in our pockets and there was time to spend it. Sailing became a pursuit within the reach of practically everyone. The war had spurred on technological advances which soon began to show up on Cup boats: plastic, aluminium, titanium, terylene, computers, and a mass of electronic gadgetry, were just some of the products of the space age that have been employed by the Americans, Swedes, French, Australians and British to defend or try to wrest away the America's Cup in the post-war period. The Americans have always been two steps ahead in the employment of such material, which is one of the reasons the Cup has stayed bolted down in the New York Yacht Club. The other is that the Americans have proved themselves to be either better sailors, better boatbuilders, or better sailmakers – and sometimes all three – than any challenger.

There are other factors: a good business sense is essential (the 1958 defence was run, it was said, like IBM), experience is invaluable, the will to win a prerequisite. Britain, who challenged in 1958 and 1965, really had none of these except experience.

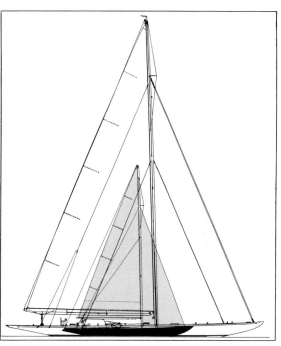

The transformation in America's Cup boats between 1937 and 1958. This is the 1958 defender, Columbia, *superimposed on* Ranger, *the 1937 J-class defender* (Sparkman and Stephens)

She is a sporting nation *nonpareille*, but, unfortunately for her, sportsmanship really has nothing to do with the America's Cup and probably has not since Lt. Henn sailed to America in *Genesta* with his wife, his monkey, his dogs, and his potted palms. Her one asset, experience, has been dissipated by failing to make an adequate challenge in 1958, failing to learn from this disastrous experience in 1964, and by subsequently giving up 12-metre racing altogether, and turning to ocean racing. Britain has some of the best yachtsmen in the world – you only need to look at the ocean racing and Olympic records to realize that – but racing in a class and match racing are different skills (though great match-racing helmsmen have come from the ocean-racing ranks).

Australia, France and Sweden lack Britain's only asset: experience. But while a business sense and a will to win are an attitude of mind experience can be gained and Australia, at any rate, is gaining it fast. As the 12-metre racing world develops her great problem will be her isolation from Europe and America. That leaves France and Sweden. Sweden is still an unknown factor. She has only challenged once (1977) and was eliminated in the preliminary trials. Backed by Swedish industry with a formidable international yachtsman Pelle Petterson in charge, *Sverige* could be a force to be reckoned with in 1980. Could be. France's experience goes back further, to 1970, and the millionaire ballpoint pen manufacturer, Baron Bich, who is in charge of that country's challenge for the Cup is a very determined man indeed. He is very rich, which is normally incidental as money in any challenge – even Britain's abortive ones in 1958 and 1964 – is something so totally taken for granted as hardly to be worth mentioning. I mention it here because the Baron is spending his astutely, which is quite another matter. After a farcical first try in 1970 Bich learned from experience and ever since has gone about the task of lifting the Cup in a determined and organized manner. He currently owns several 12-metres and has been sailing in America against Americans ever since the last challenge. It seems that his clash with the International race committee in 1970 has given him the impetus he needs. It is not just for the glory of France, that *France III* is racing. The Baron wants blood. He may not get it but at least he is in the right frame of mind.

By contrast, the 1958 challenge was organized by a group described by one yachting journalist as 'a group of kindly, elegant, elderly British gentry, whose sense of loyalty and gallantry was infinitely superior to their sense of competition and their critical understanding of boat speed'. The seventeenth challenge grew out of a series of discussions in 1946 and 1948 between Captain John Illingworth and a number of American yachtsmen, and subsequently talks between the Commodore of the New York Yacht Club, Henry Sears, and the Commodore of the Royal Yacht Squadron, Sir Ralph Gore, and others, in the mid fifties. As retaining the J class was quite out of the question economically, Illingworth, an ocean-racing man of vast experience and talent,

had, in the earlier discussions, proposed a new type, basically an ocean-racing design, 'boats that, after the challenger trials, defender trials and Cup races were completed, would still go on to give their owners pleasure and racing interest in other fields'. It was agreed in principle with the then Commodore of the New York Yacht Club, DeCoursey Fales, that when the Cup was revived it would be raced between this type of yacht. The stumbling block was that the Deed stipulated a minimum waterline length of 65 feet, much too big for any existing ocean racer then or since, and the Club could not at that time see its way to altering the Deed. However, when Sears raised the question again in the mid fifties, the Club were quite willing, indeed eager, to apply to the American Supreme Court for the Deed to be changed so that the minimum waterline length became 44 feet (the loaded waterline of a 12-metre), and that any challenger was no longer required to get to the defending club's designated race course on her own bottom.

The 12-metre was, in retrospect, the obvious choice for the Club, as the largest extant thoroughbred racing yacht and therefore in the tradition of America's Cup boats. By today's standards the 12s are huge and enormously expensive, and really quite useless for anything else except challenging for and defending the Cup. Charlie Barr, Lipton, and all the others would not have minded the choice. Indeed, Barr would probably have approved of the choice as he admired the sturdiness of the early 12s. 'These are the best built little vessels I have ever seen,' he remarked while watching a race between 12s in Britain that took place in half a gale, 'We have no yachts of their size in America which would stand that sea without breaking up.' Their longevity is now proven. The first British 12, *Heatherbell*, built in 1907, was still afloat when the seventeenth challenge took place and almost half the hundred or so 12s built between these two dates were still around at that time, 1958, in Norway, Sweden, Germany, Italy, England and America.

The Royal Yacht Squadron were interested in challenging but did not want to commit themselves to a challenge at that stage; when the prospect of making a challenge was announced to club members later that year not all were by any means in favour, for the rot in British metre racing had already set in, and British showing in the 1952 Olympics had been poor. Nevertheless, Hugh Goodson, the owner of the 12-metre *Flica II*, decided to form a syndicate; once the American Supreme Court had allowed the changes to the Deed of Gift in December 1956, there was never any doubt that the British would challenge.

12-metre racing in both America and Britain was at a low ebb; it could be said that just as the disastrous challenge of 1964 killed off the class in Britain the challenge in 1958 only just saved it from extinction in America. No new boats had been built in the class since the war on either side of the Atlantic, and there was only one man alive, Olin Stephens, who had designed one. In Britain all the 12s but one had either been sold out of the country or converted to cruising. The exception, *Evaine*, had been laid up since 1939. In America all four remaining 12s had been converted for cruising. This lack of preparedness made Colonel Perry, the technical adviser to the Goodson syndicate who was passing through New York on the way back from winning the 5.5 metre silver medal at Melbourne, realize that if a challenge was to be made it was a case of 'sooner the better': neither side had any obvious advantage at that point but given time it seemed inevitable that the Americans would be able to outbuild any challenger. The syndicate agreed with this assessment and four designers David Boyd, Arthur Robb, James McGruer, and Charles Nicholson, nephew of the great 'Charlie', were asked to submit two models each for tank testing. It was originally suggested that one of the two designs from each designer could be in some way revolutionary but they all turned out to be orthodox except for one of Charles Nicholson's which would have had a bowsprit had it been built.

Because the model of *Flica II* had been tank tested in the Stevens Institute tank in America, and the data of this test was still available, this, too, was included in the tests that were to take place on the models at the Saunders-Roe tank at East Cowes. The plans had to be submitted by 1 April, and the tests in June established an order of merit, with David Boyd's model 'B' coming top of the class. It was not a happy choice, for the rounded forward sections of the yacht, named *Sceptre*, although a feature of Boyd's work, almost certainly slowed the hull up in the choppy confused waters off Newport. Not for a long time had a boat been so outspokenly condemned by its critics; there is little doubt now that it was the manner in which the British syndicate chose a design that caused the problems, for they showed little if any understanding of what tank testing was about. The tank at Saunders-Roe gave extremely accurate if limited information but it was in no way as sophisticated as the one at the Stevens Institute. It

did not, for instance, have a wave-making device. Yet when it was decided to develop a hull for windy conditions – a wrong evaluation in any case – the models were tested in the tank in the quite unreal conditions of a strong breeze and a glassy sea! As the superintendent of the Saunders-Roe tank pointed out, the tank had been used solely as a 'referee' instead of being an instrument in developing the fastest model. Not only were the tank tests used for the wrong purpose but, it was later revealed, woefully little time was given to them.

The nine models were tested for a total of 41 hours, or 500 runs of 5 minutes each; Allan Murray, the director of the experimental tank at the Stevens Institute, commented that the Institute would hardly have been able to test two models in that time. 'It takes 18 to 20 hours to establish data on a single model,' he commented. 'Towing in an upright position and at three angles of heel – 10, 20 and 30 degrees.' He added that the Institute had worked for nearly a year on the models of the three new American contenders. The tests on the model of *Columbia*, for instance, began in April 1957 and were still in progress in November. Olin Stephens, her designer, tank tested seven models altogether and compared them with the proven lines of *Vim*, the outstanding 12-metre he had designed for Harold Vanderbilt before the war.

Stephens's aim was to produce an all-round boat that would perform well in a breeze but which would move, too, when the wind was light, and he in no way let the tank dictate to him. 'Olin's "feel" for the reality of performance is rarely seduced by mere tank statistics,' was how the American yachting journalist, Norris Hoyt, expressed it in his book, *The Twelve-Metre Challenges for the America's Cup*. The very different American approach produced a successful defender. Though no designer can afford to produce a slow hull, producing a fast one does not automatically guarantee selection. It is as important to have a first-rate crew and first-rate sails; indeed, the least successful contender in the 1958 series, *Easterner*, was subsequently proved to have the fastest hull with *Columbia* second, then *Weatherly*, and lastly *Vim*, which with the slowest hull came within an ace of defending the Cup. It was a remarkable achievement and the fierceness of the competition for the honour to defend during that summer set a standard which every competitor has striven to maintain ever since.

Vim had the great advantage of being in commission a year earlier than the other 12s, and she had a

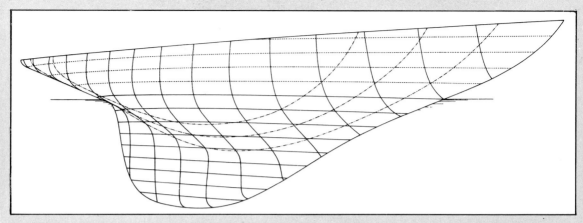

Lines of Vim. *She was built for Harold Vanderbilt who took her racing in England in 1939 and won an incredible twenty-one firsts out of twenty-seven starts. She so nearly won the defender's berth in 1958* (Sparkman and Stephens)

magnificent crew. In 1951, after sitting on a cradle in a City Island shipyard for many years, she had been bought by a shipping magnate John Matthews. He wanted, as he put it, 'a fast sporty boat for racing', and in *Vim* he certainly got that. He added a small engine but obviously kept her in other respects in full racing trim. When the Deed was changed he realized he had a contender for the America's Cup and did not hesitate to campaign her. He restored her to her original trim, fitted her out with new winches, a lightweight 'bendy' boom and rigging and in the autumn of 1957 ran a series of trials against another 12, *Gleam*. Though the racing did not prove much it was invaluable experience for Matthews. 'It made us realize,' he said, 'how much we have to learn about sailing a 12 with these new sails of synthetic materials. They're a whole lot different from cotton sails and we don't feel we know the half of it yet.'

The new Dacron sails were stronger and lighter than the old Egyptian cotton ones as well as being smoother and water resistant. Quite a bit of experimenting was done with sails on both sides. *Sceptre* ordered two huge Herbulot spinnakers from a Frenchman of the same name – it was before the NYYC banned any challenger from obtaining sails outside the challenging country – and these were one of the very few pieces of equipment which were a qualified success. *Columbia* had a very light pink mainsail made which the crew immediately nicknamed the 'purple people eater'. It was so baggy it looked, as someone said, 'as if an elephant had been sleeping in it'. But it worked and after being recut twice worked well.

Vim was back in the water the following April, and it was this early tuning up that made her such a tough competitor. Another was the excellence of her crew. On board was a future helmsman of a Cup defender (Bus Mosbacher), the sailmaker who was to dominate America's Cup competitions in that department for nearly the next two decades (Ted Hood), and a whole range of other talent, including Buddy Bombard who went on to sail on three future defenders. (Matthews's son Don started the season as skipper but by the time the final trials took place he had been replaced by Bus Mosbacher.) *Vim* was a great yacht but it was her crew and the dedication of her owner that drove her to her full potential. It was almost enough for her to outclass her three rivals. But in the end *Columbia* showed just in time what she was worth and how good her crew was.

Commissioned from Olin Stephens by Henry Sears, *Columbia*'s beginnings were not particularly auspicious. Initially Sears, though keen to get the Cup races started again – and with 12 metres – had not really intended building one himself. However, when the challenge arrived various syndicates, which had intimated they would build, suddenly evaporated. Sears, left to his own devices, decided to enter the fray.

As he said, he 'would have looked awfully damned silly to have sponsored a challenge and then have no boat to defend'; eventually, and rather late, he managed to gather a syndicate round him including Gerard Lambert and a top helmsman, Briggs Cunningham, who had sailed with Vanderbilt in *Vim* in 1939. Doubt must have crept in at some point because *Columbia* was originally called *Swift*; she was only renamed because one syndicate member felt her name would be inappropriate if she turned out to be a dud! Then, after reaching Newport, she was nearly seized by a US marshal for non-payment of a bill. But by the time she hit the water the rumour was around that *Columbia* was a fast boat. She was the one to watch.

The other two contenders launched late – *Easterner* arrived at Newport for the preliminary trials oozing caulking compound from the seams of her mahogany sides – and never really ever reached their full potential. *Weatherly* had been commissioned from the designer Phil Rhodes by another shipping magnate, Henry Mercer. But unlike Sears, Mercer was no racing man. His motives were different. Years before, as a young man, he had struck up a friendship with Sir Thomas Lipton and from then on had nurtured the ambition that if ever the circumstances allowed it he would back a contender. He decided he would enter the fray when he heard that Sears was having trouble raising funds. Mercer told Rhodes: 'I want you to handle the whole thing. Get the best builder and select the finest possible crew. And if we don't win don't worry – there will be no gripe.' Arthur Knapp – the man from *Ranger* and one of America's most brilliant helmsmen – was chosen as skipper.

Easterner, too, really came into being because of doubts about the Sears syndicate. Chandler Hovey, the one-time owner of *Rainbow* and *Weetamoe*, was one of the elder statesmen of American yachting and when Harry Morgan telephoned him to say there might be no new boat with which to meet the challenge Hovey signed up designer Raymond Hunt to produce a 12 for him. Hovey, too, had his own motives for entering the fray. As a Bostonian the rivalry with New York was something that flowed in his veins. As a syndicate member of *Yankee* he had been aboard during the last trial race in 1934 and the memory of it still rankled. Most Bostonians had thought the selection of *Rainbow* precipitate. *Easterner* was a family boat and run as such; during the summer they became known as the 'covey of Hoveys'. Even the kids had a chance to sail during the preliminary trials. It must have been great fun but it was not what America's Cup racing was about, and soon after the Preliminary Trials some of the covey were replaced by ocean racing types, and *Easterner*'s performance improved. But later Hunt left the afterguard, and there were a series of minor breakdowns. Launched late, by Cup standards inadequately managed, *Easterner* never reached anywhere near her full potential. But she was a beautiful boat, and compared with the others an unusual one, a foot longer than any of the others on the waterline and 4 feet shorter overall. Hunt gave her a square rudder and a long, squared keel. 'The final aim,' said Hunt, 'was to achieve a good boat in light weather, but at her best in a breeze – good in light weather because of relatively more sail and not excessive wetted area; at her best in a breeze because of power, ample ballast and long waterline.'

The Preliminary Trials began on 12 July – and so did the one-upmanship between rival boats that was to be brought to such a fine art in later years by Ted Turner and others. It was rumoured that the day before *Weatherly* arrived at Newport Arthur Knapp had slipped and fallen overboard. So when *Weatherly* hove in sight *Columbia*'s crew dressed themselves in orange life-jackets and lined the deck at attention as *Weatherly* passed close by. Rivalry between the skippers as well as the boats was strong that year, for Mosbacher, Knapp and Cornelius Shields – who had come out of semi-retirement to steer *Columbia*'s trial horse *Nereus* and sometimes *Columbia* herself – were all old rivals in the most competitive class on Long Island Sound, the International One designs. The friendly feud between Shields and Knapp resulted in another neat piece of one-upmanship. When *Columbia*'s navigator went aboard one morning he discovered a wooden box with a glass front fixed to the bulkhead near where he worked. Across the top of the box in bold red letters ran the legend, 'In Emergency, Break Glass', and behind the glass lay a copy of *Race Your Boat Right* by Arthur Knapp Jr! The humour, in later years, was not always so gentle.

In attendance for the trials were two committees

of the New York Yacht Club, the Race Committee to run the trials, the Cup Committee to assess the contenders and finally, after the Observation Trials and the Final Trials, to pick the defender. Both committees would be working full time throughout the summer to this end. It was a serious business. The Preliminary Trials were really a shakedown for the boats and crews. All four boats raced against each other twice. These early trials seemed to show that *Columbia* was the fastest boat but the races dogged by calms and fog, were inconclusive. However, on the New York Yacht Club cruise it was a different story with *Vim* winning five out of seven races. Neither *Weatherly* nor *Easterner* won one. Officially the cruise should not have counted in the calculations of the Cup Committee but as the Preliminary Trials were so inconclusive it almost certainly must have had some influence on them.

After further adjustments, the Observation Trials began on 16 August. To confuse matters further *Weatherly* came out top, winning six races and losing only two. When the Final Trials began it was, statistically at least, still very open, with *Easterner* the only boat without much chance of success. But even she had improved enormously and was at last fully equipped and properly crewed. But after only three days of racing both *Weatherly* and *Easterner* were eliminated from the trials. *Easterner* had never really jelled and her exclusion surprised nobody, especially as she was beaten on every occasion during those first three days. The surprise was that *Weatherly*, top dog after the Observation Trials, should be eliminated so swiftly. But she too was beaten decisively during the first three days of the Final Trials, twice by *Columbia* and once by *Vim*. It was later revealed that *Weatherly*'s keel had been delivered from the foundry half a ton lighter than specified. This had affected her stability. Iron pigs added before the Observation Trials had corrected the problem. However, before the Final Trials a gamble had been taken to add yet more ballast in anticipation of stronger wind in September. It had not paid off and *Weatherly* was badly beaten by *Columbia* in the Final Trials, once by 4 minutes and once by 6, huge margins under the circumstances.

Although *Weatherly* had lost in a year of innovations and new tactics – *Vim* had worked out a new method of gybing, for instance, called the dip-pole gybe system – she had contributed a lot to improving how a 12 should be sailed. In fact so highly was her spinnaker work regarded that when she had been eliminated from the trials Knapp was asked if his

man in charge of spinnaker handling, Victor Romagna, could be transferred to *Columbia*. Romagna agreed provided his friend, Jakob Isbrandtsen on *Vim* – the 12 *Columbia* now had to beat – gave his blessing. He did and Romagna joined *Columbia*. This left *Vim* and *Columbia* to fight it out and in their first race Cornelius Shields took the helm of the new boat for the start.

One surprising thing about *Columbia* had been that, despite having a brilliant crew which included Rod and Olin Stephens, crew work had not been all that good; her starts had been, as *Weatherly*'s navigator, Carleton Mitchell put it, 'notably un-aggressive and tardy'. Now, with the 63-year-old Shields at the helm for the start and first windward legs this all changed. *Columbia* got into the groove and really went. She beat *Vim* by 4 minutes and looked invincible. Yet in the second race *Vim* came back and, with superb starting tactics, led *Columbia* over the line and covered her for the rest of the race. One-all. Mosbacher however couldn't repeat his starting manoeuvre successfully in the third race and it was two-one to *Columbia*. Everyone thought that at that point *Columbia* would be named. But she was not. Instead in an incredible fourth race in which the two boats went about no less than thirty-six times on the first windward leg, tacking, countertacking and false tacking, *Vim* won by 1 minute 35 seconds. Two-all. Then *Columbia* came back and won the fifth race. The crew of *Vim* knew that the sixth race would be their last unless they won it. Briggs Cunningham replaced Shields at the helm of *Columbia* for this race (Shields had suffered a severe heart attack two years previously and was ordered by his doctor to step down). It took place in perfect sailing conditions with an 18-knot wind. In an extra-ordinarily close duel, with *Vim* twice snatching back the lead, *Columbia* crossed the finishing line 12 seconds ahead. It had been a memorable series. Could the Cup races possibly be as exciting?

The yacht on which the answer to this question depended, Boyd's B-model *Sceptre*, was built at Alexander Robertson and Sons, of Sandbank, Argyll, Scotland, and was launched on 2 April. She was built in the utmost secrecy and even when launched her deck was screened by a canvas. The reason for this secrecy was *Sceptre*'s enormous open cockpit, which extended from near the mast right back almost to the counter. This huge open space enabled the crew to work below where the winches

Sceptre tuning up against Evaine, *1958* (Beken)

were, and kept excessive weight low. It was a brilliant idea which worked extremely well. It was about the only thing on *Sceptre* that did.

The British syndicate's first mistake had been the method of hull selection. Their second and third were an efficient method of crew and gear selection and the lack of a proper trial horse. Almost seventy volunteers were tried out between March and June, most of them from the armed services, which seemed to be the best place to find men who could afford to take the whole summer away from work. To say the least, it seems a haphazard method of picking an America's Cup crew. Absurdly, although *Sceptre* was launched on 2 April her final crew were not picked until 23 June! As Hugh Somerville put it in his book on the 1958 challenge, 'there was a certain vagueness in the actual requirements, so that an awful lot of men were tried, who, although they were very good sailormen, were not really young, quick, or tough enough for a Cup challenger's crew'.

Maitland Edey in an article headed 'Wrong Hull, Wrong Sails, Wrong Training' in *Life* magazine was more outspoken:

There are top-notch, hard-headed international yacht racers in Britain, *and* some of their boats are among the world's best. Unfortunately too few of these yachtsmen got involved in *Sceptre*'s planning. Also too few found their way aboard as crew members. For one thing, they were considered too old – in their thirties and forties. The first of the bad decisions made was that none of *Sceptre*'s deck crew should be over thirty. The priority would be brawn. The result, according to one member of the after-guard, was that the crew was 'too larky and too inexperienced. We had to spend time teaching them things they should have known when they came aboard – valuable time which should have been spent tuning the boat.'

But it wasn't just with the crew that the British management – without Perry, who had resigned because his advice had been ignored – were inept, as Edey pointed out:

'Experts' began to gather. Too often they failed to agree. Too often their advice was not really expert. Too often they failed to understand the needs of the crew. When the navigator asked for a Fathometer, they gaped at him. This is an instrument for measuring the depth of water. . . . The value of such an instrument in fog is obvious. But no Fathometer was provided for *Sceptre* until she arrived in the US and it was seen that the other 12s were so equipped. A couple of the experts even insisted that *Sceptre* would not need a compass in closed-course racing. 'You can stay with the other boat,' they told the navigator.

'You're assuming we'll always be behind?' he asked. A compass was provided.

Graham Mann tacks over towards Columbia *during the fourth race, 26 September 1958* (Darling)

Edey pointed out other defects in the challenger's equipment and training: *Sceptre* was devoid of the right light-weather sails and after the first race tried unsuccessfully to borrow some from *Vim*'s owner; no calibrating was done on the performance of the challenger's sails, so little was known about which combinations worked best under differing conditions. And so on.

Saying that *Sceptre* lacked a proper trial horse is not, perhaps, doing *Evaine* justice as she consistently beat *Sceptre* early on. Her owner, Owen Aisher, one of the great names in ocean racing and a man consistently behind Britain's post-war efforts to regain the Cup, had bought her when he heard that a challenge was in the offing. He refitted her for

racing, and in the summer of 1957 there were trials in Torbay with two older 12s which had been converted for cruising, *Flica II* and *Kaylena*. These trials were really to help the designer and others, including the short list of helmsmen, which included Commander Mann who was finally chosen, to get accustomed to 12-metre sailing. Then, the following summer Aisher took on the task, with others, of assessing crew members and this was mostly done on *Evaine*. If someone proved themselves they were shipped across to *Sceptre*. There is no doubt that the two boats sailed long and hard in the months before the challenger was shipped, but it was hardly the quality of competition which *Columbia* was subjected to. What the British boat really needed was an opponent good enough to prevent her crossing the Atlantic if she and her crew were not sufficiently fast. But this did not happen and it was never the intention of the syndicate that it should.

Even when *Sceptre* arrived in America on 12 August, there was no really good trial horse to get the challenger properly tuned. The British were lent *Gleam*, but she proved hopelessly inadequate. To start with the crew of *Sceptre* dragged lines and buckets behind the challenger in an effort to equalize the speed of the two craft. But this affected *Sceptre*'s manoeuvreability so *Gleam*'s engine was used to keep up with the British boat. Owen Aisher, who was at *Gleam*'s helm much of the time, commented wryly how convenient it was when racing a yacht to be able to do a little motoring before filling away on a new tack.

The first race, on 20 September, was watched by President and Mrs Eisenhower from a destroyer. The result never looked in any doubt – despite *Sceptre* finding a private wind at one point which drew her almost level with the defender – and *Columbia* won by 7 minutes 44 seconds. By that time, the President had left to play golf. The next race was even more disastrous to the challenger, which she lost by 11 minutes 42 seconds. Both these races took place in light winds. The British crew were more optimistic when they went out for the third as it was blowing 22 knots; much more *Sceptre*'s weather, it was thought. But this was not the case: she bucked badly in the steep seas and lost the race by 8 minutes 20 seconds. The final race – as everyone knew before it even started – was almost as much a disaster as the others, though the margin of 7 minutes 5 seconds was less than in the other three races. During it *Sceptre* broke her main boom. But instead of giving up, the boom was 'fished' with the boom crutch and spinnaker boom and the challenger carried on. She even gained slightly on *Columbia*. As she crossed the line all US Navy and coastguard ships present ran up a signal which had been sent to Nelson by Lord St Vincent when he had failed to take Tenerife. It read: 'Mortals cannot command success; you and your companions have certainly deserved it.' The *New York Herald Tribune*'s comment – 'It is a spectacle calculated to make the tea break in a cricket test seem wildly exciting' – was not so courteous. The seventeenth challenge was over, and though the British planned to have another go in 1962 they were beaten to it by the Australian press millionaire Sir Frank Packer.

If the 1958 challenge was a disaster – and it was – then the 1964 challenge can only be called catastrophic. After it, Britain did not summon up the will and the courage to try again for another sixteen years. There seems only one certainty about Tony Boyden's 1980 challenge and that is it cannot be

Sceptre, her boom jury-rigged, at the finish of the fourth race (Darling)

worse than his 1964 one. Boyden, a self-made millionaire, had been involved with 12-metres for some time; in his book *Twenty Challenges for the America's Cup*, John Illingworth mentions that he and Commander John Stewart had been working for Boyden for some years on as 12-metre challenge which included buying the pre-war Laurent Giles-designed *Flica II* and putting her back into racing trim. As the British had originally wanted to challenge in 1962 they were at least well advanced with their plans for the 1964 challenge as several syndicates had been at work after 1958. *Sceptre*, bought by Eric Maxwell who had improved her considerably, was available as a trial horse. The Livingstone Brothers, millionaire sheep farmers from Australia, had indicated they were interested in building a 12 and Lord Craigmyle, heading the Red Duster syndicate, had started tank tests and had bought the old 12 *Norsaga* for experimental purposes. The 12-metre Association was an active organization and there was a good 12-metre class in Britain which had raced consistently in the years between the two British challenges. There was even a committee, headed by the Duke of Edinburgh, busy organizing a joint Commonwealth Challenge. So it cannot be said that the 1958 challenge put the British off 12-metre racing. On the contrary it helped revive it. So what went wrong? Britain's relative lack of affluence was probably a factor, as were the old traditional attitudes that had refused to die. The fact that the younger generation preferred ocean racing was a possible reason. But there seems little doubt that Australia's intervention on the America's Cup scene put a few noses out of joint and that the British effort, timed for 1962, flagged when the NYYC hardly bothered to disguise the fact that it preferred a challenge from Australia to one from Britain, and in April 1962 Lord Craigmyle withdrew from the Red Duster syndicate which ceased functioning.

From a promising start the second British 12-metre challenge got into all sorts of problems, but initially the Royal Thames were eager to challenge with a new boat in 1963. An offer from Packer for *Gretel* to race the new challenger off Newport for the honour to challenge was quickly, and not surprisingly, brushed aside. The Club, however, refused to race in 1963. The Royal Thames requested the Club to reconsider as the British, first geared to a 1962 challenge, did not want a further year's delay, but the Club again refused as it was felt that the expense of a challenge two years running would be too much. So October 1964 was agreed upon, and the Club subsequently decided that challenges should take place only once every three years.

The other major decisions taken by the Club before the 1964 races were that the traditional alternating triangular and windward–leeward courses be abandoned in favour of the Olympic course, which entailed much more windward work for the competing yachts. *Gretel* had proved much too fast downwind for the liking of the Americans. Additionally it was decided that a prospective challenger had to be designed, tested and equipped in the country of origin. In future Dacron and the testing tank at the Stevens Institute were for home consumption only, as both (as will be seen) had helped the Australians give the defenders the fright of their lives.

The second pronouncement immediately put the

Sovereign had many faults. As can be seen here one of them was that she 'hobby-horsed' badly (Darling)

British at a disadvantage. Boyden commented after the 1964 challenge that there was a 'terrific lack of original thinking' in British design work so far as the 12-metres were concerned. Boyden had tried to procure the same type of bendy boom that was on the 1964 defending boat, *Constellation*, but, he said,

the sparmakers were unable to produce the spars that bent in the right places and went back into their proper form. The sailmakers were unable to make sails that fitted the bends, so we had to scrap everything and go back to the old methods. Those old methods were not good enough.... *Constellation* was able to go out each day with only one mainsail and no matter what wind blew they could alter the shape of the sail with their bendy spars. We had to go out with three mainsails and if the wind changed or we had chosen the wrong mainsail, it was goodbye to the race.

With a handicap like that it was a wonder that Boyden had the tenacity, if that is the right word, to continue.

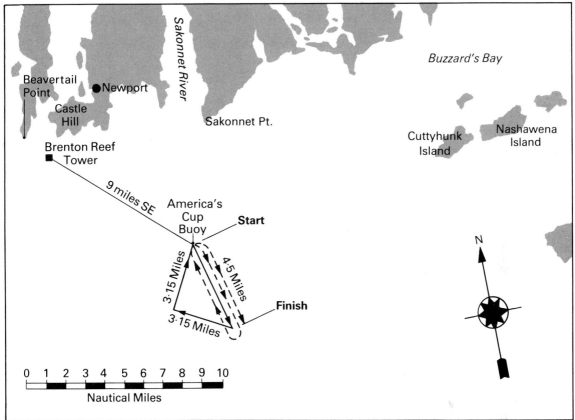

The Olympic course used for America's Cup races at Newport since 1964.

It is likely that when the British began to mount their second campaign after 1958 they had assumed they would not be cut off from the technology of other countries – the new challenger's lines, again designed by David Boyd, had already been tested at the Stevens Institute. By the time the Club's ruling on this was made known, in December 1962, the challenge was too far advanced to consider withdrawing. Indeed *Sovereign*, the new challenger, was launched in June 1963 giving her an almost unheard-of margin of time for tuning up. The trouble was that none of the other syndicates had managed to build, so again the prospective challenger was without the kind of competition that breeds successful 12s. She did, however, have *Sceptre* to tune up against; it was probably these races which made the challenging club realize that unless something was done quickly to produce a rival boat the 1964 challenge might end in even worse defeat than 1958. For a much-improved

Sceptre proved to be every bit as good as the new boat and though the trials ended – when *Sovereign* lost her mast – eleven–four in the new boat's favour, the general opinion was that *Sovereign* was nowhere good enough to compete on equal terms with the American 12s. Boyden considered ordering a second 12, and *The Times* wrote that it would be 'a national disgrace' if no Englishman stepped forward to help. There was, it could be fairly said, no great stampede but in August 1973 the Livingstone brothers stepped into the breach. Illingworth, who had been working with fellow designer Angus Primrose for some years for the Livingstones on a 12-metre design, was at last given the go-ahead to finish the design and build. But the decision came too late and Illingworth could not find a yard which could guarantee delivery. A golden opportunity had been allowed to go by, and the Livingstone brothers could only make amends for their tardiness by committing themselves to build a sister-ship to *Sovereign*, to be called *Kurrewa V*. This meant that no new design had to be tested and lofted and the builders of *Sovereign*, Alexander Robertson's, the yard which

129

Sovereign *tuning up with* Kurrewa V, *1964* (Beken)

had built *Sceptre*, could get on with the construction of *Kurrewa V* without delay.

The Livingstone brothers agreed on this plan so long as someone could be found by the challenging club to equip and manage their boat. This Owen Aisher agreed to do and announced 'an agreement to hate' between the rival boats. It was going to be, he said, the first joint challenge in the history of the Cup, and he intended there should be all-out competition for the honour to challenge. 'Although we have identical hulls,' he said, 'the boats as racing identities have many dissimilarities. There is more than one way to skin a cat or organize a 12.' John Parkinson, however, in his *History of the New York Yacht Club* comments that the decision was 'unfortunate and unimaginative' and certainly it did little to further the cause of 12-metre design in Britain. That David Boyd should be chosen again to design the new boat, after the disaster of *Sceptre*, appeared particularly inept, but Boyd's design at least had had the advantage of having been tested at the Stevens

Institute before the ban on the use of the American test tank had been imposed. Besides no one else in Britain had 12-metre design experience. What is more reprehensible was the method of crew selection – it was decided to use rugger players as it was thought toughness and fitness the best qualifications – and the attitude of the managers of the British challenge, methods and attitudes so astutely summed up by Norris Hoyt at the end of this chapter.

The close racing of 1962 had stimulated enormous interest in the Cup in America and two new boats were built for the 1964 challenge. *Constellation*, designed by Sparkman and Stephens and built at Minneford's, was run by a syndicate headed by Walter Gubelmann and Eric Ridder. *American Eagle*, built and designed by Bill Luders for the Aurora syndicate headed by Pierre 'Pete' du Pont, were the two new entries. Two older boats also entered the fray: *Nefertiti*, redesigned by Hood and with the famous sailmaker at the helm, appeared a strong contender at the beginning of the season, while *Columbia*, now sold to Californian Patrick Dougan, with Briggs Cunningham and a new bright young sailmaker and champion sailor, Lowell North (of whom more later) aboard, also looked a force to be reckoned with. *Easterner* was still around, too, but only took part in the Observation Trials. Although this formidable array of talent originally came about to fight off the British challenge, during the summer of selection races the emphasis was different from previous years simply because it was apparent that *Sovereign* in her early races with *Sceptre* had not been markedly superior and because it had somehow got about that in the tank tests *Sovereign* had not performed well.

Constellation, the favourite to defend, in fact started off the season appallingly badly, consistently losing to *American Eagle*. So badly did she perform that Norris Hoyt suggests that it was all part of Ridder's tactics. The two older boats were proving themselves no match for the new ones, and without fierce competition from *Constellation* how could *American Eagle* get tuned to the perfection she needed? Whatever the reason until the final trials it certainly looked as if *American Eagle*, with North American sailing champion Bill Cox at the helm, would be chosen to defend. However, in mid season Bob Bavier, Ridder's relief helmsman, took over the wheel more often and from then on 'Connie' began to improve. She was a remarkable boat with several innovative features and was equipped with a 'bendy' mast, as well as a 'bendy' boom, both of which allowed her mainsail to be set to perfection whatever the weight of wind. Once her crew got themselves together *Constellation* began to win races against the 'Bird' and the fight for the honour to defend soon became a needle match between these two. 'Beat the Bird' bumper stickers began to appear in Newport. The reply were rolls of lavatory paper stamped 'Prevent Constipation'.

What is so remarkable about the 1964 trials is the complete reversal of form that occurred in the two main contenders. In the early and midsummer races *American Eagle* led her opponent sixteen races to six, having won fourteen in a row. Then, as Bavier began to steer more, she won the last three races on the New York Yacht Club cruise against *American Eagle*. They did not count in selecting the defender, of course, but it improved the morale of the crew no end and confirmed the syndicate's feelings that Ridder had to hand over the helm to Bavier completely. This he did and *Constellation* then won the vital second race in the Final trials against *American Eagle* after the other two contenders had been eliminated. This second race was the vital one, for in the first race, which *Constellation* had won, *American Eagle* had broken her jib luff wire. It was not enough for *Constellation*, at this point, to win; she had to prove to the Committee that she was consistently superior. Bavier wrote later:

The crowning moment of my America's Cup summer in 1964 was neither the first race in which we beat *American Eagle* after many losses, nor the first time I was entrusted with the job of *Constellation*'s helmsman, nor the day we were selected, nor the first start against the challenger, *Sovereign*, in the match itself. These were all pinnacles of excitement and satisfaction, but the real peak was achieved in a race in which I didn't sail too well but still won.

This second race Bavier was to describe in his book *A View from the Cockpit* under the chapter heading 'Breaking Eagle's Heart', and that is just about what he did, forcing *American Eagle* into the fiercest tacking duel ever seen in the history of the America's Cup. The 'Bird' tacked forty-two times in the final 4½-mile leg while *Constellation* tacked forty times, grinding down her opponent and winning by 1 minute 8 seconds. *American Eagle* only won one more race, and by that time Bavier knew he had the faster boat.

The early races between *Sovereign* and *Kurrewa V* had shown they were closely matched but once at Newport *Sovereign* proved she was the better boat though she was equipped with inadequate sails. Another weak link was *Sovereign*'s helmsman, Peter Scott, who though a brilliant dinghy helmsman had had no match-racing experience of America's Cup calibre. The son of Scott of the Antarctic, Peter

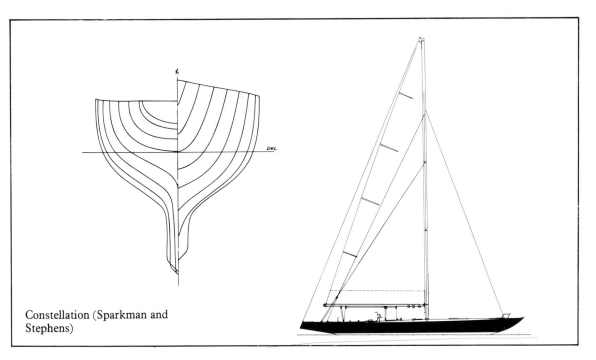

Constellation (Sparkman and Stephens)

Three minutes before the start of the second race on 17 September 1964 (Darling)

Scott was the kind of brilliant amateur all-rounder which Britain excels at producing. Not only an Olympic helmsman, he was a noted explorer, champion glider pilot, painter, author, naturalist – and a naval hero who won the DSC, while commanding a patrol boat during the Second World War. If ever there was a gifted man at the helm of an America's Cup challenger it was Peter Scott. But unfortunately, racing in the America's Cup is not for the all-round genius but for the man who can do one thing and one thing only: to maximize his boat's speed through the water – and that Scott did not appear to do. He was soundly criticized in the press – not necessarily the best judge of such things – for his performance, but it is more than likely that he was persuaded against his better judgement to steer the

challenger. Illingworth advised Scott to take the helm and his comment on Scott's selection makes the reader wonder if the British were trying to win the most important trophy in international yachting or whether they were still fighting to uphold the traditions of the British ruling classes: 'Judging that he would be a good skipper in the leadership sense and, also important, was able to get on with the owner, I advised him then to accept the post of helmsman,' and this after Scott had confessed that his racing experience was rusty and limited to inshore events, and that he had no doubt there were better men available!

The races themselves were a charade with *Sovereign* losing one of the races by the largest margin – 20 minutes 24 seconds – since *Mayflower* beat *Galatea* way back in 1886. The other three were also lost by large margins and Olin Stephens commented sadly when it was all over: 'It's too bad for all

of us who have put so much into it – we've put in so much that there isn't a contest left.'

Norris Hoyt summed up the second British 12-metre challenge succinctly:

The 1964 series was a classic example of how challengers lose. On the challenging side were the worst of both worlds – a self-made man arbitrarily directing his operation, supporting a boat with inadequate sails and a crew of football players. Her skipper was a small boat champion who came to the toughest match race in the world entirely innocent of match racing. Their companion challenger *Kurrewa V* had the same sails, virtually the same hull and an adequate crew of ocean-racing types. Her skipper was remote, Olympian, and superior to the crew in the icy manner of an absentee landlord on a tour of inspection. Both managers acted like lords of the manor; both crew were drilled like troops. The challenge was in the best tradition of empire and it lost against modern management.

Ouch!

Constellation *winning the fourth and final race on 21 September 1964. Note the beautiful curve of her mainsail, and her 'bendy' boom* (Darling)

1962/1967

In October 1959 the Royal Sydney Yacht Squadron threw a party to say goodbye to the Governor General of Australia, Sir William Slim, who, during his farewell speech, announced that it had been decided the Squadron would enter a challenge for the America's Cup in 1962, to mark the Squadron's Centenary year. The syndicate was to be led by Frank Packer (later Sir Frank) and the veteran American 12, *Vim*, had been chartered as a trial horse for the challenger.

The Australian challenge, as has been mentioned, did not much please the British, and the Royal Thames, which had been planning to be the challenging club in 1962 asked the Club if they would consider a Commonwealth challenge instead. The Duke of Edinburgh wrote to the Australian Yachting Federation suggesting a co-ordinating committee, and altogether a lot of cables and letters flew around the world. But the Club stood firm on its acceptance of the challenge and so did Packer. The Australians wanted to go it alone. 'After all you've had a long uninterrupted run,' Sir Frank cabled Illingworth, who had been on his way to New York to arrange the British challenge when Packer, hearing of his impending visit, cabled an official challenge ahead of his arrival. 'Maybe we won't do any better, but every now and again you have to give the young fellow in the family his head. . . .' It was just as well 'the young fellow' did get his head because it was undoubtably the Australians who put life back into the Cup. And they did do better. Much better.

At the same time as Packer was arranging for *Vim* to be chartered, Frank and John Livingstone indicated to the NYYC that they, too, were interested in challenging – as indeed they had been in 1958. But they had doubts about building a 12 in Australia and asked the Club if a new challenger had to be built in the country of the club challenging. It did, the Club

replied, but made no mention that this applied to the challenger's sails and other gear. The Livingstones did not proceed at that point but Packer must have picked up the fact that the Club were being open-minded about what did and what did not have to originate from the challenging country for he promptly requested that his designer, Alan Payne, be allowed to use the test tank at the Stevens Institute and that his sailmakers, Joe Pearce and Peter Cole, be allowed to import American Dacron for the new challenger's sails. Both these requests were granted by the Club, which, many journalists subsequently felt, had grown so secure in its possession of the Cup that it had quite overlooked the enormous potential advantages it was giving away. But that was said after the 1962 races. It is much more likely that the Club knew just how much to give away to this new challenger without endangering the Cup. If it had given nothing away there would always have been the possibility that the 1962 challenge would have proved as big a fiasco as 1958 – and then what would happen to the Cup?

In May 1960 one of the Sydney Squadron syndicate members, Bill Northam, who was in London, received an invitation from the Royal Thames to discuss the possibility of a coordinated challenge from the Commonwealth. Northam described the meeting in a letter to Packer which has become famous in Australian yachting circles:

I had received a note from the Secretary for me to attend, and unlucky me arrived two-and-a-half minutes late and I walked into the room and there were twenty blokes, mostly Lords and Earls, and at the head of the table my old cobber the Duke. I don't mind telling you I started to feel nervous, as nobody told me he was to be present. However, he left his chair despite the stony stares at me and walked over and shook me by the hand and said he was glad I could attend and I sat down at the opposite end of the large table like a shag on a rock, facing HRH at the other end.

The meeting opened as per the agenda enclosed and for a long time I looked at a lot of necks, nobody even troubling to look my way, and I chipped in when HRH asked me whether we had changed our minds with regard to elimination tests and I swear you could have heard a pin drop when I took it upon myself to say NO and believe me he really grinned and asked why not. I explained that it was in my opinion too late to alter. Owen Aisher (a big shot) and Lord Craigmyle surprised me by saying 'hear hear'. Then we got cracking.

He directed more questions at me than anyone in the room and I swear that at the finish I had 95 per cent on our side and it was unanimous that Australia was the logical challenger and we had all their good wishes and definite offers to help.

Lord Craigmyle, the bloke that has given £40,000 for the tank testing, is the big guy behind the Red Duster outfit and is nearly in Australia to help us train with his 12 metres and apparently I saved a sticky meeting and we all had lunch and a few snorts and everyone was happy and I finished up in a corner with HRH and we had a long friendly yarn.

The elimination tests Northam referred to had been suggested by the Royal Thames to the NYYC as a method of selecting the next challenger – rather as is done nowadays – but the Club replied that as it had accepted the Australian challenge this was a matter for the Australians to decide. The Australians, as Northam implied, had decided not.

Obviously everyone was leaning over backwards to avoid friction. The NYYC went so far as to say that if it beat the Australians it would accept a 'prompt' challenge from the Royal Thames or any substitute British club. Furthermore the Club said that if it was beaten then the British could have first crack at retrieving the Cup. (This was quickly followed by the Royal Sydney Yacht Squadron confirming that it would be agreeable to a match between itself and any British club in 1963 or 1964.) And in future if challenges were received within thirty days of the last challenge the Club would regard them as being received simultaneously.

The spectator fleet in the 1960s

Gretel, the new challenger, was built at the Lars Halvorsen yard in the Sydney suburb of Ryde, and was launched on 28 February. She suffered as had earlier challengers from an inadequate tuning-up period, for the early trials with *Vim* were inconclusive and in America, like *Sceptre*, she only had *Gleam* as a trial horse. Despite the generosity of the NYYC in allowing Payne to use the tank at the Stevens Institute, and for Dacron to be imported, Australia faced a difficult task. Payne, the only full-time naval architect in Australia at the time, had to use a good deal of ingenuity and persuasion to get the boat he wanted. Experimentation always takes place in any new yacht but the number of changes made on *Gretel* was really phenomenal. The layout of her cockpit was radically altered on her arrival in America; two weeks before the races began her mast was restepped 19½ inches forward to correct weather helm; while winches, according to Illingworth, 'came and went like autumn leaves', though in the end she was fitted with American-made Barients. She also had a mass of sails to experiment with (some from other American 12s), probably far too many for the time available to assess them properly. There was also trouble with Sir Frank Packer. An autocrat who ran his publishing empire with a despotic hand – it was known by his harassed employees as 'Packerstan' – Packer could not leave well alone and continually made arbitrary decisions about the day-to-day running of the challenge. Jock Sturrock, the skipper, was never given his head and allowed to get on with it, but had to endure Packer's continual ham-fisted interference. 'His bluster and brass,' wrote Norris Hoyt, 'was a stalking horse for a mind as devious and sly as a barrel of snakes', and Packer used both for all he was worth. 'Alcohol and delusions of grandeur,' he said were his reasons for challenging for the Cup when asked by an American journalist. So at least he had a sense of humour (when the Queen visited Australia in 1952 they were on a dais together and Packer leaned forward and said, 'You're costing us a lot of money, but we're very pleased to see you here'), but a sense of timing and tact he did not possess. This lack precipitated last-minute changes in the crew; on the very morning of the first race he changed the navigator, substituting one with a knowledge of the Newport waters for one with none.

The Americans took the challenge from 'Down Under' very seriously. Here Columbia *(US 16),* Weatherly *(US 17) and* Easterner *(US 18), race against one another as they often did during the summer of 1961 (Darling)*

Australian supporters on the way out to the course (Darling)

Weatherly *and* Gretel *neck and neck*

It was not surprising that the first race was at least partially lost by a tactical error when the navigator held *Gretel* on the wrong tack for 2 minutes.

In America it looked at first as if there would be no new defender built but fairly late in the day the Commodore of the Boston Yacht Club, E. Ross Anderson, decided to form a syndicate. First he chose Hunt; when he pulled out Hood was chosen. Hood had never designed a 12 before, had no formal training in naval architecture, and had previously designed only five boats, all ocean racers. The result was *Nefertiti*, a quite radical 12 in that she was a very beamy, lightweight boat with a short keel and a large foretriangle. She proved fast in a strong breeze but had rather too much wetted surface to hold her own in light airs. Her helmsman, Don McNamara, sailed her brilliantly but tangled with the N Y Y C Race committee rather too often for his own good: 'An aggressive, hopelessly explosive, tactless, and highly talented helmsman', is Norris Hoyt's description of him. 'The "stormy petrel" of Boston.'

All three of the remaining 1958 contenders turned out again, but this time the results were very different. *Columbia* had changed owners and crew, and had not sailed too much between the two challenges. It showed. *Easterner* and *Weatherly*, on the other hand, had remained with the same owners in the years between the challenges, and *Weatherly* with the same skipper, Arthur Knapp. Both yachts improved their performances remarkably and *Easterner*, often with Mosbacher at the helm, really began to show her potential. Knapp, however, still felt *Weatherly* was not fast enough to defend and after the 1961 season had tried to persuade Mercer that a new boat was the best answer. Mercer, however, had spent money improving his boat at Luders yard and stuck with her; Bus Mosbacher took over *Weatherly*'s helm for the 1962 season, Mosbacher having realized that Chandler Hovey could never bring himself to make the *Easterner* campaign other than a family affair. Thereupon *Easterner*'s designer took charge – which he should have done in 1958 –

and took 5.5 metre champion George O'Day aboard as helmsman, though later O'Day moved across to *Weatherly* as Mosbacher's tactician.

Easterner, with the fastest hull of the three, new sails, more weight on her keel, and the formidable combination of Hunt and O'Day – one magazine dubbed them 'the keenest and most dangerous pair of strategists afloat' – looked, at the beginning of the trials, a force to be reckoned with. But it did not turn out that way, with *Easterner* doing no better than she had in 1958; and as the season progressed it also became clear that *Columbia* was not up to her old form. This left *Nefertiti* and *Weatherly* to fight it out as both *Easterner* and *Columbia* were eliminated from the final trials after six races. Then *Weatherly* took the next three straight from *Nefertiti*. *Nefertiti* could reach faster than any of the other contenders but in winds of around 16 or 18 knots – the average velocity at the time of year – she could not get the better of *Weatherly* to windward and in those last three races the wind never reached more than 8 knots. Important, too, was that Mosbacher had a

In the second race on 18 September 1962, Sturrock initiated a tacking duel, which showed he had the faster boat. Thereafter Mosbacher avoided mixing it with Gretel. *'The Aussies had a better boat,' Mosbacher said after the races, 'with much better winches and bigger men, while our gang was called Mosbacher's midgets. If they had made us tack and tack and tack, they would have beaten us.'* (Darling)

settled crew around him, people he knew and had sailed with before. 'I guess,' said Henry Mercer, when *Weatherly* was named defender, 'this proves it takes four years to get a 12-metre tuned up.' Future challenges showed how right he was.

The first race took place on Saturday 15 September. The start was delayed by over an hour as a much-reduced coastguard patrol desperately tried to herd back the enormous spectator fleet of around 500 craft, which included President Kennedy in a destroyer accompanied by two more destroyers. He did not stay to see the finish either, which must have been an enormous relief to the competing yachts. As one newspaper succinctly put it, 'Why anybody with an ounce of sense thinks a destroyer, let alone three,

139

has any business within five miles of two sailing craft defies comprehension.'

Jock Sturrock won the start, but after the tactical error already mentioned *Gretel*'s back stay parted and Mosbacher won by 3 minutes 45 seconds. It was not a disgrace but it was not particularly encouraging either. It told both skippers a number of things about their opponent, notably that though *Gretel* could foot faster than *Weatherly* she could not point as high. However, she was faster downwind and her crew work was just as smart as the Americans. Inevitably, Halvorsen the navigator, was taken off by Packer but instead of putting back the original navigator, Terry Hammond, he chose Archie Robertson, the spare helmsman ('Looking for a quick learner?' Norris Hoyt wondered.) Again Sturrock won the start, by a length, in a westerly gusting up to 25 or 30 knots, and after a few minutes initiated a tacking duel which Mosbacher broke off when he realized the Australians, using their cross-linked coffee-grinders to good effect, were gaining. But when he came back he crossed well ahead of *Gretel* which told him that, without a yardstick, Sturrock did not know his boat well enough to get her going at her fastest. One of the attributes of world-class helmsmen is that they have minds like computers, and Mosbacher stored that piece of information safely away and used it with good effect in the remaining races.

Sturrock then tacked too short for the mark – the navigator again – but managed to round only 12 seconds behind *Weatherly*. On the run back *Gretel* lost another 2 seconds, Norris Hoyt who was broadcasting the race expressed his astonishment that *Gretel*, supposedly at her strongest point of sailing when reaching, did nothing with her vang or her sheets to try and increase her speed. Consequently after the race Mosbacher took him aside and told him firmly that his job was reporting the race not giving tactical advice. 'This was the biggest poker game in the world,' he told Hoyt, 'and if he ever gets a notion that he can beat us on any point of sailing, he might just sail off by himself and do it.' Then he gave Hoyt a drink.

As it was, Sturrock did not sail off by himself exactly – not in Mosbacher's sense anyway – but on the final leg of the second race, moments before *Weatherly* ran into trouble with her spinnaker, *Gretel* found a private wave, mounted it and literally surfed past the luckless defender, with the Australian crew giving a whoop of joy which must have startled the Americans out of their wits. Stanley Rosenfeld, the yachting photographer, wrote.

They gybed around the mark 14 seconds apart. *Gretel* was first up with her spinnaker and then it happened. Spawned far out in some distant disturbance a fast-moving swell, combined with a local wind wave and perhaps some chance wake of the spectator fleet, crested under *Gretel*'s stern. It carried her along on a surfing sleigh ride, doubled her speed over the bottom. She surged ahead at about 14 knots, her crew suddenly screaming, and as her bow lifted on the wave a rooster-tail streamed from her shrouds as though behind a racing speedboat. As often happens with these swells a second and third helped her along as *Gretel* passed *Weatherly* to windward and went on to win.

It was a magnificent win by a 47 second margin, and *Gretel* broke the course record. 'Surfing a 12 metre is the one art in which Bus Mosbacher is inexperienced,' said one newspaperman in the long postmortem that followed.

The delight of the Australians knew no bounds, and the news of the victory rapturously received 'down under' (the first item on the Cabinet agenda next morning was to discuss the wording of a congratulatory cable). After the race, so great was the crowd round *Gretel* that the pontoon where she was berthed began to sink, obliging the photographers and reporters to carry on with their work ankle deep in water.

By contrast the third race was a sad anti-climax. Instead of racing the next day when the wind was still strong the Australians asked for a lay day. When they came to the line on 20 September the wind was a mere 10 knots, and fading. The third race showed both sides what the first had proved: that *Gretel* was the faster boat, even in light airs, and that Sturrock did not know her well enough to take advantage of that fact. The Australians lost this race by 8 minutes 40 seconds which was pretty disastrous, but they had been as much as 24 minutes behind at one point and it could have been worse.

The fourth race was better. In fact one Australian yachting writer, with understandable hyperbole, called it the 'most thrilling America's Cup finish in history'. It was certainly a close and exciting one. This time Sturrock did not get the better of the start and on the first leg did not seem to know which genoa to use. *Weatherly* turned the first mark 1 minute 26 seconds ahead, but on the second leg the Australians lopped 31 seconds off that. As the yachts turned for the final leg, a square run, the wind picked up to 16 knots and *Gretel* began to make little surges forward, closing on the defender all the time. It was obvious to everyone that unless the American boat did something *Gretel* was going to pass her well

before the finish. In his graphic description of what happened next, Hoyt wrote:

But Mosbacher was a student of history as well as performance, and he used the trick with which Sherman Hoyt had twice robbed Sopwith and *Endeavour* of certain victory. He sharpened to a reach away from the finish and set a genoa. At first, Sturrock hoisted his genoa inside his spinnaker and accelerated, eating away at Mosbacher's lead at almost a third better speed. For 2 minutes he was actually closer to the finish line that *Weatherly*, but he sharpened still more on to Mosbacher's course, took down his spinnaker, and dropped speed. Mosbacher gauged his move exactly, set spinnaker, dropped genoa and ran for the mark. The wind had faded back to 10 knots, and

Gretel surfing down on Weatherly *during the second race. The Aussies overtook the defender and won by 47 seconds* (Darling)

Inset: *We've done it! Coming in from the course after the final race on 25 September 1962. Mosbacher's at the helm* (Darling)

Sturrock went back to spinnaker and chased Mosbacher. But Mosbacher's play for time had worked, and now there was not enough space left to close the gap. The wind was down to 8 when *Weatherly* crossed the line, 26 seconds ahead of *Gretel* in the closest finish yet in an America's Cup contest. Steadily gaining in the final minutes, *Gretel* would have won on a course a hundred yards longer.

141

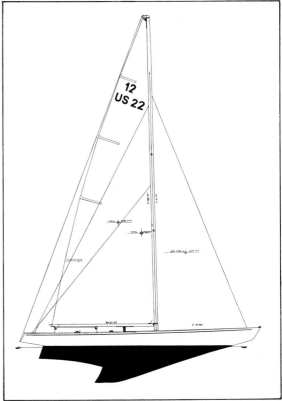

This really was a tragedy for the Australians and anyone who knew anything about match racing could not understand why Sturrock had allowed it to happen. He was, after all, an Olympic medallist and a helmsman of vast experience. But then so had been Sopwith. After that race Mosbacher was asked if he had been worried. 'Are you kidding?' he replied. 'I'm going to bed.'

This fourth race, although *Gretel* lost, caused an even bigger stir in Australia. It was thought – and not only in Australia – that *Gretel* was now beginning to find her form and was still very much in the series with a chance. However, it was not to be and *Gretel* lost the fifth race by 3 minutes 40 seconds. The Australians had not won the Cup, but they had certainly put life back into the races.

Among the foreigners watching *Sovereign* being hopelessly thrashed in 1964 were Sir Frank Packer, Alan Payne and Payne's assistant, Warwick Hood.

In heavy seas and brisk winds Intrepid *(in the background) and* Dame Pattie, *with their jibs in stops, get ready for the first race on 12 September 1967* (Darling)

Immediately the races were finished Sir Frank handed in another challenge, for 1967, and this was soon followed by another from Australian businessman Emil Christensen who was supported by a number of Australian commercial interests.

The effect of the new conditions, stipulating that all sails, sailcloth, rigging, tank testing and so on had to originate in the challenging country was mitigated by a 'grandfather' clause, which meant that the new conditions were not retrospective and only applied to future designs.

The 'grandfather' clause was just the kind of loophole the wily old Sir Frank Packer needed and he declared that he was going to 'repair' *Gretel* below the waterline. In fact he got Alan Payne to redesign the underbody completely while still retaining all the sails and equipment acquired from America in the 1962 challenge. The other syndicate had to start from scratch. Christensen commissioned Payne's assistant, Warwick Hood, to build a new design, and the result was *Dame Pattie*.

The new challenger's main problem was finding sailcloth which came up to the same standard as the Americans. After a great deal of research the Australian firm, Bradford Cotton Mills Ltd, produced a new synthetic cloth called Kadron from which Joe Pearce made *Dame Pattie*'s sails. Though stronger and lighter than anything previously used in either America or elsewhere, it did not perform remarkably well and probably did not measure up to the advance the defenders had made in the same area.

In the seven races of the First Trial series both yachts suffered gear failure – *Dame Pattie*'s mast went overboard during one trial race – but the newer boat skippered by Jock Sturrock, who had had enough of Packer, won the series 6.1.

Although the alterations to *Gretel*'s hull had increased her windward performance, and she still proved herself extremely fast downwind, she was not as well managed. Sir Frank again made last-minute crew changes, with Gordon Ingate taking over the helm from Trygve Halvorsen after the third race. *Dame Pattie* won all three races of the second series, and was promptly chosen as the challenging yacht. In due course she was shipped to Newport where she was helped to tune up by the Hood-designed *Nefertiti* which the Australians had chartered for that purpose.

The Americans that year lined up an impressive array of 12s to fight for the honour to defend. The 1964 defender, *Constellation*, under the aegis of the

Strawbridge syndicate, came out again, this time with Bob McCullough at the helm, as did *American Eagle*, now skippered by George Hinman. Competing for the defending berth, too, were old-timers *Weatherly* (Briggs Cunningham), and a completely redesigned *Columbia* skippered by West coast helmsman, Bill Ficker. Ficker, a Congressional Cup winner and a World Star Class champion, was unknown on the East Coast which up to that time had had virtual monopoly of America's Cup racing. He was a sign of things to come.

But despite this impressive array of talent interest centred on the new Sparkman and Stephens design, *Intrepid*, ordered by the Strawbridge syndicate. Olin Stephens, her designer, has always stressed that in his opinion there is no such creature as a 'super' boat or a 'break-through' yacht, that the essence of advancement in 12-metre design is the cumulative effort of a lot of people and the almost imperceptible improvements in design, rigging, sails, or crew – and occasionally all four. It was an inching towards perfection, not by leaps and bounds. That having been said, it must surely be true that if ever Olin Stephens proved himself wrong it was with *Intrepid*.

The man behind the building of *Intrepid*, Bill Strawbridge, had become interested in the America's Cup when, more or less by accident, he had been involved in the 1964 challenge by offering his power boat as *American Eagle*'s tender. When things began to go wrong with the *Eagle*'s campaign Strawbridge found himself involved in the politicking that inevitably goes on when a very expensive machine with a lot of people's money in it starts losing races. He commented: 'I became involved in some inside politics. Perhaps I opened my mouth more than I should, but what I said seemed to work and helped steer around a few problems with the afterguard. I guess Olin heard about this. He had lunch with me in Newport after the '64 races and he said, "I understand you've gotten interested in this America's Cup business. If there's anything I can do to help you in the future, don't hesitate to call me."'

The following February Strawbridge commented it was silly the way the whole thing had been done in '64. Two boats were built on a crash program and it cost a lot more money than I thought it should have. Properly run, properly organized, it could be a much easier operation and less expensive. Why wouldn't it be a good idea to get started on the 1967 Cup Defender right now?

But Stephens demurred. He already had two other enquiries for building a 12, from Detroit and from

California, and he was not sure whether he should build more than one boat. Who would be in the syndicate and who would sail the 12 Strawbridge wanted him to build? Who was the best man for the job, Strawbridge countered, and, without hesitation, Stephens said: 'Mosbacher.' But when Strawbridge approached Mosbacher, Mosbacher felt he couldn't commit himself that far ahead. But Strawbridge was obviously not a man who gave up easily and he eventually got together the nucleus of a small but impressive syndicate.

The money to start was now available but the vital ingredient of top talent was still missing. Eventually Burr Bartram, one of the syndicate members, suggested a meeting at his house to which Bus Mosbacher and Olin Stephens were asked. Strawbridge explained the dilemma to Mosbacher. 'Olin can't commit himself until you say you'll sail the boat. You've stung him pretty badly twice and he doesn't want to find himself in opposition with you again.'

Eventually a compromise was reached. Mosbacher still wouldn't commit himself because his father was ill and the family business interests had to be looked after, but he did say that if he sailed with anyone it would be with Strawbridge. After the 1967 series Mosbacher confessed that he never did officially say 'yes' and that he'd 'sort of backed into it'. It became a family joke; almost a year after the races when he told his wife, Pat, that he was lunching with Strawbridge she said, 'Are you finally going to come out and tell him you'll sail *Intrepid*?'

The matter of helmsman settled, so far as Stephens was concerned, tank testing began. But Strawbridge still had to find other members to bring the total syndicate financial commitment up to the required $700,000. It was slow going. In those days the money spent was not tax deductible and the number of individuals capable of giving $50,000 upwards for the pleasure of seeing a 12, of which they only owned a fraction, winning the America's Cup – or being eliminated by the eventual winner – was strictly limited even in a country as large and as rich as the United States. Eventually, however, sufficient members – including Harold Vanderbilt – were rounded up.

But, hard as large sums of money were to come by, Strawbridge and his associates were nevertheless very choosy about whom they approached. 'We were very careful about whom we asked,' Strawbridge said, 'because we didn't want anyone in the syndicate who would try to take over the organization and running of the boat. We turned down two

or three people for just this reason.' In fact Strawbridge himself became the boat's manager and an agreement was drawn up between himself and the syndicate which virtually gave him complete control of the campaign though the syndicate, provided enough of them agreed, could sack him.

One of Strawbridge's first moves was to charter the 1964 winner, *Constellation*, from Baron Bich for $25,000. The syndicate then spent far more than that again to get her into proper shape and to race her through the season, but Strawbridge thought it a good investment. It meant a second highly trained crew was always available, as was an alternative boat if anything happened to the new one.

By early 1966 the financial arrangements had been straightened out and then began the task of getting the boat built. The Vietnam war made it impossible for the mast extrusions to be built by an aircraft manufacturer so some other equally expert source had to be found. The new boat was to have a titanium rig and this had to be specially produced. 'We contracted separately for everything,' said Strawbridge, 'the boat, the masts, winches, rigging, booms, mast fittings, and sails. Even little parts like backstay sheaves and genoa tracks had separate contracts.... Everything came hard, but the yard did a heck of a good job and the boat, in spite of a raise in wages, didn't cost any more than *Constellation*.'

For the design of the new boat Stephens came up with the idea of separate keel and rudder – or kicker as it was called – which he and others had already used on ocean racers. Dick Carter notably had used such a design for his successful ocean racer, *Rabbit*, on which he had also used a trim tab – an additional rudder on the end of the keel – to cut down on leeway caused by the shorter keel which decreased lateral resistance. Stephens consulted with Carter and tank tested the results of their discussions. He tried seven completely different models for *Intrepid* before coming up with the right combination. By that time the original budget for tank testing of about $25,000 had been exceeded by $5000 or more, but this did not stop Strawbridge encouraging Stephens to continue until he found the right model. Money was important but more vital still was time. Because he had started early Strawbridge could afford to make sure the designer was not over-pressurized at the early stages. Even so the building schedule got

Sturrock initiated a tacking duel after the start of the second race on 13 September 1967 and managed to hold Intrepid *until a wind shift caught him on the wrong tack, enabling the Americans to forge ahead* (Darling)

Jock Sturrock at a post-race press conference. Australian syndicate manager Emil Christensen is on Sturrock's right, and Bob Bavier on his left (Darling)

The third race, 14 September 1967, with Intrepid *well ahead of the Australian challenger* (Darling)

behind for it took Stephens time to come up with a model that was that much faster than *Constellation*. 'Every boat is a compromise,' says Stephens, 'that you're forced into by the calendar and the clock,' but more – though not enough, there's never enough – time was available to think through all the problems of *Intrepid* than there ever were with *Constellation*.

The whole approach to the problems that arose, thanks to Strawbridge, was also different. With *Intrepid* the crew were allowed to have their say about deck layout and as a result the whole emphasis of deck work was shifted forward and away from the helmsman – and the possibility of distracting him and interfering with his view – and below, where the coffee grinder winches were placed. Both increased the boat's stability, and placing the coffee grinder winches below was undoubtedly a breakthrough of its kind. Vic Romagna also insisted on having two spinnaker hatches instead of the usual one, and this eliminated the danger of spinnakers fouling as they were being changed.

Placing the winches below was something of a departure. Not only was it new for 12s – though not for America's Cup boats, of course, as *Enterprise* had been so equipped – but also it enabled experimenting with a low boom, something Mosbacher had in mind when planning the new deck lay-out. A low boom, also not a new idea, was certainly new to the 12s. When Halsey Herreshoff did some experiments at MIT on Stephens's behalf he found that even when closing only half the gap between the boom at normal height and the deck a considerable improvement in performance resulted, as it increased the aspect ratio of the mainsail.

The low boom was one of *Intrepid*'s vital secrets, but it would have been easy for the Australians to spot it. So when both sides went through the normal procedure of inspecting each other's boats on official measurement day the Americans had to think of a way of concealing the low boom. They came up with a classic ploy of one-upmanship. They distracted the Aussies from the boom by taking off even more winches than they had already removed, and replaced some with clamps. The Australians did not like the idea of *Intrepid* being measured without any winches and said so in fairly forceful terms. Thereupon the Americans promptly put all the winches back, diverting the Australians' attention from the boom to the winches while at the same time hiding how many of the winches had actually been replaced by clamps. But this diversionary tactic was to have nasty repercussions.

The trials for the American contenders started right at the beginning of the season and were followed by the Observation Races which took place in Oyster Bay. *Intrepid* showed top form in all these early clashes, losing only one race in the Observation trials (and that because she rounded the wrong mark). Once it was seen that *Intrepid*'s 'kicker' was working practically all the other boats, including *Sceptre* (racing with the Americans during the New York Yacht Club Cruise), added one. But it did not seem to make much difference to the normal order of finishing. The Cruise that year was plagued with fog alternating with strong winds, and in a 25 knot breeze, gusting to 30, both *Constellation* and *Intrepid* were dismasted. This was the second mast to go on *Intrepid* and it caused a lot of anxiety. Mosbacher, for one, let his thoughts be known quite forcefully. 'Were I on the selection committee,' he commented crisply, 'I sure as hell wouldn't pick any boat that had a mast falling out every two weeks.' The problem was found to be with the spreaders and was soon put right, but the worries of campaigning remained especially when the normal rumour about the challenger being fast went around.

The Final Trials started on 16 August. *American Eagle* and *Constellation* were soon eliminated, leaving *Columbia* and *Intrepid* to fight it out (*Weatherly* had not entered). The new S & S design then went on to beat the older in two straight, and that was that, *Intrepid* having established a nineteen to one lead.

While the selection trials were taking place the Australian challenger was tuning up with *Nefertiti*. Once or twice after the selection trials had taken place, and much to the displeasure of the NYYC, the 'Dame' had paced herself against *Columbia* and seemed her equal if not slightly superior.

On official measurement day the Australians in the person of Warwick Hood registered a formal protest with the America's Cup Committee that *Intrepid* had been improperly measured. Mosbacher, who had known Hood was unhappy about the removal of the winches and had requested Olin Stephens to clear matters up, was furious that Hood had made a formal complaint instead of talking with the defenders face to face. He was equally angry that Jock Sturrock, the Australian skipper, had not approached him direct, 'a man I thought I had known fairly well and had considered a friend for five or six years, hadn't had the courtesy to discuss the problem with me'. Mosbacher felt the Australians were accusing him of cheating. He was

The most dramatic moment of the 1967 challenge came when a Coastguard helicopter capsized a small boat that had blundered on to the course during the third race. The helicopter caused Intrepid *some problems as well* (Darling)

additionally riled that a day was lost by the defender being remeasured but had demanded that the challenger be remeasured too, which she was.

Those last days before the first race were tough ones for *Intrepid* just because she was the favourite and because of the war of words and nerves that was taking place between the defender and challenger. Said Mosbacher of those days: 'Sometimes at night I walked up and down in my bedroom saying, "It's only a game; it's only a sport. It's only a game."' 'Bus is a tough leader,' commented George O'Day, 'and he was harder to work with in '67 than he was in

'62. He was more short-tempered and he couldn't tolerate as much. This is not an easy sport. A lot of people think sailing a 12 is easy, but not the way Bus does it.'

The remeasuring was smoothed over and though Mosbacher did not appear at a certain cocktail party, photographs were taken of him and Jock Sturrock shaking hands. However, when the first race was over Mosbacher sailed straight for his berth instead of waiting for the challenger to finish, as tradition demanded. There was obviously little love lost between the hard-driving American and the tough Melbourne skipper, who was described by one American as having 'about as much old-world charm as a Queensland crocodile'.

But tough as the Australians were in the days before the races, once started they did not prove themselves to be in the same league as the Americans. The 1967 challenge differed radically from the first Australian effort not so much because of what the Australians did or did not do – though the crewing was poor compared with the earlier challenge – but in the strength of the opposition they met. In 1962 it had not taken them – or the Americans – long to realize that *Gretel* was a faster boat than the retread *Weatherly*. But five years later there was not the slightest doubt after the first 15 minutes of the first race that the Americans, despite the Australians having a wind totem on their mast, a gift from a tribe of Aborigines, had produced the faster boat. 'We absolutely killed them,' Toby Tobin one of *Intrepid*'s crew noted. 'They couldn't point or foot or tack with us, and their sail-handling was less competent, and their sails didn't hold up in the breeze.' After the second race the wind totem was removed from *Dame Pattie*'s mast, but the Americans won in four straight. The really only lively moment in the whole series occurred when a coastguard helicopter tried to drive a sailing boat from the course, and only managed to capsize it. It was obliged to rescue the boat's occupants, and then it backed off – right into *Intrepid*'s course. The downdraft hit the defender which was obliged to take avoiding action, but it made absolutely no difference to the result of the race.

France, and then Sweden, join in

1970/1974/1977

Within the stipulated thirty days of *Intrepid* thrashing *Dame Pattie*, the NYYC received challenges from Australia, Britain, France and Greece. All these challenges were therefore regarded as simultaneous. Australia, the first to send a new challenge, was asked to arrange selection trials off Newport between the different nations. An impartial international committee would then select the yacht to challenge. The Greeks and the British (the Royal Dorset Yacht Club) dropped out, leaving the two millionaire challengers, Baron Bich and Sir Frank Packer.

Bich had watched the 1967 races and had gone home determined to enter the fray. He had become involved in the 12s not through any boyhood ambition to win the Cup but through his predilection to overspend his fortunes – perhaps a prerequisite for anyone involved in the America's Cup. 'I am one of those men who always spend more than I earn,' he explained, 'and when my children [he has nine] wanted to go sailing on a Mediterranean holiday five years ago, I bought them a 12-metre.' The holiday boat he bought was *Kurrewa V*. Perhaps not up to much as a potential challenger, *Kurrewa V* must have been a cut above the average even in the exotic yachting harbours of the Riviera, and the Baron – and presumably his children – all fell in love with her, renamed her *Levrier des Mers* (*Greyhound of the Sea*), got to know the excitement of sailing a 12. From this sprang the Baron's final determination to challenge for the Cup, though his designer, Andre Mauric, had been working on a 12-metre design since the mid-sixties.

His first problem was lack of 12-metre know-how in France, but this had applied to Australia, too, and they hadn't done all that badly, so it did not deter Bich. He solved the problem at least partially by commissioning Britton Chance Jr to design him a 12

which he then had constructed by the Swiss boatbuilder Herman Egger. The result was *Chancegger*. To show he wasn't doing anything by halves Bich also bought *Sovereign* and the 1964 winner *Constellation*.

As Bich had to have a potential challenger designed and built in France *Chancegger* gave Mauric the latest in American thinking, an excellent potential trial horse (though, in the event, *Constellation* was preferred) and a superb model against which to test Mauric's new design in the tank. Mauric incorporated nearly all the new American thinking in his design, *France*, including the trim tab, the shortened keel, the kicker, and the 'bustle'.

The bustle, an idea Olin Stephens introduced with *Intrepid*, took account of research done by Pierre DeSaix who now ran the test tank at the Stevens Institute.

What Stephens had achieved with the kicker on *Intrepid* was to reduce significantly the resistance of the water to the boat's hull by reducing the wetted surface of the keel by something like 40 square feet. Wetted surface creates drag which is, of course, directly related to the boat's speed. Less drag means more speed. Water next to the hull flows less quickly than that further off, an effect known as laminar flow. There is nothing that can be done to prevent this effect and so long as the water flows evenly minimal resistance is caused. But the laminar flow begins to be disturbed – and drag therefore increases – when the hull of the boat begins to curve back to the stern. DeSaix discovered, by attaching bits of thread to his tank models, that the laminar flow was

For the 1970 challenge two new American contenders, Heritage *and* Valiant, *were built. But neither proved a match for the 1967 defender,* Intrepid, *though in the Observation race here* Valiant *is leading* (Darling)

In 1970 the French challenged for the first time and a series of elimination races were held, the winner of which became the challenger. Here, the French boat, France, *is just slightly ahead of* Gretel II *during one of these races* (Darling)

Inset: Gretel II *supporters*

interrupted just at the point where the quarter-wave on a 12 appeared.

Stephens made use of this information by incorporating in *Intrepid*'s design a fuller aft section which minimized the disturbance of the laminar flow and had a rather bulbous appearance, and this quickly came to be called the 'bustle'. It was just as quickly taken up by the designers like Chance when it came to designing new 12s after the 1967 challenge.

Having a number of boats gave Bich the chance to train up the best possible crew and to get the

potential challenger up to a reasonable standard of efficiency and competitiveness. He also found three top-class helmsmen: the elder statesman of sailing in Europe, sixty-seven-year-old Louis Noverraz; Poppy Delfour, the French 505 Champion; and Jean-Marie Le Guillou, a 5.5 metre Champion. But what the French challenge suffered most from were poor sails. These were cut from Ferrari cloth by the Nantes sailmaker Gaston Burgand, but they never really came up to the standard required. However, though *France* may have suffered from the quality of her sails she never suffered from a lack of them. No less than twenty-seven mainsails were shipped over for the races against *Gretel II*, the new Australian challenger, as well as fifteen spinnakers. Each spinnaker had the crest of a different French province on it, which must have helped the Australians identify more easily what size and weight of sail was being used. Bich eventually went to Newport with three 12s, *France, Constellation* and *Chancegger*, about sixty men, two chefs, and a supply of French food and wine. But the French effort suffered from the same defect as Australia's 1962 challenge: the man in charge would keep on interfering and making crew changes.

In Australia Payne began work on the new boat, *Gretel II*. He incorporated several new features including collapsible spreaders, which enabled the genoa to be sheeted home harder, and twin wheels, one on each side of the cockpit, to improve the helmsman's view for trimming the headsails. *Gretel II* had her tuning problems; her mast was shifted forward 18 inches and 1600 lb of lead shaved from her keel. But her single largest problem, the perennial for any challenger, was the lack of competitive racing. This was made worse by the fact that *Dame Pattie* had been sold – to Canadian George O'Brien – and the only modern trial horse available was *Gretel*. Reports from Australia, mainly via Packer's Consolidated Press newspapers, said the older boat was beating the newer one, but when the time came it was *Gretel II* that was shipped to Newport. The consensus was that Packer was just being his wily old self, but the truth is that *Gretel II* did not get her final rig from her designer until she had arrived in Newport and this must have affected her early performance.

At least for this challenge Packer had appeared to make up his mind to appoint a skipper, thirty-seven-year-old Jim Hardy, and let him get on with it. That, anyway, was how it looked to the world when the Australians arrived at Newport and started tuning up against *American Eagle* with a millionaire TV network owner from Atlanta, Ted Turner, at the helm. But it did not turn out that way.

Turner, of whom more, much more, later was a new phenomenon in the history of the America's Cup. No sooner had the West Coast started to be involved than middle America appeared on the scene too. There were doubtless some who felt that the private preserves of the privileged few were being encroached upon, or – in the case of Turner perhaps – trampled over. But Turner, having proved himself in ocean racing – he was the only man to have won the SORC twice – was eager, very eager, to get in on the America's Cup. In 1970 he only managed to get a whiff of the action – his effort to get *American Eagle* entered in the Trials was too late – but in 1974 he was at the helm of the contender, *Mariner*, and in 1977 he skippered the winning boat *Courageous*, which he now owns and will be racing in 1980.

The selection races between the two potential challengers took place in very light winds with Baron Bich behaving towards his crew as capriciously as Packer in the Australian camp in 1962. Noverraz took the helm of *France* for the first race and led the Australians for most of the way before running into a calm patch. Hardy saw what had happened and managed to sail round it, and went on to win. But it was a close race, which either side could have won, and Hardy must have faced the next race with some trepidation. But then the Gallic temperament intervened on behalf of the Australians for the Baron, for no discernible reason, replaced the seasoned Noverraz with Poppie Delfour (the third helmsman, Jean-Marie Le Guillou, had left the French camp some time previously, piqued by the Baron's autocratic behaviour). This, all the commentators said, was a bad decision, and *France* lost the second race. But again it was close, with the two boats exchanging the lead several times.

Noverraz took over again for the third race but again lost. This made it three–nil out of a series of seven. The Baron himself then took the helm of the French boat, as he had said he would and sent a message to Hardy saying, 'Don't be too kind. Treat me as a skipper.' After all he'd spent more than any other challenger – reportedly four million dollars – so he probably felt he was entitled to a bit of the action. Sadly, fog rolled in over the course making the race more of a test of the navigator's sense of direction than the helmsman's skill. Even more sadly the Baron – or rather his navigator – got lost and *France* had to abandon the race. The press wrote rude words and the Baron got upset. The word 'abandon' in French is not a nice one to use about a sportsman and Bich accused the International Race Committee of 'dishonouring' him. The Committee, he maintained, should not have allowed the race to proceed. The Committee retorted that the coastguard had not requested that the race be postponed, but this was surely just a case of trying to pass the buck. The race should never have been started. To make matters worse for the French the spectator fleet were allowed to get between the Australian boat and *France* thereby blocking out the sound of the bells on the marks. The French navigator, incidentally, was Eric Tabarly who seemed to be able to find his way about without much difficulty normally.

The selection trials over, the French helped the Australians get ready for the challenge itself. Further races were held, some against *France* and some against *Chancegger*, with *Gretel II* winning each time. It could have been this tuning that made the 1970 challenge one of the closest in the history of the Cup but there is no doubt that Payne also produced a very fast boat indeed. He had closed the technology gap in a quite remarkable way. The Americans, on the other hand, had reached one of the plateaux amongst the peaks of 12-metre design.

In designing 12s for the America's Cup, the Americans lead the way but slow down every now and again which enables others, the Australians, to catch up occasionally, and perhaps even inch ahead. But design, of course, is only one of the elements that hold the Cup in New York. With the other two elements, sails and tuning, which includes crew work, challengers have always significantly lagged behind. No one but the Americans have the breadth of experience in match racing 12-metres.

Four American 12s were again in contention, though *Weatherly* was included more to make the numbers than from any real hope that she had much chance. She was eliminated early but acquitted herself well. *Intrepid*'s syndicate manager, Bill Strawbridge, knew that he would be up against a faster 12

in the new Sparkman and Stephens boat, *Valiant*, so he asked Britton Chance to update the 1967 defender. It was a clever move, and Chance's alterations made the older boat faster than the newer S & S design. Strawbridge's other decision was a good one too. With Mosbacher in Washington as chief of protocol he chose the 1967 skipper of *Columbia*, Bill Ficker, to helm *Intrepid*. Ficker put together a keen but inexperienced crew which in the early trials looked the weak link in an otherwise formidable combination. But despite the respect that the *Intrepid* camp inspired, early money must have been on the two new boats, *Valiant* and *Heritage*.

Valiant was designed by Olin Stephens for the Vice-Commodore of the N Y Y C, Bob McCullough, while *Heritage* was built by Charley Morgan who, like Turner, was a newcomer to America's Cup racing. Morgan had tried to put together a syndicate

The Australians ran into problems during the first race on 15 September 1970. Firstly, after rounding the first mark, there was a spinnaker snarl-up which eventually broke the spinnaker pole; and then her foredeck boss slipped on oil

for the 1967 series without success, so for 1970 he decided to go it alone and build his boat. He was well placed – not only a brilliant helmsman but, until 1966 when he sold it for a fortune, the owner of one of America's most successful yachtbuilding firms, the Morgan Yacht Corporation.

Heritage was a beautiful yacht and had a good crew, but she was launched late and suffered the usual problems of a new contender on the America's Cup scene. She lost consistently but managed to chalk up a few victories before being eliminated along with *Weatherly*, leaving *Valiant* to fight it out with *Intrepid*. Unlike 1967 none of the 12s stood out in 1970 as superior in the Preliminary or Observation Trials, but in the Final Trial *Intrepid* showed her superiority by beating the newer boat by six races to one. 'Ficker is quicker' read the bumper stickers and lapel buttons all over Newport. Not

which had been washed out of the winches, and fell overboard. Gretel II, *having lost 2 minutes because of the first accident, now lost a further 2.* Intrepid *won by 5 minutes 52 seconds* (Darling)

since 1901 had a previous defender been chosen again to defend the Cup, and, as in 1901, the defender very nearly blew it. In neither case do the statistics really show how close a call it was, though the first race in 1970 was a complete *débâcle* for the Australians.

When *Gretel II* rounded the weather mark for the first time she failed to hoist her spinnaker properly and broke the pole, and by the time everything was disentangled *Intrepid* was well ahead. Then real disaster struck when *Gretel II*'s foredeck boss got swept overboard and more time was lost picking him up. The spectator fleet didn't help either and Strawbridge commented afterwards that the management of the course 'was the worst ever'.

The second race had to be abandoned because of fog. *Intrepid* was leading at the time, which was just as well. If the Australians had been there might have been more cause for friction. (In the first race both yachts had crossed the line with protest flags flying, the first time this had happened since the 1934 series, proof of the tension in both camps, though both protests were subsequently dismissed.) But in

The incident that caused the biggest row since Endeavour *luffed* Rainbow *in 1934.* Intrepid *has squeezed through the gap between* Gretel II *and the committee boat which marked the end of the starting line, but the challenger hits* Intrepid, *and damages her bow. The Race Committee later ruled against* Gretel II. *They were certainly in a position to see what was going on!* (Darling)

any case friction there was when the second race eventually got under way, with a collision occurring just after the start gun. Again the protest flags were hoisted and this time the Race Committee held an enquiry.

Gretel II won that second race – Hardy having been taken off the helm by Packer for the start and replaced by Martin Visser – but her protest failed and the race was awarded to *Intrepid*. The furore was immediate and intense. The press accused the Club of partiality. Packer threatened to go to the Supreme Court. The Club received as many as 500 letters nearly all accusing it of partiality, though one man did say it was all the fault of the Committee boat and if that had not been in the way there would not have been any problem! Maybe the Australian Navy was

even put on alert, but there seems little doubt that the Australians were not as well versed in the rules as they should have been. Some years later the then-chairman of the Race Committee, B. Deveraux Barker, commented that he remembered

How astounded we on the committee were at the Australians' very primitive knowledge of the racing rules. Here at the very highest level of international competition, and in match racing where instinctive reactions to changing rule situations are vital, were men with a 'junior programme' knowledge of the rules. Bill Ficker tore them apart at the hearings.

The racing rules are complicated and sometimes open to interpretation. The problem, put simply, was barging at the start line with *Gretel II* hitting the American defender, both boats claiming the right of way.

After the collision *Intrepid* crossed the line at a good speed while *Gretel II* was almost stopped. Nevertheless Hardy sailed a perfect race, picking up all but 42 seconds of the time lost at the start, closing that gap to 30 seconds on the second windward leg, with Olympic champion, Dave Forbes at

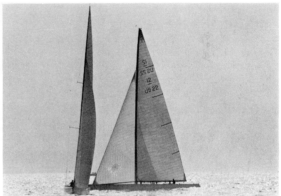

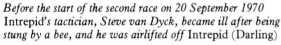

Before the start of the second race on 20 September 1970
Intrepid's tactician, Steve van Dyck, became ill after being
stung by a bee, and he was airlifted off Intrepid (Darling)

The third race on 22 September 1970 was sailed in a 20
knot wind. But Gretel II *was a light-weather boat and on*
this day she could not catch Intrepid (Darling)

The fourth race on 24 September 1970 took place in light
airs. A 90 degree wind shift on the last leg forced the
defender to tack under the stern of Gretel II, *and* Intrepid
never managed to make up this lost ground (Darling)

the helm, pulling past *Intrepid* half a mile from the
finish, crossing 1 minute 7 seconds ahead. It was a
magnificent win much appreciated by the huge spectator fleet, though *Intrepid* must have been partially
incapacitated when she lost her tactician Steve van
Dyck minutes before the race was due to begin.
Earlier that morning he had been stung by a bee,
which caused a violent reaction. He was taken off by
helicopter and replaced by *Intrepid's* navigator Peter
Wilson, Toby Tobin going aboard to replace
Wilson.

The protest was heard the following morning.
After studying aerial photographs, the Australians
were disqualified, though many commentators cast
doubt on the Committee's interpretation of the evidence. One thing was for sure, as stated by Norris
Hoyt 'the Australians were better advised to win the
America's Cup by outsailing *Intrepid* than by trying
to beat the NYYC Race Committee'. But the wide
condemnation of the Committee's judgement forced
the Club to agree in future to an international
committee to hear protests, something which should
have been done after the 1934 series.

Ficker, by astute sailing, won the third race and
seemed likely to take the fourth and wrap the series
up when he led by over a minute at the final mark.
But then the wind dropped from 12 knots to 6. In
these very light conditions *Gretel II* showed how fast
she was, and she closed to within 100 yards of
Intrepid. Then the wind shifted through ninety
degrees. At the time both boats were tacking parallel
with the finish but the windshift favoured the
Australians and enabled them to lay the line. They
won by 1 minute 2 seconds.

The final race – for that's what it turned out to be – was a thriller, 'one of the most brilliant ever sailed', according to Hoyt. Hardy who had started *Gretel II* for the fourth race did the same for the fifth and won the start. The wind was light and both competitors used every trick they knew to get ahead and stay there, but in the end the Americans' superior knowledge of wind patterns and the cunning of their skipper put them across the line 1 minute 44 seconds ahead of the Australians. Ficker really was quicker.

A 'Ficker is Quicker' button. In 1977 someone produced a 'Beat the Mouth' button which didn't make Ted Turner too happy. But no one did (Darling)

The 1970 challenge was a watershed in the post-war history of the Cup. Before, technical advances had often been slow and unobtrusive. Sometimes, the use of exotic material and new technology had not been particularly successful. There had been real advances in hull design, notably *Intrepid*'s kicker and bustle, but that breakthrough had been more a crystallization of ideas than a sudden innovation. But after 1970 came the aluminium 12s, on-board computers, Kevlar sailcloth, and 101 smaller, advances. Not all were successful but space-age technology had come to the America's Cup.

The seventies also brought other perhaps more inevitable changes: Ted Hood's undisputed leadership as a sailmaker was challenged by younger men like Lowell North, John Marshall and Robbie Doyle, who all worked, as did Hood, with cloth that had dropped in mainsail weight from 12 oz per yard in 1964 to 7.6 oz in 1970, with double-ply mainsails and triaxial headsails, making the battle for better sails an unending one; the East Coast dominance of the Cup, already loosened by the West Coast, was finally broken altogether by a young man from the Middle West, Ted Turner; and in 1970 two challengers appeared on the horizon where before there'd only been one.

In January 1970 the Club had extended the period of submitting simultaneous challenges from thirty days to ninety days after the last race of the previous challenge. After the 1970 races no less than eight clubs from five countries – Britain, Canada, Australia (two clubs), France (three clubs) and Italy – submitted challenges for the 1973 races (later postponed to 1974), though this was eventually whittled down to two again, Australia and France. But in 1977 there were three challenging countries, France, Australia and Sweden, and in 1980 there are four, the three 1977 countries plus Britain. As the competition gets hotter, potential challengers are acquiring the competitive edge essential if a challenger is ever to succeed, and the Americans are having to find new means to fight off the increasing pressure.

The start of the seventies was also a watershed in that the tenor of the campaign changed. The personalities involved in the America's Cup challenges in the mid- and late-seventies made them strident affairs with a lot of politicking and bluster. Take, for instance, Baron Bich's campaign. Bich obviously took to heart the criticism after the 1970 races that he had not elected one skipper and allowed him to develop a winning team. So for the next challenge he appointed the Danish Olympic helmsman Paul Elvstrom to run the show. It seemed at first a master stroke. Elvstrom was a brilliant helmsman, the only man who has won four Olympic gold medals in yachting; his prestige and experience, combined with increasing French know-how and unlimited resources, made the Gallic challenge a force to be reckoned with. The Baron, a latter-day Lipton, was determined to win, and Mauric was hard at work on a new 12. But as the months passed and Elvstrom's campaign methods started to take shape, questions were asked and criticism of Bich and his choice was voiced by the French press and French yachtsmen. For one thing it was rumoured that Elvstrom intended having a Scandinavian crew on board, not a French one. This not unnaturally infuriated all ambitious French helmsmen, like Jean-Marie Le Guillou, who felt that a French challenger should have a French crew. When one Frenchman tried to get a berth aboard *Constellation*, which Elvstrom was using for experimental purposes in Denmark – for instance he wanted to steer the new French 12 with a tiller so he had one rigged on *Constellation* – he found the mixture of Scandinavian nautical language used by the Norwegian, Swedish and Danish crew was a barrier impossible to break through.

The new Australian challenger, Southern Cross *(KA 4), her first time out, with the two Gretels* (Gretel II *on right*)

Alan Bond

Elvstrom made several other tactical blunders which the French press were quick to seize on. One of the worst was when he decided to return the other two Bich 12s in Denmark, *Chancegger* and *France*, to Le Havre as he did not require them for his early experiments. They were towed via the Kiel Canal and the North Sea. A gale struck the first night out and *France* sunk. Luckily she went down in shallow water and was raised, but the resulting publicity did Elvstrom's cause no good at all. To make matters worse for 'The Great Dane', as he was nicknamed, he began to be beaten in international races by Frenchmen who were determined above all else to prevent Elvstrom maintaining his position as Europe's leading yachtsman. The vital ones, the 1972 Olympics and the 1973 Half-ton World Cham-

Southern Cross. *Cuneo is at the wheel*

pionships, were sailed as grudge matches, and Elvstrom was beaten in both by Frenchmen who were more concerned to beat the Dane than to win. Word also got about that Elvstrom was tank-testing his own design in Denmark. Besides looking as if he did not trust Mauric to produce the best possible boat, Elvstrom could have jeopardized the whole campaign if it could subsequently have been proved that the new French 12 incorporated any of his ideas.

But the final blow in the campaign to topple Elvstrom came when articles appeared in magazines about the Dane's mental fitness. He had a history of nervous illness which in the past had afflicted him while racing, a fact too well known in yachting circles for Bich not to have known of it; but having it revealed in public for the first time at that particular point gave Bich's critics additional ammunition.

Pressured by his own doubts about his choice, and by the French press, Bich, in October 1973, finally

acted. First, he told Elvstrom that he was out, and then he informed Herman Egger to stop building the new 12. The 1974 French challenge which had once looked so promising and so dangerous had come to nought. But wisely Bich did not give up entirely. Instead he put the salvaged *France* in charge of young Jean-Marie Le Guillou and sent them both to Newport for the experience. As it happened, the experience wasn't a pleasant one as *Southern Cross* thrashed the French boat four–nil in the selection trials for the challenger.

While the French challenge campaign was being both metaphorically and literally sunk by political in-fighting, the Australian campaign headed by Perth property developer, Alan Bond, took a different form with the aggression, more constructively, being aimed at the enemy, the N Y Y C.

Bond decided that a bit of tough talking would set the right tone for his challenge. As he didn't think much of the Club's Race Committee, or the new international committee set up for adjudicating on

160

Courageous (Darling)

protests, he would send to Newport along with his challenger *Southern Cross* a videotape camera crew to record any rule-breaking incidents where the Club might be tempted to find for its own side – as most Australians were convinced had happened after the second race collision in 1970. He also announced he would be taking his lawyer with him to Newport. These pronouncements could not have endeared him to the Club, but Bond was probably only saying what a lot of people had been thinking for a long time.

The other potential challenger from Australia, Sir Frank Packer, withdrew his challenge when the races were postponed a year and he died before they were held.

Both *Gretel* and *Gretel II* were bought by Bond and sent to Perth where they helped tune the new Bob Miller-designed 12. Bond was a great fan of Miller, thought him a genius and gave him the job of

designing *Southern Cross* over the more obvious candidates, Alan Payne and Warwick Hood. Miller produced a radical boat, extremely narrow forward and with long overhangs at either end and with a different rudder shape that Miller had been working on for years. Many of Miller's refinements had already appeared on his successful ocean racers. Despite the economic climate Bond spared no expense in making his challenge the most thorough yet devised. For instance, he built an enormous concrete boat-house costing $200,000 in which to keep the three 12s, and surrounded it with wire fencing and guard dogs to discourage snooping reporters. The three 12s raced throughout the Australian summer of 1973/74 with 1972 Olympic Dragon class champion, John Cuneo, at the helm of *Southern Cross*. But before *Southern Cross* was even launched Cuneo had already raced in over eighty matches in *Gretel* against *Gretel II*. Then *Gretel II*, with Jim Hardy at the wheel, raced and raced against *Southern Cross* off Perth and then off Newport. The 1970 challenger was still a very fast boat and the outcome was by no means clear cut, though *Southern Cross* had the edge to windward. When the Australians went to Newport they were fit and well trained, and convinced they had a winner. With them went four and a half tons of meat, 24,000 cans of beer, and a thousand bottles of wine.

Once at Newport Hardy showed he had the edge over Cuneo and was given the helm of the mustard-coloured yacht (Yanchep yellow it was called) and went on to win the trials against the French challenger with consummate ease.

The number of challenges that flooded in from overseas after the 1970 races had put the Americans on the alert. Bill Strawbridge was the first to inform the NYYC that he intended forming a syndicate and building a new Sparkman and Stephens boat. Then George Hinman came in with another syndicate and ordered *Mariner* from Britton Chance.

The West Coast syndicate, which owned *Intrepid*, indicated they would be in, and Gerry Driscoll replaced Chance's alterations with a new wooden underbody from S & S plans that closely resembled the new Strawbridge boat, *Courageous*. This made her the lightest boat in 1974, for Driscoll was able to invoke the 'grandfather' clause (as Packer had with *Gretel*) so *Intrepid* could keep her lightweight rigging of titanium, a material now banned by the Club. Driscoll had become involved in the America's Cup scene in 1964 when he had crewed on the old 12-metre trial horse, *Nereus*. In 1967 he was the chosen helmsman for the revamped *Columbia* but stepped down after a crew dispute. In 1970 he had tank tested his own design for a 12 but could not put together a syndicate to build it. Now in 1974 he was to be at the helm of *Intrepid*.

Another West Coast syndicate were also interested but later dropped out. This particular syndicate won a ruling in court that would have enabled its campaign to be tax deductible, and George Hinman decided to use the same perfectly legal dodge, which meant funnelling all the syndicate funds through the King's Point Merchant Marine Academy with the Academy owning *Mariner* after the races.

The other two 1970 contenders, *Valiant* and *Heritage*, suffered from the fact that when it was decided that the much lighter material aluminium could be used it was also decided that there should be no weight compensation in the new boats. Aluminium made the hulls of the 12s as much as 15 per cent lighter so this percentage could be added as ballast making the 12s much stiffer. Using it virtually ruled out both these 12s from having any chance whatsoever of defending. *Valiant* was revamped and used as a trial horse for *Mariner*, but *Heritage* continued to lie at her moorings at the St Petersburg Yacht Club.

All syndicates were slow off the mark in building and were doubtless relieved when the British, still in the running at that point to challenge, requested a year's postponement to give them more time for building in the new material, a request that would, perhaps, have not been granted if it had not been for the economic recession. *Southern Cross* was already out sailing at the end of 1973 while in America the building of neither *Mariner* or *Courageous* had even started. To make matters worse the 1973 oil crisis hit America and stocks tumbled on Wall Street. Strawbridge requested the Club for a further one year postponement. This was quickly refused but not quickly enough to keep Bond from commenting long and loudly that the Club were up to some new trick to hold the Cup.

Strawbridge had work stopped on *Courageous* anyway, announcing that he did not think it appropriate to continue in the present economic climate. This was possibly right but it was also well known that the syndicate – which had not gone for tax-exempt status – was having a hard time raising money (George Hinman, on the other hand, having arranged that all contributions for his campaign were tax deductible, had nearly gathered all of the

one million dollars he required). The Club was somewhat put out by the syndicate's withdrawal and after discussions Strawbridge was encouraged to continue. It could have been a disastrous break in an already late schedule but neither Sparkman and Stephens nor the builders stopped work, preferring to continue on their own until the situation became clearer. What was serious however was that in the two-week pause before the project was recommenced the skipper, Bill Ficker, an architect by profession, had committed himself to business contracts and was therefore unable to continue. He left the syndicate and in his wake so did two other vital members of the afterguard, Steve van Dyke and Peter Wilson. This development must have unnerved Strawbridge, for he put the running of the syndicate in other hands. The new men in charge persuaded the skipper of the 1964 defender, Bob Bavier, to take over the helm. Bavier built up a good team which included Ted Hood, who started out as the sailtrimmer and windward helmsman, but ended up being the main helmsman. With this crisis weathered the *Courageous* campaign began to jell.

The *Mariner* campaign, however, never really got itself together. In many ways it was a classic example of how it should not be done. Yet at the beginning it had all the hallmarks of being the most formidable group to appear on the scene for years. Headed by George Hinman, an immensely experienced and highly respected yachtsman who had been involved, one way or another, with every challenge since 1958, the team had the experience, the talent and the drive to make *Mariner* the 1974 defender. So what went wrong? The chosen skipper, Ted Turner, and the designer of *Mariner*, Britton Chance, never hit it off. Turner was a proven ocean-racing skipper but Chance was convinced after early discussions with Turner that it was not the skipper who was going to win *Mariner* the defender's berth, but a radical breakthrough in design. But the design took too long to test in the tank. Though *Mariner* was eventually launched only two weeks behind schedule Chance soon realized that he had taken too big a gamble and that it had not paid off. *Mariner* was slow. Chance blamed Turner's tactics. Turner blamed Chance's design. Hinman probably thought it was both. When *Mariner* should have been reaching her peak she was sent back to Bob Derecktor's yard and her radical stepped after end was replaced by a more conventional one. While the other contenders were racing in the July Observation Trials, Turner had a small plane fly over them trailing a

Southern Cross's *cockpit. Note the lucky horseshoe*

banner which announced: MARINER WILL
RETURN. It was a typically flamboyant Turner
touch, but when *Mariner* did return she kept losing.
Hinman then replaced Turner with *Mariner's* tactician, Dennis Conner, and things got better but not
much and *Mariner* was eliminated early. A hugely
expensive campaign had failed.

Valiant went early too, which left the West Coast
Intrepid and the new *Courageous*. Bob McCullough,
the new boat's syndicate manager, then invited
Dennis Conner to join *Courageous*, and Conner, who
had marginally improved *Mariner's* performance by
starting her brilliantly, was given the wheel of
Courageous for the starts after which Hood took over
for the windward legs and Bavier for the downwind
ones. The arrangement must have had its awkward
moments but, of course, historically it was not
unusual for a defender to have more than one skipper on board.

The final trials showed nothing to choose between
the two boats in light airs and the scores were
remarkably even – much too even for the comfort of
the Selection Committee. Then on almost the very
last possible day, with the score at four races each,
Courageous beat *Intrepid* in a very strong wind, and

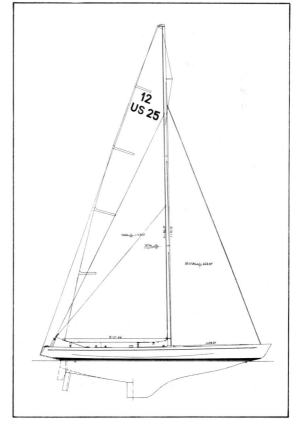

Mariner, *showing how she was altered during the 1974
season* (Chance)

163

was chosen to defend. The 1974 selection trials had shown once again what superb racing was produced by the American contenders.

By contrast the Cup races were disappointing. Despite Alan Bond's loud pronouncements on the superiority of his boat and crew – and his one-upmanship of protesting this and that and then the other – *Southern Cross* proved a terrible disappointment. She was beaten by large margins, the last race being the worst: 7 minutes 19 seconds. 'I was amazed,' Bob Derecktor commented after the races, 'I know a lot of those guys. Five of the guys on their crew are the best sailors you could find anywhere. I would be happy to have any of them on my crew. I don't know what happened. It was so bad I couldn't bring myself to ask them,' and when someone asked Jim Hardy how he slept after losing the first race he said: 'Like a baby. I woke up every two hours and cried.' However Dennis Conner for one, felt that the races were by no means the walkover they appeared to be. The first two were close, he maintained, and could easily have been won by *Southern Cross*. If she had won them, perhaps Bond would not have made the crew changes which threw away the last two races.

Bond said he would be back, and in 1977 he was. Bich challenged once more and *Gretel II* was also on the scene again, managed this time by an Australian syndicate headed by Gordon Ingate, who challenged through the Royal Sydney Yacht Squadron. For the first time in the history of the Cup two clubs from the same country were putting in separate challenges. The British via the Royal Corinthian Yacht Club again entered a challenge, this time on behalf of John Livingstone, and again withdrew through lack of funds. The newcomers were the Swedes who challenged through the Royal Göteborg Yacht Club with *Sverige* designed and sailed by the Olympic yachtsman, Pelle Petterson. The money for this challenge was subscribed by a large syndicate of business interests.

The Americans might have regarded this invasion of foreign 12s with some trepidation. So much rivalry between not only clubs but nations must surely breed, they may have reasoned, the very kind

France II *passing Castle Hill, Newport, after a practice sail. She's using a spinnaker belonging to* France I (Darling)

Inset: Sverige *pinning* Gretel II *down after the start of one of the elimination races. The Swedes eventually won by 46 seconds* (Darling)

of competition that was needed to produce a boat and a crew and a set of sails that would, after nearly 130 years, take away the treasured Cup from the New York Yacht Club. If the Americans did think this they showed no sign of it, as one of their first announcements was that *Intrepid* would not be racing again. Too much money was needed to alter her to the requirements for the 1977 challenge, as the NYYC had decided after the 1974 series to encourage the type of 12 that was more seaworthy and which could after its competitive days be converted for ocean racing. So they made self-draining cockpits obligatory, restricted deck openings and decreed that those remaining should have hatches, and also that all winches must be on deck. *Intrepid* was subsequently bought by the *Enterprise* syndicate as a trial horse.

Two other syndicates announced they would build new boats, one from the West Coast, headed by Edward du Moulin, the other from the East with the establishment figure of Alfred L. Loomis in charge. Both syndicates could claim tax exemption as they were channelling their syndicate's money through charities. The West Coast boat *Enterprise* was to be skippered by Lowell North, the East Coast one, *Independence*, by Ted Hood. *Courageous*, skippered by Ted Turner, started out as the trial horse for *Independence* – but it did not end up that way.

Courageous was altered for the 1977 challenge by having her waterline length shortened by 6 inches. This was not to improve her performance – though it certainly seemed to do it no harm – but to make her conform to the 12 metre rule without penalty; in 1976, after Sparkman and Stephens had given her lines to Ted Hood to help him develop *Independence*, Hood discovered that *Courageous* was underweight. S & S had already informed him that by their calculations *Courageous* must have been about 300 lb underweight during the 1974 races but Hood estimated that the error was probably much larger. He had *Courageous* weighed and found to everyone's horror that *Courageous* must have been as much as 1800 lb underweight even though her designer's certificate had allowed 700 lb for miscalculation. The formula for a 12 does not, of course, state a maximum displacement but given the length of *Courageous*, and her measured sail area, the figure declared on the certificate was the minimum allowed without penalty. As she weighed less than that she sailed the 1974 races without penalty on a waterline 6 inches too long and with 84 square feet too much sail area. It was an easy mistake to make, especially as aluminium tends to shrink when welded.

Ted Turner enjoys the press conferences as much as he does winning. Next to him is tactician Gary Jobson (Darling)

Loomis and Hood were old friends, and Loomis had no liking for the brash fast-talking Turner. ('Now I know why you called your boat, *Northern Light.*' Turner told the tall syndicate manager. 'Why?' asked Loomis. 'Because you're the Big Loom, that's why.' The nickname stuck and Loomis and Turner spent much of the campaign at loggerheads.) But Turner gave as good as he got on the water and off it, beat his newer stable-mate, *Independence*, as well as the other new boat, *Enterprise*, in the Trials and so was selected to defend. Plenty of people around did not like it – Turner had been turned down twice for membership of the NYYC before being elected – but there is no doubt the man from Atlanta had proved himself the best. Yet Turner was not one of the computer revolutionaries, one of a new-wave electronic

yachtsmen. He liked sailing by instinct and, unlike Lowell North, for instance, who designed his sails by computer and who got more than a little help from a mini-computer on board *Enterprise*, relished the human element in driving a yacht to her maximum. 'I'm not much on this electronic stuff,' he's been quoted as saying. 'It's not my style to run up a lot of statistics. I have a wife and five kids, a ball club, a basketball team, a television station – I don't intend to spend all my time fiddling around with numbers.' The distinguished writer John Hersey who got this quote from Turner had a very different and totally fascinating response from Lowell North, showing perhaps, the way America's Cup racing will be in the 1980s:

North seems tired. He has been getting boat speed out of *Enterprise* but has been making tactical errors. It is a down time. But when he starts talking about computers, the

mask of control dissolves, a radiant face comes out from the cover of caution, and the hands begin to move with the arcane logic of flow charts. This sailmaker–sailor's tongue seems to have levitated into a higher language. 'The greatest problem at present is the interface between your sensors and the computer. The wind-direction sensor will give you readings of two-tenths of a degree eight times a second. The optical decoder has 1800 slits – five slits for every compass degree. You're going back and forth two or three degrees in waves, and you have distortions from heeling, upwash – so with such sensitive devices there's gross overkill, when you're trying to get an absolutely accurate true wind direction. First you work it out theoretically. Fudge the distorting factors. Calculate. Then tack. Average the two, and you have it.... We have a special tacking program to tell us how we're doing coming about. It averages over ten seconds. You get five two-second boat speeds, and five two-second compass readings' – the pairs of North's outspread fingertips approach each other – 'and matches them up and plots your progress through the tack and gives you a delta of the

The second race, on 16 September 1977, was the closest of the series. On this final beat Australia *matched the defender for speed but eventually lost by 1 minute 3 seconds* (Darling)

amount lost in the tack. You can then compare with other tacks when you've turned sharper or slower and work out the most efficient tack in given conditions.

The temperaments of North and Turner are very different, and North clashed with the skipper of *Courageous* when he refused to sell his sails to Turner, because Turner was in the same syndicate – though in a rival boat – as Hood. Hood and North were rivals, business rivals more than sporting rivals. North, anyway, had promised that in return for big development money he would make sails exclusively for the *Enterprise* syndicate. It seemed reasonable, but Turner took it as a personal affront. At one cocktail party the two stood toe-to-toe and it

Courageous leads Southern Cross *on the last leg of the third race, 17 September 1977* (Darling)

looked as if fists would fly. Roger Vaughan, who was present, reported the confrontation in his book *The Grand Gesture*:

'You know, Lowell,' Turner said, 'I always thought you were a good guy. And I've been a good customer for years, right?'

North: 'That's right, a very good customer.'

Turner: 'Well, I'm not going to be a good customer anymore. I want you to know I'm going to do everything I can to work against you for the rest of my life.'

Later Turner asked Vaughan if he should have hit North. Not a very enjoyable party.

While the Americans were fighting it out on land as well as on the water, the Australians, French and Swedes were sorting themselves out into some sort of order. The elimination series for the four challenging clubs, the Yacht Club d'Hyeres, the Royal Göteborg and Royal Perth Yacht Clubs, and the

Royal Sydney Yacht Squadron, were run by the French club. After a few preliminary races which served more as a warm-up than a serious assessment of the competing boats' capabilities it was decided to sail off *Australia*, which had emerged as the superior boat, against *France I*, *Gretel II* against *Sverige*, the winners of these semi-finals to meet and race for the honour to challenge. Both the semi-finals and the finals were to be the best of seven races. *Australia* thrashed *France I*, which Bich had raced in preference to *France II*, but the fight between *Gretel II* and *Sverige* was a very even one which showed just how fast the Australian boat still was. The two Australian boats met only once in competition at Newport and then the older boat trounced *Australia*.

The Swedes won the first race, lost the second, and the third when they were dismasted, squared the series two-all for the fourth, lost the fifth, won the sixth, and then the seventh in convincing style.

In the finals against *Australia*, however, *Sverige* was badly beaten four–nil.

Australia's deck layout (Darling)

These selection trials must have helped give *Australia* the kind of tuning every challenger has always needed. But to put the series in perspective remember that the challenger raced sixteen times, mostly against inferior boats, while the defender raced twice that many times, nearly all the time against boats nearly her equal. The 1977 elimination races for the defenders were extremely close though *Courageous* dominated the Preliminary Trials winning seven–one, her only defeat being to *Enterprise* by only 8 seconds. The Observation Trials, a three-way affair with each boat taking a day off in turn, really ended with no one yacht emerging as superior. In the Final Trials *Independence* was eliminated first after being beaten by *Courageous* by 1 minute 20 seconds. What really caused her elimination, however, were two previous races against *Enterprise*, which beat her both times by narrow margins after both boats had tacked in the two races 135 times and gybed 31 times.

Courageous, dominating the Final Trials, raced and beat *Enterprise* only once before being chosen to defend. It was personal triumph for Ted Turner. It was rare for a skipper of an unsuccessful contender of a previous series to come back and be chosen to defend – Mosbacher had done it in 1962 after sailing *Vim* in 1958 but no one really thought of *Vim* that year being defeated in the normal sense of the word – and it was quite unknown for a sacked skipper to reappear on the scene. But Turner was a very different man in 1977. Instead of having a boat he knew was slow and a syndicate management all at odds with one another Turner now had a boat of his choice and the right crew as well. This time no one, but no one, was going to stop him.

The *Courageous*–Turner team had come about because Loomis asked Turner to sail *Courageous* to tune up Hood's *Independence*. If *Courageous* turned out faster then Hood would skipper her in the Final Trials. Millionaire Turner refused and made a counter-offer. He would pay for the 1974 defender's alterations provided the boat was his to sail. No second best for Turner. Loomis, perhaps gambling that Hood and the new boat would prove superior, agreed. It must have caused a tremor through the yachting establishment, and many people thought that Turner would never be selected however fast he sailed his boat. 'If he is selected,' quipped Don MacNamara who had voted against Turner's admission to the Club, 'he will be the first skipper in the history of the Cup to appear on the starting line wearing a muzzle.'

It was the disastrous 1974 *Mariner* campaign that caused Turner's success in 1977. If ever a man thrived in adversity it was Turner. It was for him a very basic motivation that sparked a ruthless competitiveness and a combative spirit. His tactician in 1974, Dennis Conner, and the man who took over the wheel of *Mariner* when Turner was sacked, has remarked that this is both an advantage and a disadvantage. 'His kind of aggressive leadership works well when times are tough, but it can be counter-productive when things are going well.' Turner's tactician in 1977, Gary Jobson, who proved the perfect counterfoil to the mercurial Turner, showed just how counter-productive this attitude could be when he described an incident aboard *Courageous* during the races against *Australia*:

I was getting some publicity toward the end, and it caused Ted to play mind games. During that second race I told him to tack. He said no. I really knew we should tack, so I was pushing. We had those kinds of disagreements all along. It's normal. But that day he said either I could do it his way or he would get someone else who would. I told him to feel free, but in the meantime, we should tack.

When the summer was over and *Courageous* had won, it was generally acknowledged that Jobson had been brilliant in picking the wind shifts. Turner's answer as to why *Courageous* won was four-fold: 'One, I had the most experience sailing big boats. Two, I was the best organizer and leader. Three, I didn't make a lot of changes. I just concentrated on sailing. And Doyle made us great sails.' No mention of Jobson.

The actual races were, as usual, an anti-climax with *Courageous* winning four straight and *Australia* never looking really competitive. The times were closer than some of the previous disasters, between 1 and 2½ minutes, but the challenger never really looked like winning and indeed after the starts never even led at any point in any one of the four races.

Immediately after the races Turner asked the Trustees of the King's Point Fund to sell him *Courageous* and expressed the wish that he be the only man in modern Cup history to skipper a Cup boat to two successive victories. Vanderbilt had done it no less than three times and Charley Barr had also done it three times, but that had been a long time ago and they'd done it in different boats. Anyway Turner doesn't care much about the historical side of things. Why should he? It's the here and now that counts.

Loomis thought Turner could have had the

decency to discuss the purchase of *Courageous* with him first, but it was not likely that Turner cared much what Loomis thought. Turner was popular – at least with the press – while no one cared much for Loomis. When the celebrations took place on *Courageous* after her victory the traditional dunking of all those involved took place. But Loomis was ignored. In the end he had to jump in the water himself. One thing is for sure as that one incident perhaps showed. The rule of the East Coast establishment is slowly losing its grip on the America's Cup. Some time in the eighties we'll probably see Ted Turner on the America's Cup selection committee. That is, if he's still not racing the winning boat.

In his lively book, *Showdown at Newport*, published in 1974, Jeff Hammond predicted that the end of the 12-metre class was at hand. He could be right of course and many people would be only too pleased if the America's Cup was raced for by ocean racers. But right now, in September 1979, it doesn't look that way at all. At the time of writing the world's first 12-metre championship is taking place off Brighton, in the English Channel. The yachts competing are by no means the best in the world, but at least there are six of them including the Dutch boat, *Windrose* (ex-*Chancegger*), and the new British challenger, *Lionheart*. In America Baron Bich already has *France III* racing, and there are two new American 12s. If numbers are anything to go by, therefore, the 12s are very much on the increase in popularity. And as the number increases so does the competition. This means that the 12s outside America, and their skippers, crews and designers – and maybe, who knows, even their owners – are going to get better and better. So let me make my prediction. The New York Yacht Club is going to lose the America's Cup in the 1980s.

Australia, *with the US Coastguard training ship* Eagle *in the background* (Darling)